Autorenkollektiv

Analytical Problems

Autorenkollektiv

ANALYTICAL PROBLEMS

Mit 83 Abbildungen und 16 Tabellen

AKADEMIE-VERLAG · BERLIN
1981

Die Originalausgabe erscheint im Springer-Verlag
Berlin · Heidelberg · New York

Vertrieb ausschließlich für die DDR und die sozialistischen Länder
Akademie-Verlag Berlin

Erschienen im Akademie-Verlag, DDR-1080 Berlin, Leipziger Straße 3—4
Lizenznummer: 202 · 100/536/81
Gesamtherstellung: VEB Druckerei „Thomas Müntzer", 5820 Bad Langensalza
Bestellnummer: 763 005 0 (6643) · LSV 1215
Printed in GDR
DDR 96,— M

Table of Contents

Mass Spectrometric Methods for Trace Analysis of Metals

Ute Bahr and Hans-Rolf Schulten

Institute of Physical Chemistry, University of Bonn, Wegelerstr. 12, D-5300 Bonn 1, Federal Republic of Germany

Table of Contents

1 Introduction

Today, mass spectrometry is widely used. Its field of application ranges from structural analysis of organic and inorganic compounds, the main area of mass spectrometry, to the study of reaction kinetics, measurements of isotopic abundances and quantitative determinations in biochemical, medical and environmental investigations. The analysis of metals on trace (ppm) and ultratrace levels (ppb, ppt) is one of the longest employed mass spectrometric applications. Determination of metal isotopic abundances[1], investigations of terrestrial minerals and meteorits[2], and decomposition and fission products in nuclear physics[3] have been analyzed on a large scale, due to the availability of commercial mass spectrometers.

During the last three decades, trace analyses of elemental impurities in materials such as semiconductors, superconductors, nuclear reactor components[4] have become increasingly important, because very low amounts of these elements fundamentally affect the quality of the material. Recent developments of instrumental and methodic conditions of mass spectrometry allow precise and accurate quantitative investigations down to the ppb-range from a total of microgram amounts of samples. The lower limit of detection, the easier handling of the instruments available and the efficient and fast processing of modern data systems are a few of the reasons that have expanded the applications of mass spectrometric techniques in the last years to metal analysis in biological, medical and environmental samples. The global biological consequences of the dispersal of poisonous metals such as lead, mercury, cadmium, thallium etc. in the environment have resulted in an urgent need for reliable data collections of trace metals in human tissues, body fluids[5], in the atmosphere and hydrosphere and in soils[6,7].

Because of its extraordinary high sensitivity and specificity mass spectrometry has become a standard tool besides other powerful analytical methods for the trace analysis of metals, such as emission spectroscopy, atomic absorption spectroscopy, neutron activation analysis or electrochemical methods.

The rapid development of mass spectrometric technology and the wide field of applications exclude a complete and comprehensive discussion of mass spectrometric possibilities for trace analysis of metals. Therefore, this report will give a brief outline of the principles of mass spectrometry (MS) and the fundamentals of qualitative and quantitative mass spectrometric analysis with emphasis on recent developments and results. The classical methods of analysis of solids, i.e. spark-source MS[4,8] and thermal ionization MS[2], as well as newer methods of metal analysis are described. Focal points in this survey of recently developed techniques include secondary ion MS[9], laser probe MS[10], plasma ion source MS[11,12], gas discharge MS[13] and field desorption MS[14,15]. Here, a more detailed description is given and the merits of these emerging methods are discussed more explicitly. In particular, the results of the FD techniques in elemental analyses are reviewed and critically evaluated.

2 Principles of Mass Spectrometry

As reported elsewhere in more detail[16)], a mass spectrometer consists of three major components: an ion source for producing a beam of gaseous ions from a sample, a mass analyzer (in Fig. 1 a magnetic field) for resolving the ion beam into its characteristic mass components according to their mass-to-charge ratios, m/z[1], and an ion detector for recording the mass and the relative abundance and intensity[1] of each of the ionic species present (Fig. 1).

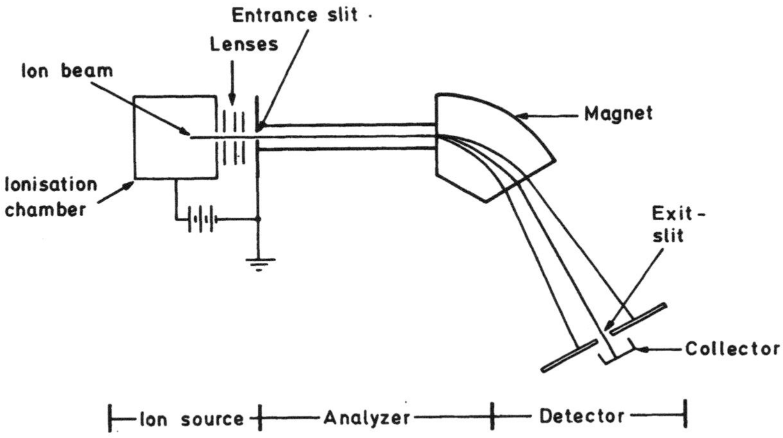

Fig. 1. Schematic diagram of a mass spectrometer (for explanations see text)

2.1 Ion Source

Special methods for producing ions will be described in Section 4. The common principle of these methods involves the production of gaseous ions from a solid sample. In general, singly charged positive ions will be formed, but also multiply charged or negative ions can be produced. Before entering the mass analyzer of a magnetic instrument, the ions produced in the ion source are accelerated by passing through a potential of some thousand volts. On the flight path the ion beam is focused onto the entrance slit of the analyzer by a series of electrostatic lenses.

2.2 Mass Analyzer

The analyzer must be operated at low pressures, in general below 10^{-6} mm (Hg) to prevent collisions between the ions produced and the neutral molecules of the

[1] See "Recommendations for symbolism and nomenclature for mass spectrometry" from IUPAC[18)]

residual gas, mainly nitrogen, oxygen and water. These collisions would deflect the ionic species from their flight path and would prevent an exact separation of the different mass peaks. For mass separation, the commonly used methods involve deflection in a magnetic field (single focusing) or in a combination of electrostatic and magnetic fields (double focusing), separation by different velocities (time-of-flight mass spectrometer) or in alternating electric fields (quadrupole mass spectrometer).

2.2.1 Single Focusing Instruments

In the presence of a magnetic field perpendicular to the direction of the motion of the ion beam, each ion experiences a force at right angles to both its direction of motion and the direction of the magnetic field, thereby deflecting the ions to a circuit. The radius of the circuit is proportional to $(m/z)^{1/2}$ (Eq. (1)) so that the magnetic field is sufficient for mass analysis of an ion beam:

$$r = \frac{1}{B}\sqrt{\frac{2mU}{z}} \tag{1}$$

(B = flux density, r = circulation radius, m = atomic mass unit, U = accelerating voltage of the ions, z = number of electronic charges).

Mono-energetic ions with various masses and/or different charges pass the magnetic sector with different circular paths. The radius of a circular path from an ion with large mass number is greater than that of an ion with lower mass number (Fig. 2).

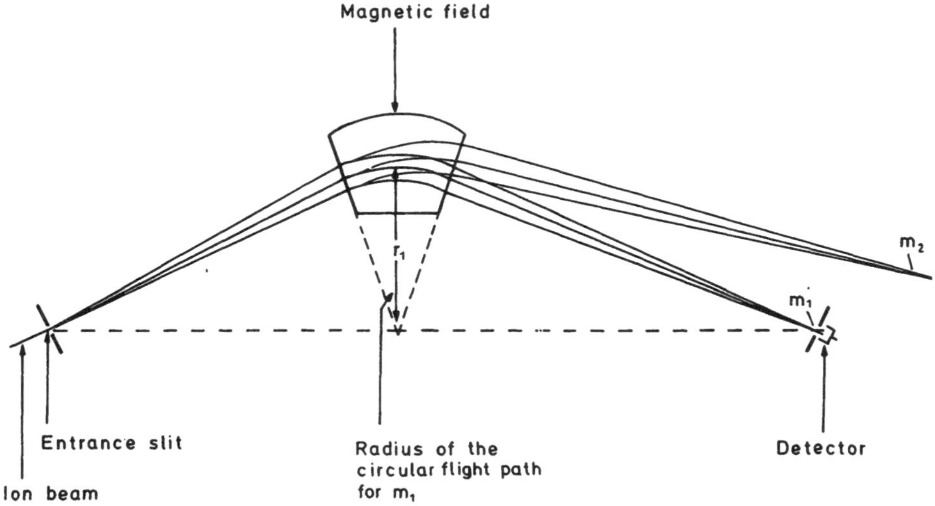

Fig. 2. Single focusing principle. In a magnetic field ions are deflected to a circuit with a ratio proportional to $(m/z)^{1/2}$. So the ions m_1 and m_2 are separated according to their mass-to-charge ratios. In addition to mass separation, the ions with same m/z ratios but with small differences in their directions are focused at the same point.

By using a magnetic scan, i.e. a continuous change of the magnetic field at constant accelerating voltage, the ions with different masses pass the exit slit one after another. Depending on the type of ion source, the ions entering the mass analyzer reveal a certain degree of inhomogeneity in their direction. Besides mass separation, the magnetic field displays a focusing action like that of a cylindric lens so that ions having the same m/z ratio and the same velocity are focused on the same point.

2.2.2 Double Focusing Instruments

The thermal energy of the ions, the instability of the accelerating voltage and the construction of the ion source produce an ion beam with more or less large energy spread. With an energy spread of more than 10 eV the ion beam must be focused before entering the magnet by use an electric sector field. The deflection radius of ions in a homogeneous electric field perpendicular to the direction of motion of the ion beam is given by

$$r = \frac{2U}{E} \tag{2}$$

(E = electric field strength).

In a particular arrangement of the magnetic and electric sectors (Mattauch-Herzog geometry) simultaneous double focusing for all masses can be achieved in the same plane[17)], permitting the use of a photographic plate (Fig. 3).

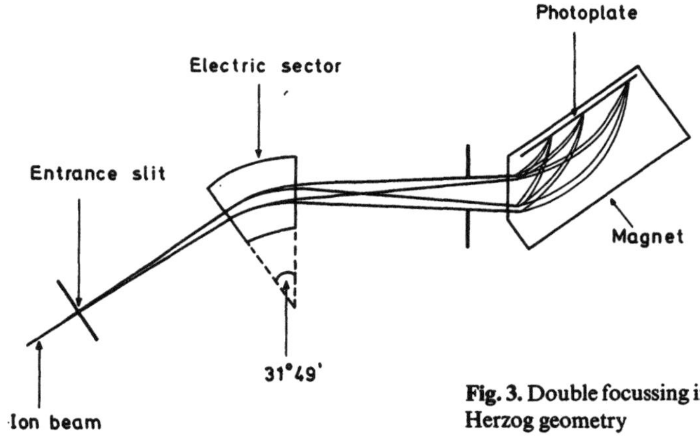

Fig. 3. Double focussing instrument of the Mattauch-Herzog geometry

2.2.3 Resolution

Double focusing instruments produce ion beams with a small energy spread and a mass resolving power of about 100,000 can be achieved. Single focusing instruments only display resolution powers of about 1000. A resolution of 1000 means that signals for the ions at m/z 1000 and m/z 1001 can just be recorded separately. Resolution is usually defined in "10 percent valley definition", which implies that two adjacent ion peaks of equal intensity are to be considered as separated when the valley between them is not greater than ten percent of the peak height.

2.2.4 Time-of-flight Mass Analyzer

In a *time-of-flight mass spectrometer*, mass separation results only from the mass-dependent velocities of the ions. Linear time-of-flight instruments employ neither electric nor magnetic fields. After acceleration, a beam of mono-energetic ions passes a field-free tube. Ions of different masses will pass the space at varying velocities and can be registered as a function of their time of flight. This kind of mass analyzer needs a pulsed production of ions for which the spread in time must be much smaller than the approximate time of flight of the ions.

2.2.5 Quadrupole Mass Analyzer

In a *quadrupole mass analyzer* the ions are stimulated to oscillations in an electric quadrupole field. The quadrupole field has a dc voltage and a rf voltage component and mass scanning is accomplished by varying both types of voltage while keeping their ratio constant. Thus, ions with varying m/z ratios can be detected. The assignment of the mass numbers to the ion signals is uncomplicated as there is a simple correlation between voltage and detected ion masses so that a linear mass scale can be achieved. In addition the resolution, which is approximately proportional to the transmission (ratio of collector ion beam to entrance ion beam) can be varied in a simple mode by changing the voltage ratio.

2.3 Ion Detection

The use of a particular detection- and recording-unit mainly depends on the intensity and stability of the ion beam. The three major types of ion detectors include Faraday cup, electron multiplier and photographic plate.

2.3.1 Faraday Cup

Ion beams of the order of 10^{-6} to 10^{-3} A can be detected with a *Faraday cup*. The ions are captured in a metallic collector (Faraday cup) and the voltage drop across a large resistance placed between ion collector and ground is measured. Double collector systems are often used for recording two different ion species simultaneously, a technique which allows the determination of the ratio of isotopes with high precision. The major advantages of this detection system are the elimination of errors caused by fluctuations of ion currents, registration of changes in isotopic ratios during measurements and the shortening of the analysis time.

2.3.2 Electron Multiplier

An *electron multiplier* can amplify an ion current up to a factor of 10^7. Each ion which impinges on the metal surface of the first dynode of the multiplier causes the emission of a number of secondary electrons. These are accelerated to another electrode inducing consecutive, additional electron emission thus producing a cascade of electrons.

This process is repeated several times, using ten stages or more. The multiplication factor depends on the material and number of the dynodes and of the voltage between them. After amplification the signals can be registrated with a recorder, oszillograph or on-line with a computer and stored on magnetic tapes or disks.

2.3.3 Photographic Plates

Recording with *photographic plates* is possible if the mass spectrometer focuses ions of different masses in a plane. This is achieved by double focusing instruments of the Mattauch-Herzog geometry. The photographic plate integrates simultaneously the ions received from all masses within a certain mass range. For example, if the ratio of the lowest to the largest mass is 1:36 all signals from m/z 18 to m/z 648 can be recorded using a particular magnetic field strength and accelerating voltage. Ions produce a latent image on the ion-sensitive emulsion of the photographic plate. As in black-and-white photography this image is developed and fixed and shows more or less black, sharp lines, according to the intensity of the ion beam. Some thousand ions are enough to produce a visible line on the ion-sensitive emulsion of the plate[19].

3 Principles of Qualitative and Quantitative Mass Spectrometric Analysis

The outstanding sensitivity and the high specificity of mass spectrometry allow qualitative as well as quantitative analysis.

3.1 Qualitative Analysis

The qualitative determination of a metal is realized by comparison of the mass spectrum of the sample with those of a reference sample. Using low resolution mass spectrometry the sample must have a simple composition to prevent superposition of atomic ions and cluster ions from the components. An alternative possibility is the identification of a metal from a more complex sample using high resolution mass spectrometry. High mass resolution enables a precise mass determination in the ppm range, i.e. ± 0.1 m.m.u. (millimass unit) at 100 m.u. (mass units). Complex mixtures frequently require pretreatment prior to mass spectrometric analysis. The definite identification of the metal is a prerequisite for quantitative analysis.

3.2 Quantitative Analysis

Assuming constant instrumental conditions, the intensity of an ion current is a measure of the quantity of a sample. To determine the absolute amount of a sample, the intensities of an ion signal from a sample and a standard must be compared. This may be achieved as follows:

3.2.1 Quantitative Analysis with an External Standard

The standard is measured mass spectrometrically at different concentrations and the signal intensities are plotted against these concentrations. Utilizing this standard curve, the concentration of a sample can be determined. The disadvantage of methods working with an external standard is the separate treatment and measurement of sample and standard.

3.2.2 Quantitative Analysis with an Internal Standard

More precise is a method using an internal standard. The sample is spiked with a known amount of a reference sample and both sample and standard are treated and measured simultaneously in the mixture. Most precise determinations can be obtained using compounds labelled with stable isotopes as internal standards (isotope dilution analysis), since they exhibit different mass spectra but completely identical chemical properties. For details and examples of applications of the isotope dilution method see Ref.[20]. Because of the limited sample availability the time of measuring the ions must be utilized optimally. One possibility is the fast repetitive scanning over a preselected mass range by varying either the magnetic field strength or the accelerating voltage.

Another method involves "selected ion monitoring", in the course of which the chosen ionic species are focused on the detector by variation of the accelerating voltage. Again, multiple detectors are used to obtain most precise results. Here, often two ion beams are recorded simultaneously to prevent errors resulting from fluctuations of the ion currents and to increase the intensity. A detailed comparison of the different methods has recently been described[21]. Evaluation of a quantitative mass spectrometric determination and a comparison with results from analytical methods can be effected under three aspects: First, *accuracy* which means the deviation of the measured value from the real value; second, *precision* (defined as standard deviation) which is a measure of the reproducibility of a result repeating the analysis of a sample; third, *sensitivity* (in mass spectrometry defined as coulomb/μg for solid samples) that characterizes the ratio of signal height to sample amount used for analysis.

4 Mass Spectrometric Methods for the Trace Analysis of Metals

4.1 Thermal Ionization Mass Spectrometry

The first thermal ionization source was developed by Dempster in 1918. The solid material to be analyzed is applied to a hot metal filament and ions are produced by thermal surface ionization[17] at a temperature of ~2000 °C. A commonly used thermal ionization source is the three-filament ion source, developed in 1953 by Inghram and Chupka[22]. This ionization source consists of two parallel filament strips for the sample and an ionization filament in a plane perpendicular to and between the other two filaments. Fig. 4 shows a sectional view of this kind of ion

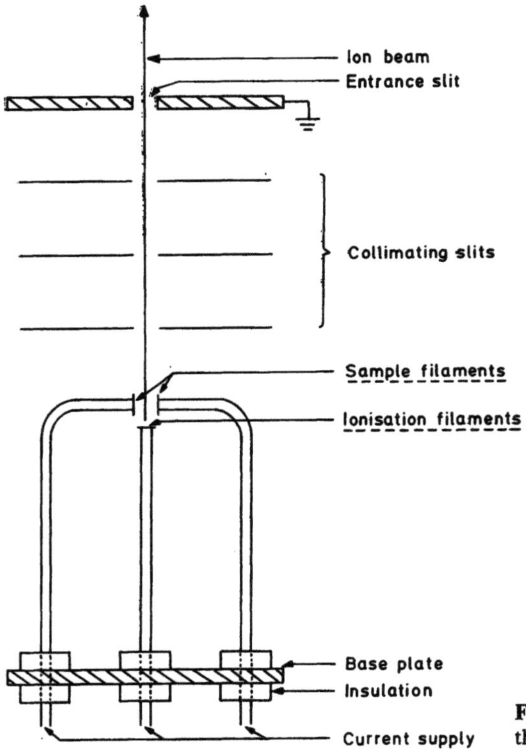

Fig. 4. Schematic diagram of a triple filament thermal ionization source

source. The filament consists of a high-melting metal with a high work function like tungsten, tantal, platinum or rhenium. In Table 1 are listed the melting points and work functions of the most frequently used metals.

The dissolved or suspended sample is applied to the filaments by a syringe and evaporated to dryness. By heating these filaments the sample is vaporized and im-

Table 1. Melting points and work functions of metals which are often used as filament strips in thermal ionization sources[23)]

Metal	Melting Point (°C)	Work Function (eV)
W	3990	4.54
Re	3180	4.97
Ta	2996	4.13
Ir	2443	4.57
Rh	1960	4.57
Pt	1769	5.55

pinges the ionization filament, which is heated to a very high temperature and the metal vapor is dissociated into atoms. The metal atoms transfer an electron to the ionization filament because of its high work function. In the first step of this process, the ionization energy of the atom must be afforded while in the second step an energy amount that is equivalent to the work function of the metal is gained. Mostly, the work function is smaller than the ionization energy and the process needs thermal energy to take place. This is the reason for heating the filament. The ionization yield β for one element, that is the ratio of the number of positively charged particles n_+ to the number of neutral particles n_0 evaporated from the filament, depends on the ionization energy I of the element, the work function W of the filament and on its temperature T and is described according to Langmuir and Saha[24)] by

$$\beta = \frac{n_+}{n_0} = \exp\left[e\,\frac{(W - I)}{kT}\right]. \tag{3}$$

The thermal ionization source is useful for an exceedingly large number of metals and metal compounds having first ionization potentials below approximately 9 eV (Table 2).

Table 2. Ionization energy (in eV) of some metals which are often determined as trace metals by mass spectrometry[23)]

Cs 3.89	Tl 6.12	Mg 7.64
K 4.34	Cr 6.76	Cu 7.72
Li 5.4	V 6.8	Fe 7.9
Sr 5.69	Ti 6.83	Sb 8.64
In 5.79	Sn 7.3	Pt 8.96
Al 5.98	Pb 7.42	Au 9.23
Ca 6.11	Ag 7.57	Hg 10.4

Because of the very high second ionization potentials only singly positive charged ions are formed and the interpretation of mass spectra is simple. Surface ionization is routinely applied to sample analysis in the range of micro- and nanogram. At best, sample amounts of 10^{-14} g can be detected. Because of the low energy spread by the ions formed, single-focusing instruments can be used for analysis. Applications of thermal surface ionization include determination of isotopic abundances in mineralogy, age determination in geology[25)] and analysis of fission products in nuclear chemistry. An example for the thermal ionization MS is the determination of calcium impurities in high-purity compounds and in feldspars by Heumann et al.[26)]. Calcium must be separated from the matrix before mass spectrometric measurements because of the superposition of ^{40}K with the ^{40}Ca isotope. This superposition depends on the much higher ion yield of potassium under the conditions of thermal ionization mass spectrometry. For analysis, a two-filament thermal ionization source with rhenium filaments is used. Calcium is applied as $CaCl_2$ after mixing with ^{44}Ca labelled standards. For one analysis about 1 μg of calcium is needed. As shown in this study, the enrichment of the standard greatly affects the precision of the result from an isotope dilution analysis. Table 3 shows the results of calcium determinations in alkali salts with a low enriched standard.

Table 3. Determination of calcium in alkali salts by isotope dilution mass spectrometry using an enriched ^{44}Ca standard[26)]

Compound	Experiment No.	Ca-content (ppm)	Standard diviation	
			S_{abs} (ppm)	S_{rel} (%)
KCl (ultra pure)	1	3.2		
	2	2.9		
	3	2.5		
	average	2.9	0.35	12
KNO_3 (pure)	1	1.0		
	2	1.0		
	3	1.4		
	average	1.1	0.2	18
$NaNO_3$ (pure)	1 and 2	<0.2		

In the determination of metals from biological and medical matrixes, thermal ionization mass spectrometry is seldom used[27)]. Disadvantages of thermal ionization MS are the great fluctuations in the results, caused by different instrumental requirements. Isotope fractionation resulting from vaporization of the sample and the dependence of this process on temperature are the main sources of error. However, the development of computer-controlled sample preparation and measurements have minimized these errors[28-30)].

4.2 Spark Source Mass Spectrometry

The method of spark source MS was developed by Dempster in 1935[31]. During the last two or three decades, this technique was utilized in the trace analysis of impurities in high purity elements, such as semiconductors, superconductors, nuclear reactor components and magnetic, thermoelectric or luminescent materials. There is an urgent necessity for the determination of trace elements in these materials, because they are characterized by the presence or absence of particular elements in the ppm or ppb range.

The principle of spark ionization is as follows: A spark is formed directly between two electrodes, consisting of or including the sample material to be analyzed. In the *radiofrequency spark source* a potential of about 100 kV is generated in the form of short pulses, which produce a spark discharge between the two electrodes. In the *vibrating arc source* an arc discharge is produced by breaking a current-carrying contact between two electrodes. This discharge can be repeated rapidly by an oscillating motion of the electrodes (Fig. 5).

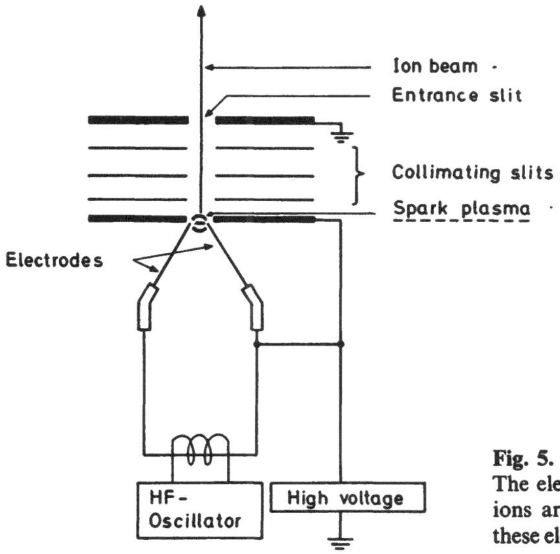

Fig. 5. Schematic diagram of a rf spark source. The electrodes contain the sample material and ions are produced by spark discharge between these electrodes[17]

Because of the high energy density on the surface target of the arc discharge, a definite amount of sample is abruptly vaporized. This kind of rapid vaporizing causes only a small segregation of the components of the sample and the chemical composition of the surface area is reproduced exactly. At very high arc energies the mass spectrum is a sum of the mass spectra of the single elements of the electrode materials. If only singly positive charged ions are formed, the resulting spectrum can readily be used for quantitative determinations. Often, multiply charged atomic ions as well as singly charged cluster ions are formed, for example from iron the Fe^{+}, Fe^{2+}, Fe^{3+}, Fe_2^{+}, Fe_3^{+} ions.

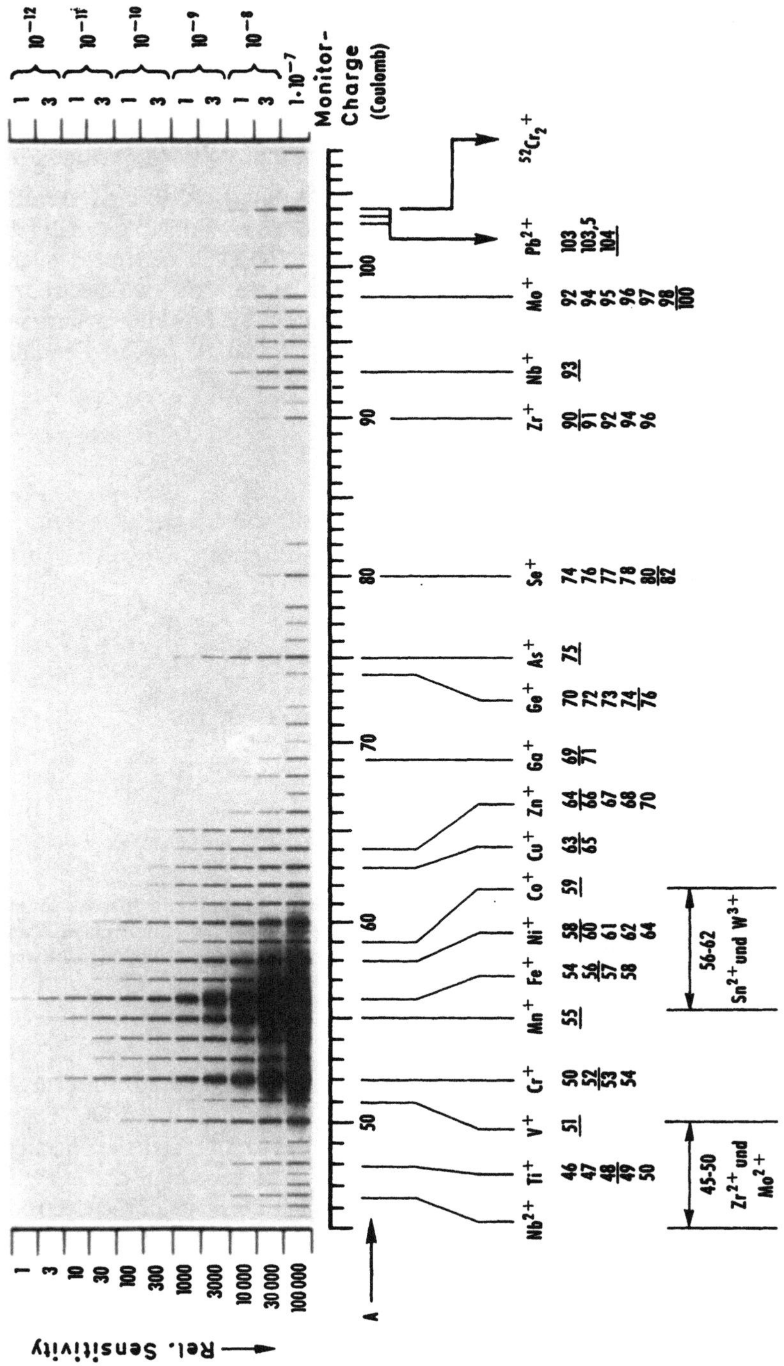

Fig. 6. Rf spark mass spectrum of a high duty steel sample. It shows eleven spectra with graded sensitivities caused by different exposure times[32)]

If signals of multiply charged ions superimpose signals of atomic ions from trace elements, then trace analysis can be disturbed. To ensure a more efficient mass resolution of the ions generated by spark source mass spectrometry, double focusing mass spectrometers are used. Fig. 6 shows a photographic detection of a mass spectrum of a high-duty steel sample (16% Cr–10% Ni). Different exposure times produce eleven spectra with graded, step-like blackenings[32].

Registration of ions with a photographic plate is quite expensive and time consuming and, in addition, qualitative and quantitative interpretations are sometimes difficult. Thus, more and more efforts are being made to use spark source mass spectrometry with electric registration[33]. This technique is applied to the analysis of all trace metals with a precision of about 5%. The main applications are in metallurgy and geology for simultaneous determinations of many elements in a sample, in particular when this is impossible with other methods. At best, concentrations at $1:10^8$ can be registered. The sample consumption is about 1 mg for one analysis.

For several years, multi-element analysis of biological materials and environmental samples have been performed using spark source MS[34–36]. One example is the analysis of ashed mammalian animal blood by high-resolution spark source MS[37]. Sample electrodes are prepared from a standard of low-temperature dry-ashed human blood. The samples are mixed with very pure graphite applying a technique of preparing sample electrodes under high pressure in slugs[38]. The mass spectrometric results and the concentration range as reported by the International Atomic Energy Agency are shown in Table 4.

Table 4. Concentrations of some metals in animal blood determined by spark source mass spectrometry. Comparison of the concentration ranges of some elements obtained by the International Atomic Energy Agency (IAEA) with values from mammalian animal blood as reported by the United Kingdom Atomic Energy Commission (UKAEC)[38]

Element	IAEA Animal blood 66/12		UKAEC Mammalian blood (Mean values)
	SSMS Values	IAEA Range	
Na	1930		1990
Mg	59		41
Al	0.32		0.37
K	2250		1690
Ca	44		60
Cr	0.07	0.02–0.56	0.023
Mn	0.35	0.08–0.38	0.026
Fe	1050	835–3270	475
Cu	2.4	0.77–3.3	1.07
Zn	10.2	11.5–22	6.5
Ag	0.02		0.19
Sn	0.009		0.13
Sb	0.002		0.0047
Hg	<0.006		0.0065
Pb	0.4		0.27

All values in μg per g wet weight.

As shown by this example, the samples mostly must be ashed (dry or wet) to prevent a superposition of metal ions and organic ions in the mass spectrum. Heavy metals such as Pt, Au, Hg, Tl, Pb and Bi have been detected from blood, homogenized liver and urine without prior ashing, in concentrations below 1 ppm[39)].

In spite of the wide field of applications, disadvantages of spark source MS are the great instrumental expenditure of using double focusing mass spectrometers and the time- and labor-consuming interpretation of the photographic plates. Besides this, there are difficulties in producing electrodes, for the samples must often be treated before mixing with the matrix element.

A higher accuracy of the results may be achieved by automatic evaluation of the photoplates, using an absolute calibration method working without standards[40)].

4.3 Special Methods

In addition to the ion sources described, there are other mass spectrometric methods for trace analysis of metals. Some of them are only used in exceptional cases and others are still under instrumental and methodological development.

4.3.1 Electron Impact Mass Spectrometry (EIMS)

In this method the sample is vaporized in a micro-oven placed in the ion source or out of a Knudsen-cell. Many metals can be analyzed qualitatively and quantitatively by this technique as metal organic compounds (see Refs.[41,42)]). The metal chelates have lower volatilities than the metals and in many cases the mass spectra reveal higher sensitivities for these compounds compared with the analysis using direct evaporation of the metal. The latter technique of direct metal analysis by EIMS is only applied if the ionization energies of the metals are too high for thermal ionization mass spectrometry[2)].

4.3.2 Secondary Ion Mass Spectrometry (SIMS)

This mass spectrometric method for trace analysis is mainly used in multi-element analysis of surfaces and thin films. Also, microscopic distributions of elements in depth concentration profiles and in adsorption processes are determined[9,43)]. A stable ion bombardment by a primary beam of a few kV is capable of ionizing atoms and molecules from the surface of a solid sample (about 100 Å deep).

The principle of this process is shown schematically in Fig. 7a. Mass spectrometry of the secondary ions provides a sensitive multi-element analysis of fresh surfaces. Figure 7b shows the spectrum of a vanadium surface containing zirconium near the surface[44)]. With a current intensity of 5×10^{-8} A a surface area of 0.1 cm^2 was bombarded with 3 keV Ar^+ ions. Only 100 seconds were required for recording of the spectrum. In this time a monomolecular layer of vanadium oxide was analyzed which corresponds to a weight of about 10^{-8} g. Zirconium in the surface is identified by registration of the mass lines 90, 91, 92 and 94. These lines represent the naturally occuring isotopes of this group IVa element. In the secondary ion

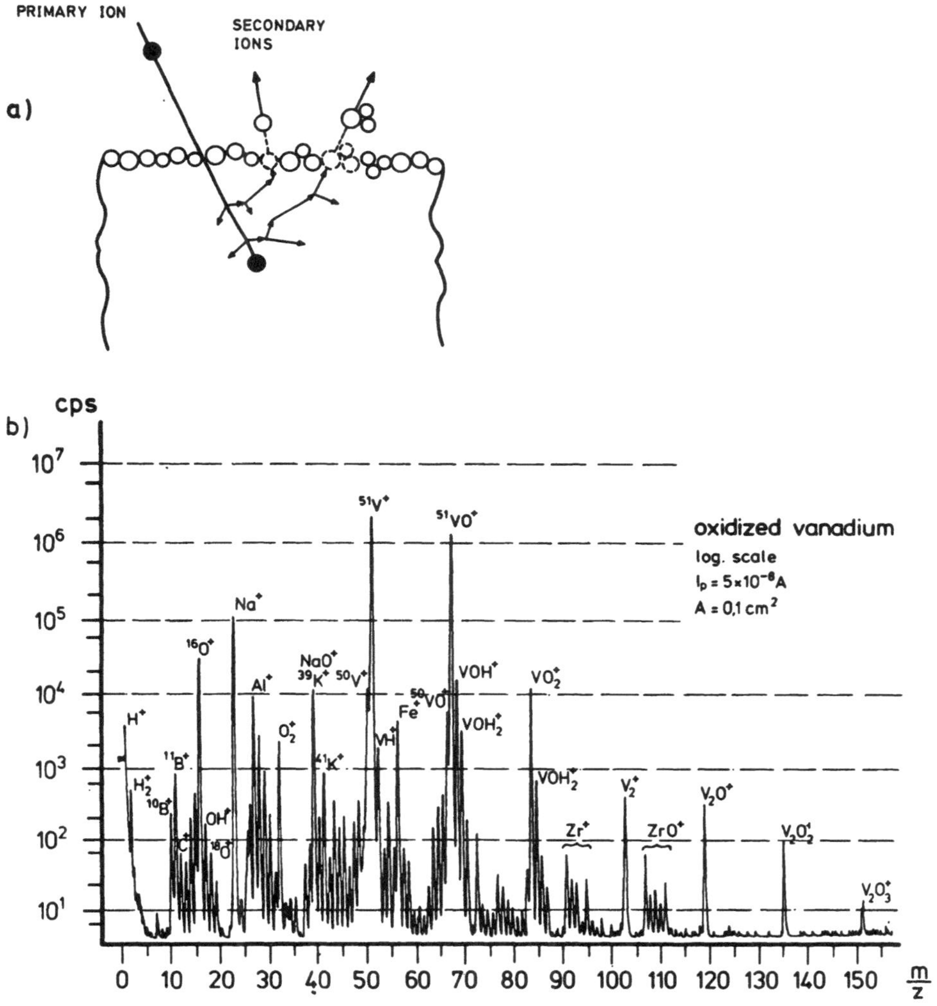

Fig. 7a. Energy transfer from a primary ion to the ejected secondary particles[43]. **b** SIMS analysis of a mono-layer of a vanadium surface which contained zirconium. An enhancement in sensitivity can be achieved by recording the relevant mass range for zirconium only (m/z 90–m/z 95)[44]

spectrum they appear as Zr^+ and together with oxygen as ZrO^+. The ratio of the intensities of $V^+:Zr^+$ is about $5\times10^4:1$. This means, if the same ionization probabilities for vanadium and zirconium from an oxidized surface are assumed, that 20 ppm of zirconium can be identified in a mass spectrum which extends from mass 1 to 100. Since just one layer of the metal surface is analyzed the total amount of Zr in this analysis can be calculated to be 2×10^{-13} g.

Difficulties of SIMS are the complexity and large dynamic range of the ion beams produced. This may complicate the identification of the positive ion spectrum and cause sometimes an insufficient reproducibility of the results. Important advantages, however, are the small energy spread of the secondary ions (about 10 eV), so that single focusing instruments can be used and the fact that the sample can be analyzed at room temperature. On the other hand a very high vacuum of approximately 10^{-9} Torr is necessary to obtain a primary ion beam of high intensity and to avoid surface contamination.

4.3.3 Gas Discharge Mass Spectrometry

Gas discharge, one of the oldest known ionisation methods[45] has been used lately as a promising method for mass spectrometric analysis of trace elements in solids[13]. Hollow cathode or coaxial cathode ion sources have been described for the analysis of conducting solids and solution residues[46,47]. Ionization takes place by use of a discharge gas, usually argon, between a cathode, containing the sample, and an anode. In contrast to rf spark source mass spectrometry, the ion flux is extremely stable and the obtained ion currents are of high intensity. The observed fluctuation is ±1–2%, so that good isotopic ratios can be obtained from a single scan. The sensitivity for trace elements is below the ppm level (see Fig. 8).

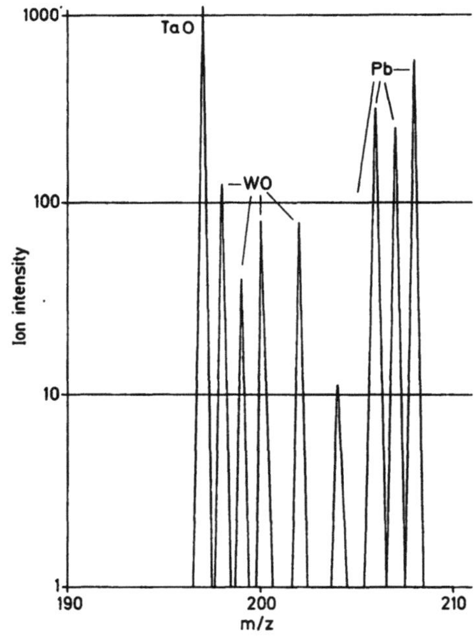

Fig. 8. Spectrum of 60 ppb lead in stainless steel, determined with a hollow cathode ion source[48]

With co-axial cathode ion sources, multi-element isotopic dilution analyses have been performed and results with a precision of 2–5% with electric detection can be obtained[47]. However, more work is needed to reduce interferences caused by the high internal energy of the ions produced.

4.3.4 Laser Probe Mass Spectrometry

Very promising is the development of a laser probe mass analyzer for metal analysis of high spatial resolution[10,49]. Foils or thin sections of less than 2 μm are evaporated and ionized by pulsed laser beams in vacuum. Lasers (rubin or Nd-YAG) with power densities between 10^7 and 10^{11} W/cm^2 produce, when optimally focused, a spatial resolution higher than 1 μm. Time-of-flight or double focusing instruments are used for mass analysis.

The laser ion source can be used for trace analysis of all elements down to the sub-ppm range. The main advantage of this method compared with spark source mass spectrometry is that little sample preparation is required so that minute sample amounts which are difficult to handle can be investigated. A mixture of the sample with the conducting material, such as graphite is not necessary, because the conductivity of the sample has no influence on the ion production.

The spot of sample analysis can be varied by manipulation of the sample so that the distribution of an element in the sample can be examined. The laser probe mass spectrum recorded by Heinen et al.[49] (Fig. 9) illustrates the determination of iron traces in a cell of an uterus gland of a pregnant animal.

4.3.5 Plasma Ionization Mass Spectrometry

In this method[11,12] designed for the analysis of inorganic solutions, ionization occurs at atmospheric pressure.

The sample solution is injected into the ion source, dispersed in a carrier gas and ionized by an electric discharge between two electrodes. A quadrupole analyzer is used for the resolution of the ion beam.

An example for plasma ion mass spectrometry is the investigation of a silver solution at a concentration of 3 mg/l [11]. When a sample of this solution is nebulized, the spectrum shown in Fig. 10 is obtained.

The isotopic peaks of silver $^{107}Ag^+$ and $^{109}Ag^+$ suggest a high sensitivity for this metal. Metal impurities of $^{23}Na^+$, $^{63}Cu^+$ and $^{65}Cu^+$ are detected besides peaks due to organic ions. Furthermore, corresponding to m/z 19 (OH_3^+) and m/z 30 (NO^+) which come from nitrogen, oxygen, carbon dioxide, and water present in the carrier gas argon are found. The method of plasma ion mass spectrometry is very sensitive and only small amounts of sample are used. The detection limit for some metals (Ag, As, Co, Pb) is below 1 ppb.

4.3.6 Field Desorption Mass Spectrometry (FDMS)

FDMS[14] is a soft ionization technique which expands the applicability of mass spectrometry to highly polar and/or thermally labile compounds and therefore has found numerous analytical applications in biochemical, medical and environmental research[50-53]. Although originally designed and developed for ionization of organic compounds of low volatility the technique has unexpectedly proved to be a powerful tool in the analysis of a large number of metals.

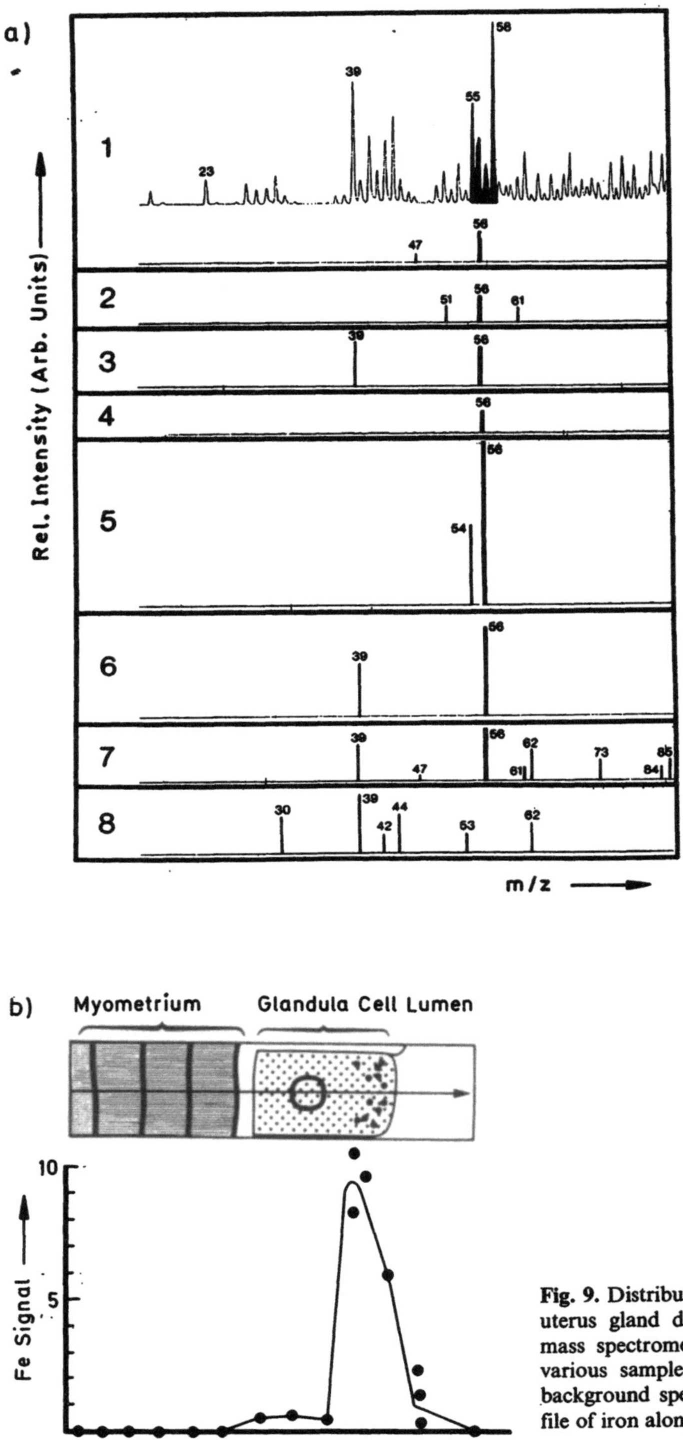

Fig. 9. Distribution of iron in a cell of an uterus gland determined by laser probe mass spectrometry[49]. **a** Mass spectra of various sample spots diminished by the background spectrum. **b** Abundance profile of iron along the gland cell

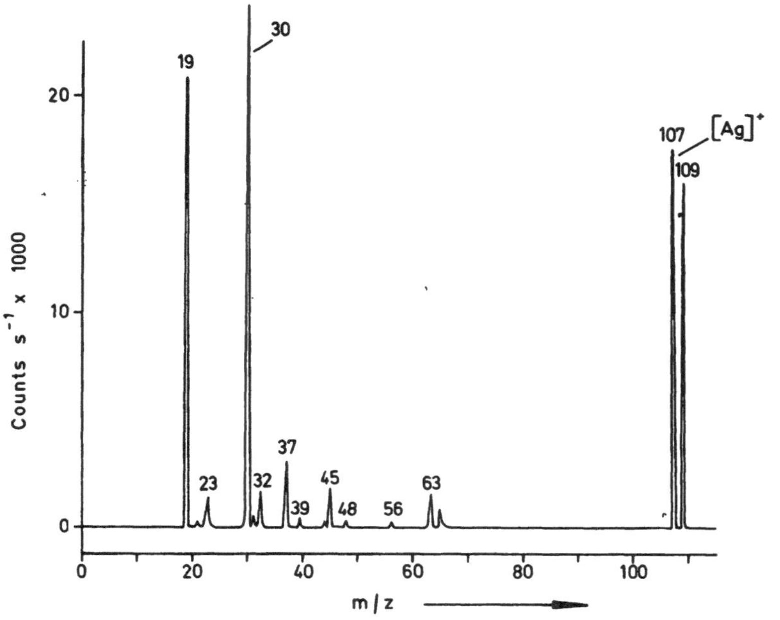

Fig. 10. Mass spectrum of 3 mg/l silver solution obtained by an atmospheric pressure ion source[11]

The extraordinarily high sensitivity of FDMS for alkali metal ions was discovered already during the early investigations of organic salts[54]. The mass spectra obtained always revealed the signals of sodium and potassium ions to be several orders of magnitude more intense than all organic ions when the spectra were recorded on photoplates and the emitter temperature was raised to red heat[55]. These observations prompted studies to exploit the potentialities of the technique in the trace analysis of metals and led to the development of FDMS as a novel method for the identification and determination of metal cations. Since these investigations were carried out in the authors' laboratory during the last three years, and this is the first survey of metal analysis by FD, it appears appropriate to describe in more detail the principle, experimental techniques and results obtained in the following.

The principles of field ionization and FDMS have been treated comprehensively for organic molecules.[14] For the desorption of metal cations under similar conditions (high electric field, activated emitter) two points have additionally to be considered. Firstly, a large number of metal cations desorb at considerably higher sample (emitter) temperature than organic ions. Thus, with growing input of thermal energy the original concept of FD is increasingly superimposed by high-temperature effects. Secondly, because the metal traces have to be determined preferably in medical or environmental samples, destruction of the complex organic matrix is necessary in order to avoid overlapping of metal cations and organic ions. In this respect, the original aim of FD analysis, namely soft ionization and detection of intact, large, organic molecules is completely reversed.

The experimental technique for the trace analysis of metals simply involves the production of an emitter of acceptable quality. In general, 10 μm tungsten wires are activated at high temperature with benzonitrile [54] in a multiple activation device. As the result of such an activation process, the tungsten wire is covered with dendrites of partially ordered pyrocarbon. Due to the small radii of curvature of the tips of the microneedles, the field strength is enhanced to a level suitable for FDMS. These emitters are mechanically stable, which is important for repeated use; they can also be chemically and thermally strained. This property is a prerequisite for the pyrolysis of the organic matrix and desorption of the metal cations, and last not least, the surface area of the emitter is sufficient for sample application.

The sample can be easily applied by dipping the activated emitter into a solution or suspension of the substance. The amount of sample, i.e. organic matrix plus metal, deposited on the emitter should be in the range of 10 μg to a few ng. Diluted solutions which are supplied by a microsyringe can be concentrated most effectively by evaporation of the solvent under the control of a stereomicroscope as illustrated in Fig. 11. Furthermore, this method enables the transfer and deposition of known amounts of sample solution onto the emitter surface and thus provides essential experimental conditions for quantitative determinations.
In order to reduce the analysis time and to facilitate the handling of the FD procedure, also for non-experts in mass spectrometry, a simplified ion source is employed.

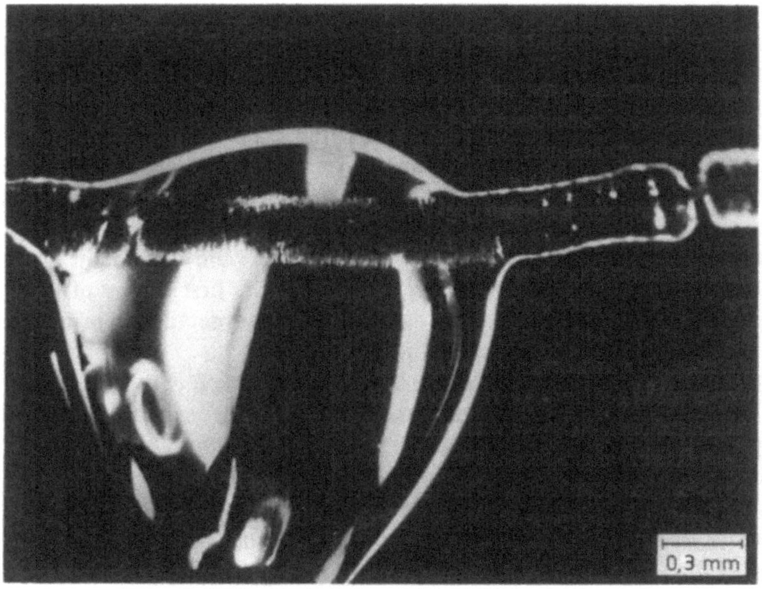

Fig. 11. Syringe technique: the sample solution or suspension is supplied with a 10 μL microsyringe to the activated emitter wire. The microscope photographs show a magnification of approximately 1:35[56])

As shown in Fig. 12 the emitter is adjusted mechanically using a micromanipulator or pushed in a predetermined, fixed position and the focusing of the ion beam can be performed by changing only two electrical potentials. In routine use the negative potential of the cathode is fixed and the positive potential of the emitter and one focusing lens of the collimating system are varied. More experimental details of the FD method for trace analysis of metals such as emitter heating, ion recording, use of external and internal standards, sensitivity and detection limit will be given in connection with some recent applications in the following.

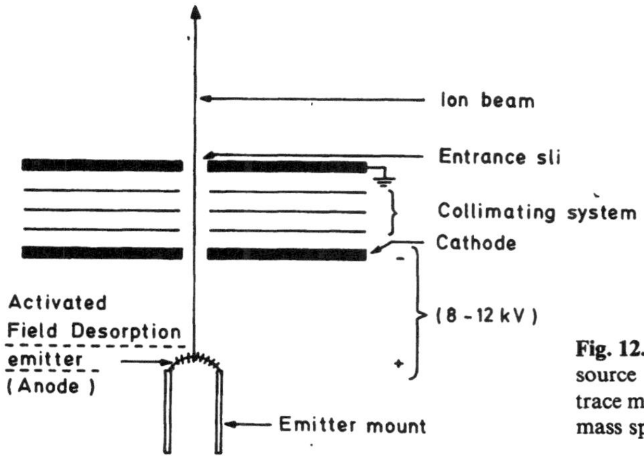

Fig. 12. Schematic drawing of an FD ion source for fast and simple analysis of trace metals in a single focusing magnetic mass spectrometer[17)]

4.3.6.1 Determination of Cesium Using an External Standard

After the first qualitative studies of lithium-, sodium-, calcium-, and silver-halides and other inorganic salts with complex anions had revealed the types of ion occurring in FD mass spectra and the high sensitivity of the method for metal cations had been demonstrated[55)] the principal question arose whether quantitative data could be obtained. If so, it was essential in the use of FDMS as an analytical technique for metals to evaluate the sensitivity, precision and accuracy for these determinations. Since pilot tests showed an extraordinary sensitivity for cesium the first approach to the quantitive determination of metals by FD was started with this alkali metal.

Quantitative determination of the monoisotopic element cesium can only be performed by using a radioactive isotope or a different alkali element as an internal standard or by establishing a calibration curve as an external standard. A plot of such a curve is given in Fig. 13 for $[Cs]^+$ [57)]. For measurements, a number of standard solutions of CsCl in CCl_4 are prepared and analyzed. The resultant values are displayed with an error of 22% corresponding to 2σ (σ = standard deviation).

This plot correlates the sample amount applied to the FD emitter with the peak area of the evaporation profile. The range of sample amounts covered by this curve extends from 1000 to 0.3 pg of cesium corresponding to 7.5 pmol to 2.3 fmol.

When a linear extrapolation to smaller sample amounts is applied, a detection limit for $[Cs]^+$ of about 10 fg is derived from the calibration curve in Fig. 13. However, measurements in this range of concentration could not be performed since no solvents

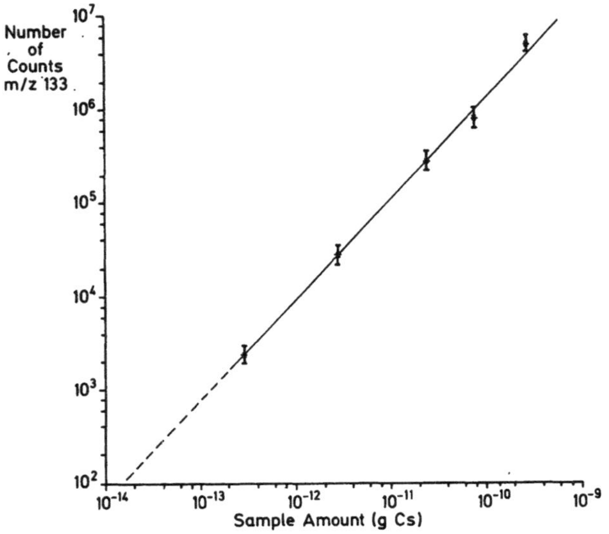

Fig. 13. Calibration curve for quantitative determination of $[Cs]^+$ correlating the sample amount with the peak area of the evaporation profile obtained by FDMS and single ion monitoring of m/z 133. For these measurements, a number of standard solutions of CsCl in carbon tetrachloride were prepared and analyzed. The values of the analyses are displayed with an error of 20% corresponding to 2σ (σ = standard deviation)[57]

containing less than about 1 μg/l cesium were available. The original trace for the detection of about 350 fg of $[Cs]^+$ by field desorption and single ion monitoring is shown in Fig. 14. It can be derived that this sample amount corresponding to 2800 counts is by far more than the detection limit since the noise level is only about 20 counts/s[57].

From Figs. 13 and 14, it can be derived that the sensitivity of the FD method for alkali metal ions exceeds that for organic compounds. The observed sensitivity of about 10^{-9} C/μg is of the same order of magnitude as that of conventional EIMS for the detection of organic compounds. One of the reasons for this phenomenon is that the particles that are to be detected are already present as positive

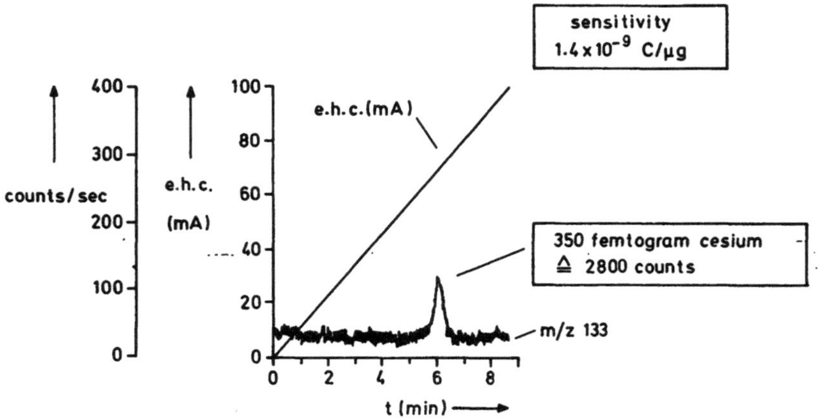

Fig. 14. Evaporation profile of about 350 fg $[Cs]^+$. The emitter heating current is raised from 0 to 100 mA linearly with 0.19 mA/s[57]

ions on the emitter surface. Field desorption of these monovalent ions from the matrix on the emitter is obviously much more efficient than field desorption of organic compounds. For organic compounds, the processes of thermal decomposition and evaporation of neutral molecules that do not undergo ionization compete effectively with the ionization process, whereas this is not valid for field desorption of metal cations.

The increase in sensitivity in the alkali metal ion series from lithium to cesium corresponds to the variation of the lattice energies and desolvation energies of the alkali elements. These energies decrease from $[Li]^+$ to $[Cs]^+$ thus favoring the desorption of $[Cs]^+$ as compared to that of $[Li]^+$. This effect is also reflected in the observation that $[Cs]^+$ desorbs at a lower emitter temperature than $[Li]^+$.

In order to test the capacity of FDMS for quantitative trace analysis, cesium was determined in a number of samples. Solvents, body fluids, and environmental samples were investigated by single ion monitoring of m/z 133 and measurement of the peak areas of the evaporation profiles by ion counting. The results of these analyses are compiled in Table 5.

Table 5. Determination of cesium in spectrograde solvents, body fluids, and environmental samples by field desorption mass spectrometry using an external standard[57]

		Counts[a]	Concentration Cs
Solvents	Water dist. (1 μl)	8,100	0.9 pg/μl
	Carbon tetrachloride (1 μl)	29,000	3 pg/μl
	Methanol (1 μl)	5,100,000	350 pg/μl
Body fluids	Human blood (0.2 μl)	34,000	18 pg/μl
	Human saliva (0.2 μl)	720,000	300 pg/μl
Environmental samples	Drinking water (1 μl)	18,000	2 pg/μl
	Seawater (0.3 μl)	666,000	165 pg/μl
	Natural aerosol (1–3 μg)	760,000	65 pg

[a] The number of counts corresponds to the intensities obtained for the calibration measurements.

The organic solvents investigated were of commercially available quality (carbon tetrachloride, Uvasol, E. Merck AG, Darmstadt, West Germany; methanol, analyzed reagent, J. T. Baker Chemicals B.V., Deventer, The Netherlands). Drinking water was taken from the tap in our laboratory and seawater from the North Sea near the coast of The Netherlands. The aerosol was directly sampled on a FD emitter[58,59] for 2 h on the roof of our laboratory on May 13, 1977. Samples of body fluids were taken from volunteers and analyzed without further treatment.

To obtain these data the FD ion currents were recorded on a homebuilt single focusing mass spectrometer of low resolution equipped with a FD source with micromanipulator[60]. The FD ion source employed is schematically described in Fig. 12. The FD emitter (at + 8 kV) is positioned at a distance of 2 mm from the counter electrode (at — 4 kV). Only the first lens (at approximately + 2 kV) is used for the focusing of the ion beam whereas all other reflection plates are at ground potential. With an entrance slit width of 0.1 mm and an exit slit width of 0.5 mm, a resolution of about 300 (10% valley definition) is achieved. This experimental set-up considerably simplifies the operation of the FD mass spectrometer because it allows an easy, a fast and reproducible optimizing of the FD ion currents which is particulary relevant for quantitation.

The ions are detected using a channel electron multiplier (Valvo) and a combined counter/ratemeter registering unit (Ortec). The channel electron multiplier is operated at —3 kV. A linear emitter heating current (EHC) programmer is employed for the desorption of the samples. In all cases the EHC is raised at 0.19 mA/s from 0 to 100 mA (see Fig. 14). All measurements for the calibration curve of $[Cs]^+$ (see Fig. 13) are made with one FD emitter starting from small sample amounts.

For trace determinations of cesium cations the procedure is executed in two steps: First, 3 μl of a standard solution containing a known amount of cesium chloride is applied to the emitter by means of the modified syringe technique[15)] and a signal at m/z 133 is recorded. Second, between 0.2 μl and 1 μl of sample are applied to the same emitter and desorbed under identical conditions. From the peak areas of the evaporation profiles obtained in both measurements, the unknown amount of the alkali element present in the sample is calculated. Usually, one analysis (calibration + sample analysis) can be performed within 30 min. Thus, cesium in sample sizes of 0.2 to 1 μl, which contain 0.3 to 1000 pg of the element, can be determined. The accuracy of repeated measurements of a standard solution is ±10% and that of the technique for the determination of unknown concentrations ±20%. A sensitivity between 1.4 and 2.5×10^{-9} C per μg is obtained for cesium. Since a good sensitivity value for an *organic* FD ion, namely the molecular ion of cyclophosphamide, has been reported to be 1 to 2×10^{-11} C per μg[61)] it is clear that FDMS is about a factor of 100 more sensitive for the $[Cs]^+$ ion.

However, also two critical points of the technique have been observed:

a) After multiple use, the ionization efficiency of FD emitters decreases. If very small amounts of the sample are coated on the FD emitter, this detrimental effect is minimized. In the FD analysis of alkali cations, because of the high sensitivity of the technique, only minute amounts of the trace metal are required and thus a quantitative determination with an *external* standard is possible.

b) In general, with rising complexity of the matrix increasing fluctuations of the FD ion currents occur. Whereas the evaporation profiles of $[Cs]^+$ from the pure solvents exhibit a smooth shape, the investigations of the seawater, of the organic samples, and the aerosol reveal stronger fluctuations of the ion current. In the analysis of the organic samples, the coated emitter is heated to about 50 mA for some minutes *without* the high voltage applied in order to evaporate and destruct the organic material. Then the analysis is performed as with other samples. Carrying out this procedure with the high voltage applied to the emitter, it is found that, by monitoring of m/z 133, no significant loss of cesium occurs.

Because of these observations it is of interest to evaluate the capacity of the FD technique using an external standard in a very complex sample matrix and to explore the disturbing influences occurring in trace metal determinations of authentic samples.

4.3.6.2 Cesium Determination in Physiological Fluids and Tissues

The physiological medium of living cells mainly consists of alkali and alkaline earth ion solutions. The different concentrations of sodium-, potassium- and calcium-ions in the various compartments of a living organism as well as the transport of these ions through cell membranes provide the basis of all physiological processes and is therefore decisive for the function of these organisms. In the body cesium ions occur in traces only. An important toxic effect of higher cesium concentrations in the body is the blockage of potassium currents through biological membranes. However, the study of these effects requires an analytical method which is able to detect cesium concentrations in very small samples (e.g. milligrams of tissue material) down to the ppb range (1 ppb cesium = 1 μg cesium/kg)[62].

It has been shown that a concentration of 1 mmol/l cesium in Tyrode solution as the outer medium of cardiac Purkinje fibers — part of the excitable system of the heart — is sufficient to suppress the potassium outward current (pacemaker current) nearly completely[63]. When the concentration of cesium exceeds 20 mmol/l all detectable potassium currents in cardiac Purkinje fibers are blocked. Since this effect occurred within one or two minutes it was believed that cesium ions are able to block the potassium channels in the membrane from the outside. One possible explanation would be based upon the fact that cesium ions are bigger than potassium ions (diameter $[Cs]^+$ = 1.77 Å; $[K]^+$ = 1.33 Å). Therefore, if they eventually invade the potassium channels, they should be hampered in their motion or even immobilized because of their bigger size. If this was the case, cesium ions would invade potassium channels whenever they reach cell membranes and would irreversibly block them. Besides, cesium ions should not be detectable inside the cells of the excitable system, since they are unable to penetrate the cell membranes.

From the standpoint of all classical microanalytical experiments on organic cell materials containing alkali ions this hypothesis seemed to be correct. However, the only reason opposite to this was that a concentration of cesium, which would be enough to block all potassium channels (about 100 nmol/l), was too small for such measurements.

As mentioned above by means of FDMS using an external standard and the single ion monitoring mode, a cesium concentration of 135 nmol/l has been found in human blood[57]. This measurement alone leads to some doubts about the hypothesis of blockage from the outside of the membrane described above, since all channels should be blocked under normal conditions. In order to check this hypothesis and because FDMS may even quantitatively determine cesium concentrations as low as about 0.1 nmol/l, measurements with this technique have been made with untreated Purkinje fibers and heart muscle from sheep as well as human saliva and urine. In addition, experiments with Purkinje fibers and heart muscle cells have been performed after treatment of the whole heart for 1.5 respectively 30 min with a Tyrode solution containing 1 mmol/l cesium. The tissue material is homogenized and the obtained suspension deposited on the FD emitter by the syringe technique without any further pretreatment. After establishing a reliable calibration curve, cesium concentrations in untreated Purkinje fibers and heart muscles are measured in a range of 880 nmol/l up to 1070 nmol/l.

According to the calculations on channel numbers this is sufficient to block all potassium channels in the membranes. If cesium ions are able to block the potassium outward current in the excitable system of the heart at all, they do not do so by plugging the channels from the outside of the membrane. After the application of a Tyrode solution, containing 1 mmol/l cesium, for only 1.5 min and a prolonged wash-out period, cesium concentrations in Purkinje fibers and heart muscle tissues increased to values between 14 μmol/l and 19 μmol/l. After the use of a Tyrode solution for 30 min, cesium concentrations increased to 42–71 μmol/l (Fig. 15).

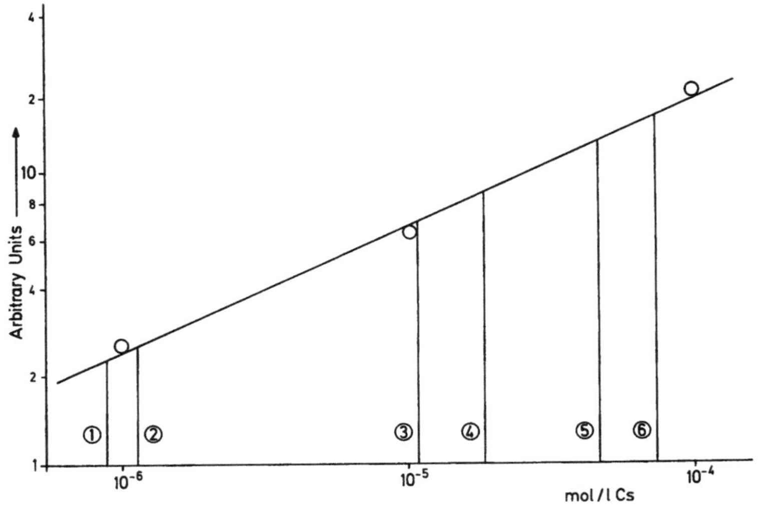

Fig. 15. Measurements of Purkinje fibers and heart muscle tissues with a typical calibration curve for $[Cs]^+$. The preparations were measured under normal conditions (see text). Ordinate: arbitrary units, abscissa: concentration of cesium in mol/l [62]

① Heart muscle
② Purkinje fiber
③ Heart muscle after 1.5 min Cs
④ Purkinje fiber after 1.5 min Cs
⑤ Heart muscle after 30 min Cs
⑥ Purkinje fiber after 30 min Cs

These relatively high concentrations measured by FDMS can also be detected by other methods with adequate accuracy, although the FD method has the advantage that tissues need no pretreatment. Parallel measurements of the same preparations by atomic absorption and emission spectroscopy have revealed no significant deviations from the authors' results.

Hence, Purkinje fibers take up so much cesium after the application of a cesium solution described above that the intracellular cesium concentration is still about 100 times higher after wash-out than under normal conditions. The speed of this take up is indicated by the measurement after 1.5 min of treatment with cesium. That cesium ions are transported very quickly through the cell membranes into the cells is not astonishing because the concentration gradient from the outside to the inside of the membrane is rather high (1 mmol/l to 1 μmol/l). If cesium ions are transported in a solvated form into the cells, one has to consider that their radius is somewhat smaller than that of solvated potassium ions. An exchange of cesium ions for potassium in leakage or pump currents would be possible. For the pacemaker outward current, however, potassium ions have to pass in an unsolvated form through special potassium channels. However, for the unsolvated ions, cesium is larger than potassium. One can imagine two possible mechanisms by which cesium can prevent the potassium transport: Firstly, blockage of potassium channels from the inner surface of the membrane or secondly, a very slow transport of cesium ions through potassium channels. If, at the inner surface of the membrane, the potassium ion concentration was about 0.15 mol/l and the cesium ion concentration about 15 μmol/l and both ions passed through the same channel system, then cesium ions would need 100,000 times longer than potassium ions to migrate through these channels. This is only valid if the pacemaker current is reduced to 10% of its normal value.

Summarizing the quantitative results obtained by FDMS using an external standard, the following facts emerge. In all cases where a reliable calibration curve can be established the method yields a precision of about 10% and an accuracy of about 20%. One can expect that the application of the FD technique will allow the determination of metal concentrations (1 μg — 1 mg/l) in environmental samples, body fluids and tissues and thus will help to explain experimentally observed effects in biosciences, e.g. pharmacology, neurophysiology and toxicology.

4.3.6.3 Analysis of Directly Sampled Natural Aerosols

A rapid sampling method for direct aerosol analysis using FD-mass spectrometer has been described[59]. In a predominantly inorganic aerosol three alkali metal cations and a number of cluster ions of intact salts have been identified under the conditions of high mass resolution ($R \geqq 15{,}000$, 10 per cent valley definition) using *photographic* registration.

The stereoscan micrograph of the FD emitter used in Fig. 16 shows the branched structure of carbonaceous needles grown on the 10 μm tungsten wire at high enlargement. The micrograph was taken after a 4-hour exposure to natural air in the jet collector, at a flow rate of $3\,l\,min^{-1}$. Numerous solid particles were caught in the dendritic emitter.

In the upper left of Fig. 16 some of the larger, probably inorganic particles can be seen to exhibit a crystalline structure. The analysis of this and similar samples has revealed that this type of aerosol consists almost exclusively of inorganic material. From the known dimensions of the emitter and a comparison with a micrograph of the unloaded emitter it is estimated that less than 1 μg of aerosol particles are impacted, which has turned out to be sufficient for analysis. This sample material was collected on a roof top of the Institute of Physical Chemistry, University of Bonn, on December 12, 1974, during the afternoon hours. A total air volume of 800 l was drawn through the collector jet at an average flow rate of $3\,l\,min^{-1}$. The weather was cloudy with showers before and after the collection period, and the visibility was good.

After exposure to the air blast the loaded field emitter is directly transferred into the mass spectrometer and pumped to 10^{-5} Torr. A trace of acetone is injected into the ion source to optimize the ion current by adjusting the emitter in front of the slotted cathode plate of the spectrometer. The mass spectrum of the sample is then recorded on a photoplate.

Forty one lines are observed in the spectrum of the aerosol 36 of which can be assigned to ions of inorganic salts and to cluster ions of these salts (Table 6). Several intense lines are accompanied by weaker signals which are attributed to less

Fig. 16. Scanning-electron micrograph of a FD emitter after direct impact of a natural aerosol from the top. Single aerosol particles are seen to be caught in the branched structure of the carbonaceous microneedles[59)]

aboundant isotopes. Five spectral lines are too weak to be precisely measured and identified. They cannot be attributed to inorganic components and are thought to result from traces of organic material in the aerosol which is pyrolyzed at higher temperatures.

The inspection of Table 6 shows that Na^+, K^+, NH_4^+ and a trace of Rb^+ are present as cations in the aerosol. Rubidium is detected as a natural trace element in potassium salts. The densitometer readings provide approximate information on the relative abundances, although ammonium compounds may be underestimated due to some evaporation of their neutral components, especially at higher temperatures. The only anions detected in the aerosol are NO_3^-, SO_4^{2-}, HSO_4^- and Cl^-. The predominance of the nitrate ion is noteworthy, stressing the importance of aerosols as a sink for NO_2 in the atmosphere. NO_2 has been shown to react rapidly with NaCl to form $NaNO_3$ and NOCl as an intermediate of presumably short lifetime in the atmosphere. The product $NaNO_3$ is most abundantly observed in the aerosol, besides some unreacted NaCl.

It is evident from these results that FDMS using photographic detection has a considerable advantage over most other analytical techniques of giving direct information on metal cations and *intact* inorganic salts present in the aerosol. The most abundant ions are "salt ions", e.g. single cations, or molecules M and clusters of n molecules, bearing an additional cation, of the general formula ($n \times M$ + cation). In addition, airborne, organic material of low volatility can also be analyzed by this technique.

Table 6. Field desorption analysis of directly sampled aerosols[59]. FD-mass spectrum of a natural aerosol, collected in Bonn, December 1974. The identified ions are arranged in groups of similar chemical nature, in the order of decreasing densitometer readings (w = weak; vw = very weak; S = saturation; i = isotopic ion)

Formula of ion	Densitometer reading	Accurate mass
H_2O^+	2.8	18.011
$(NH_4)_2SO_4H^+$	3.5	133.028
i	vw	135.024
$NH_4HSO_4H^+$	2.8	116.002
NH_4^+	2.0	18.034
Na^+	S	22.990
$NaCl\ Na^+$	5.5	80.948
i	3.8	82.945
$(NaCl)_2Na^+$	w	138.907
$NaNO_3Na^+$	S	107.967
i	3	108.946
i	3	109.972
$Na_2(NO_3)_2Na^+$	5	192.972
i	vw	193.942
i	vw	194.949
$Na_3(NO_3)Na^+$	3	277.923
$Na_4(NO_3)_4Na^+$	vw	362.900
$Na_2ClNO_3Na^+$	3.5	165.926
i	2	167.923
$Na_3Cl(NO_3)_2Na^+$	1	250.904
$Na_2SO_4Na^+$	2.2	164.921
$Na_2SO_4(Na^+)_2$	1.5	2×93.955
$Na_3SO_4NO_3Na^+$	2	249.899
$Na_3SO_4NO_3(Na^+)_2$	1.5	2×136.444
K^+	S	38.963
i	S	40.962
KNO_3K^+	2.5	139.915
i	vw	141.913
$NaNO_3K^+$	5	123.941
i	3	125.939
$Na_2(NO_3)_2K^+$	3	208.919
i	vw	210.917
$Na_3(NO_3)_3K^+$	vw	293.897
$NaK(NO_3)_2K^+$	vw	224.893
$NaClK^+$	w	84.912
Rb^+	w	96.922

In a first pilot study analyzing 1 μl human blood which was applied directly to the FD emitter sodium, potassium, calcium, rubidium and cesium were found in one analytical run[51]. Thus, it could be expected that FDMS using photographic detection should also be applicable to biological or medical samples without pretreatment.

Clearly, the advantages of photoplate registration for metal analysis include: high mass resolution, which facilitates identification; simultaneous and integrating recording of all FD ions over a wide mass range (e.g. from m/z 18 to m/z 600) which allows multi-element analysis and reliable, long-time, and space-saving storage of the obtained data. Quantitative results, however, are somewhat tedious and expensive to achieve.

Again, an external standard is used for calibration, but the corresponding ion response curve of the photographic emulsion can only be established by graded exposition of different tracks of the photoplate. Therefore, graduated amounts of the metal-containing standard have to be applied to the emitter and desorbed. The latent image generated by the metal cations is developed, similar to a photographic film, and the blackening is measured step by step with a densitometer. When the densitometer readings are plotted versus the number of ions a logarithmic scale is obtained (blackening function) which serves as a calibration curve for quantitative determinations.

The dynamic range of photographic detection is smaller in comparison with electric registration. However, the values for precision and accuracy found are more suitable than those noted for single ion monitoring (p. 27) and are comparable to results from spark source ionization. If a comparator, a data system and the suitable software were available the time consumption for the assay could be reduced drastically, but of course this means a considerable investment in instrumentation.

Summarizing the results of FDMS using external standards, electrical or photographic recording, it becomes clear that a shorter analysis time, an easier handling and a higher quality in the trace analysis of metals would be desirable. Therefore, two essential improvements have been introduced:

a) the time averaging technique by a multichannel analyzer (mca);

b) the stable isotope dilution technique for internal standards.

4.3.6.4 Determination of Lithium by FD Spectra Accumulation

As in the case of organic ions[64] the quantitative determination of metal cations is improved by integrating electrical recording in order to avoid disturbing influences caused by the fluctuations of the FD ion currents.

In order to put the quantitative trace analysis of metals on a firm methodological footing, a magnetic mass spectrometer was coupled with a multichannel analyzer. Using this approach the first FD determinations of the distribution of the lithium isotopes ^{6}Li and ^{7}Li (natural abundance 7.5% and 92.5%, respectively[65]) in some commercial lithium salts and in environmental sample were performed[66]. Measurements were carried out with a double focusing mass spectrometer (Varian MAT 731) using a mono FD ion source of our own construction and indirect heating of the FD emitter by a tunable argon laser (Spectra Physics, Model 166). The ion currents were recorded electrically and accumulated by a multichannel analyzer (C-1024, Varian), the magnetic scan of the spectrometer controlling the multichannel analyzer externally during accumulation.

The determination of the isotopic distribution of the metals presented in this contribution is a facile analytical procedure because

a) the ion currents are powerful;

b) the emitter quality plays only a subordinate role;

c) the coupling of the mass spectrometer and the multichannel analyzer can be quickly modified to accommodate a variety of analytical problems;

d) the averaging of several hundred scans requires only 10 to 30 min. An experimental accuracy of serveral tenths of a percent is achieved by accumulation of several hundred scans.

For instance, the isotopic distribution of a ^{6}Li-enriched lithium fluoride (Rohstoff Einfuhr GmbH, Düsseldorf) was determined to be 91.7% ^{6}Li and 8.3% ^{7}Li. Over 300 scans were averaged in the assay and this procedure reduced the mean experimental error to 0.3% since the LiF sample showed such a high degree of enrichment of ^{6}Li that it was suitable as internal standard for the quantitative determination of lithium. In a sample of Rhine water taken at the bank of the river, Kilometer 625 (August 25, 1977), approximately the mean natural distribution was found. The knowledge of these two distributions permits the quantitative determination of the lithium content of Rhine water by the method of isotopic dilution. Evalution of the experimental data (36.0 pg of the Li standard were added) gave a value of 8.3 μg Li/l for the water sample. The total error of this determination did not exceed 5%.

These results clearly demonstrate that FDMS, in conjunction with a multichannel analyzer, represents a powerful method for the trace analysis of metals. Obviously, the unavoidable statistical fluctuations in the FD ion currents have lost their detrimental effect on the FD assay and the signal-to-noise ratio of the signals in question has been improved considerably by spectra accumulation. In addition, it can be expected that by use of the isotope dilution technique quantitative determinations of high sensitivity and accuracy can be accomplished without prior treatment of the original biological or environmental sample.

4.3.6.5 Trace and Ultratrace Analysis of Lithium

In order to exploit the utility of FDMS as a direct (no pretreatment) analytical technique for the determination of traces (ppm range) of lithium in mineral water and ultratraces (ppb range) in tap water, wine and high-purity solvents[67], the signals are again accumulated by a multichannel analyzer (Varian CAT-1024). This device is triggered by the cyclic magnetic scan of the mass spectrometer (for a detailed description of this instrumental set-up see Ref.[68]. For stable isotope dilution the same highly ^{6}Li-enriched lithium fluoride is used as mentioned above[66]. The solid is dissolved in doubly distilled, demineralized water for preparing the standard solutions. The minute lithium content of this solvent (0.55 μg/l) is determined prior to the FD assay and considered in the calculation of the results described in Table 7.

High *precision* (2–7 %) is achieved by accumulation over 100 scans. Relative to the sensitivity of FDMS, the observed concentrations of lithium in mineral water are extremely high. The ion currents from 1-μl samples can be measured over several hours. Lithium at such levels can be determined by methods such as atomic absorption spectrophotometry (AAS) with approximately the same precision. Therefore, a comparison between the results of mineral water analyses by FDMS and AAS, gives evidence for the *accuracy* of both techniques (Table 7).

Since the solutions studied contain only minor concentrations of accompanying substances, it is possible to determine lithium from microlitre samples at levels of 10^{-7} to 10^{-4} g/l without any pretreatment. The time required for one analysis is about 20 to 30 min. In general, it is found that 1 pg of lithium present on the emitter is sufficient for a determination. This means that lithium concentrations as low as 50 ng/l can be determined in microliter samples using stable isotope dilution and FDMS.

In view of the influence of a complex matrix on the FD determination, e.g. in physiological fluids and tissues, and the importance of the use of lithium in medicine a further step was to exploit the utility of FDMS in combination with signal accumulation and stable isotope dilution (internal standard) in this field. Lithium salts are used in the chemotherapy of manic-depressive psychoses[69]. The transport phenomena of lithium through cell membranes[70] and the mode of therapeutic action in elevated lithium levels[71] are areas of biomedical research which are of special interest for the therapy of certain affective disorders. Concerning the accurate determination of very small lithium concentrations in the range of the normal physiological level, there is a special need for a reliable analytical technique, in particular, if only microliters of the sample are available.

Table 7. Trace- and ultratrace-analysis of lithium by FDMS[67]. All samples are applied to the emitter by the syringe technique without pretreatment. For one analysis 1 μl of mineral water and about 3 μl of the other samples are needed

a) Determination of lithium in three mineral waters and in a tap water sample. Comparison of the results with those obtained by atomic absorption spectrophotometry (AAS)

Sample	Concentration of Li (ng/ml) FD-MS	Standard error (%) AAS
Water 1	188 ± 7%	180 ± 5–10%
2	188 ± 4%	190 ± 10%
3	722 ± 3%	720 ± 8–10%
4	3.8 ± 6%	—

b) Determination of lithium in high purity solvents by FDMS

Sample	Concentration of Li (pg/ml)	Standard error (%)
Solvent 1	519	4
2	422	6
3	541	6

c) Determination of lithium in tour wines from different regions and of different quality by FDMS

Sample	Concentration of Li (ng/ml)	Standard error (%)
Wine 1	13.9	4
2	15.5	5
3	18.9	9
4	55.0	4

Water 1: Gerolsteiner Stern Heilwasser, Dolomitquelle, Gerolsteiner Sprudel GmbH;
Water 2: Gerolsteiner Stern Tafelwasser, Gerolsteiner Sprudel GmbH;
Water 3: Heilwasser Vulkania, Nürburg Quelle, H. Kreuter & Co;
Water 4: Tap water of the Institute of Physical Chemistry, Bonn;
Wine 1: Mehringer Zellerberg, Moselwein 1975, APNr. 17050 0533875;
Wine 2: Enclave des Papes 72, Côte du Rhône, French red wine;
Wine 3: Schloßböckelheimer Kupfergrube, Riesling 1974, APNr. 4750053/01/74;
Wine 4: Scharzhofberger feinste Auslese, Eiswein 1970;
Solvent 1: Methanol, "Distilled in glass", Burdick & Jackson Laboratories, Inc., 1953 South Harvey Street, Muskegon, Michigan 49442;
Solvent 2: Propan-2-ol, "Distilled in glass", Burdick & Jackson Laboratories, Inc.;
Solvent 3: Ethanol, 95%, for spectroscopy, Merck, Darmstadt, FRG.

Table 8. Lithium levels determined in physiological fluids by FDMS using stable isotopes as internal standards[72]

a) Plasma Li (m mol/l)	Saliva Li (m mol/l)	Urine Li (m mol/l)
0.61 ± 0.013	1.81 ± 0.09	14.43 ± 0.46

b) Volunteer No.	Plasma Li (μmol/l)	Saliva Li (μmol/l)	Urine Li (μmol/l)
1	2.43 ± 0.14	1.24 ± 0.13	4.69 ± 0.22
2	1.44 ± 0.07	0.84 ± 0.08	4.29 ± 0.14
3	1.30 ± 0.11	1.30 ± 0.03	7.54 ± 0.17
4	0.88 ± 0.03	2.79 ± 0.10	6.70 ± 0.16
5	2.01 ± 0.09	2.41 ± 0.13	15.74 ± 0.76

a) Lithium concentration in body fluids sampled from a patient under lithium therapy. Each determination represents the mean of three measurements.
b) Normal lithium levels in body fluids of five healthy volunteers.

The results of FDMS as a microanalytical method for the determination of the trace element lithium in human body fluids, such as plasma, saliva and urine are shown in Table 8.

These data demonstrate that lithium can be determined from human body fluids at the normal level of some μmol l^{-1} with a precision between 2 and 10% using only microliter amounts of sample. Since there is no possibility for interference from organic ions in the mass region where the lithium ions are detected, FDMS is a highly specific analytical procedure. Finally, the accumulation of the signals by means of a multichannel analyzer compensates for the fluctuations of the FD ion currents and thus provides quantitative data of high precision even in the analysis of complex biological samples. Thus, it has become clear that, at least in lithium determinations, the disturbing influence of the matrix is neglegible.

Summarizing the results obtained by FDMS for the trace analysis of lithium, the following principal statements can be made: The routine application of FDMS to environmental and medical samples appears feasible. As mentioned above the method can be utilized for the determination of lithium in body fluids at therapeutic levels (ppm region) as well as at the normal level (ppb region). The use of stable isotope-enriched internal standards, together with the outstanding sensitivity of field desorption for alkali metal cations and the high specificity of mass spectrometry, allows a quantitative determination of lithium in microliter amounts of body fluids, such as plasma, saliva and urine. The assay permits a determination of lithium even at ultratrace concentrations where routine spectroscopic procedures cannot be applied. The analysis of plasma requires a simple protein precipitation whereas saliva and urine can be analyzed without *pretreatment*. The *precision* of the data obtained ranges from 2–10%. At concentration levels where other analytical methods can be employed for comparison, the *accuracy* of the FD results is confirmed (see e.g. Ref.[73]). The time consumption for one analysis in routine work is about 20–30 min.

4.3.6.6 Determination of Thallium in Biological Samples by FDMS

Once the capacity of quantitative FD for alkali and alkaline earth cations was established the investigations were expanded to a wide variety of metals. One focal point in this analytical expansion of the method represents the toxic, heavy metal thallium. This metal exerts a pronounced toxic effect on mammals. Poisonings by thallium ions normally proceed very slowly; they are accompanied by loss of hair, severe polyneuritic symptoms and tachycardia, and can culminate in paralysis of the central nervous system. Atomic absorption is a common spectroscopic method for the determination of thallium concentrations down to a few ppm[74]. The direct determination of thallium from human urine reveals a limit of detection of approximately 30 ppb, whereas direct estimation from plasma and brain tissue is not successful without pretreatment.

Since thallium naturally occurs as a mixture of two stable isotopes and since isotopically enriched thallium is commercially available, stable isotope dilution appears to be the method of choice for a mass spectrometric quantitation.

In the determination of thallium by the isotope dilution technique three analyses are necessary.

a) The determination of the thallium isotopic abundances of the samples shows that there is no variation in the normal isotope ratio, within the standard deviation;
b) the isotopic abundances of the standards are calculated from an average of 8 measurements each obtained by accumulation of about 100 scans;
c) determination of the mixtures: two independent dilutions are prepared and both analyzed twice. Fig. 17 shows the isotopic abundances of naturally occuring thallium standard, and of brain tissue measured by this procedure.

For a forensic study by FDMS a mouse is fed a portion containing thallium chloride (80 mg)[75]. After the animal's death (5 h after application) the brain is removed (0.20 g), homogenized with doubly distilled water (~1 ml), and then further diluted to give a suspension (2.0 ml). For the preparation of the solution of the internal standard, isotopically enriched elemental thallium (Rohstoff Einfuhr GmbH und Handelsgesellschaft Ost, Düsseldorf, FRG) is dissolved in nitric acid (0.1 M) to give a thallium concentration of 1 mmol/l. The samples are applied by the syringe technique and the sample solution (2 μl) is used for one analysis on the average. The FD ion currents are recorded electrically as described above.

Evaluation of the data from FDMS reveals a thallium concentration in the mouse brain of 4.0 $\pm$ 0.3 mmol/kg fresh weight, which results in 0.8 $\pm$ 0.06 μmol thallium in the complete brain. Thus, only 0.3% of the total amount of thallium applied can be determined in the brain tissue.

The slow time scale of thallium poisonings and the relatively low amount of thallium found in this study indicate that the toxic metal is transported slowly into the brain tissue.

Although the desorption of thallium occurs at relatively low emitter heating currents (20–25 mA) no interference from organic ions can be observed in the investigation of the brain tissue homogenizate. For a FD mass spectrometric investigation, however, the concentration of about 90 mg/l thallium is high as compared to sample amounts usually required for an alkali metal determination. In order to as-

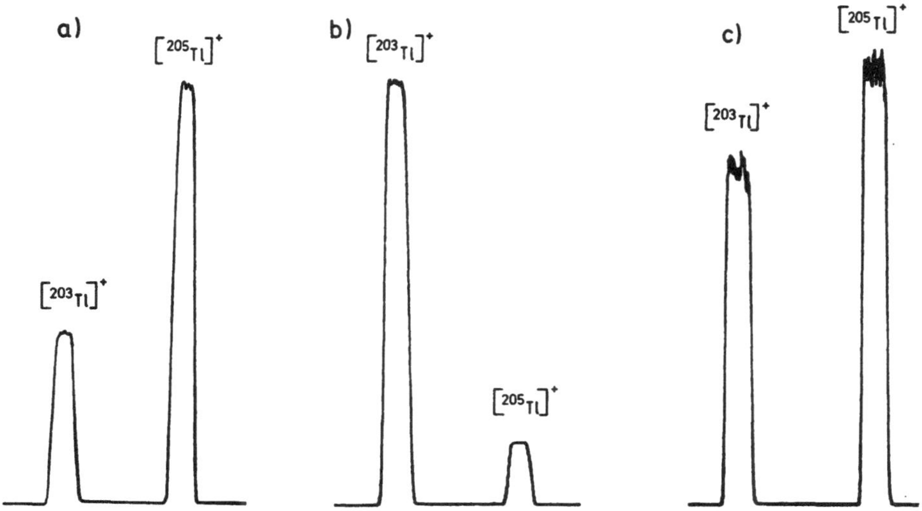

Fig. 17. Isotopic abundances of thallium recorded electrically by FDMS and signal accumulation in a multichannel analyzer. For each measurement 50 cyclic magnetic scans are performed. **a** natural abundance of thallium, theor.: m/z 203 = 29.5%, m/z 205 = 70.5%[87]; found: m/z 203 = 29.2%, m/z 205 = 70.8%, standard deviation ± 0.18, mean error = 0.08; **b** stable isotope-enriched internal standard, measurement certificate of the Russian manufacturer (supplied by Rohstoff Einfuhr GmbH, Düsseldorf, FRG.): isotope ^{203}Tl = 87.0%, isotope ^{205}Tl = 13.0%, found: m/z 203 = 87.7%, m/z 205 = 12.3%, standard deviation ± 0.46, mean error = 0.20; **c** quantitative determination of thallium traces in brain tissues. Found: m/z 203 = 43.01%, m/z 205 = 56.99%, standard deviation ± 1.28, mean error = 0.57

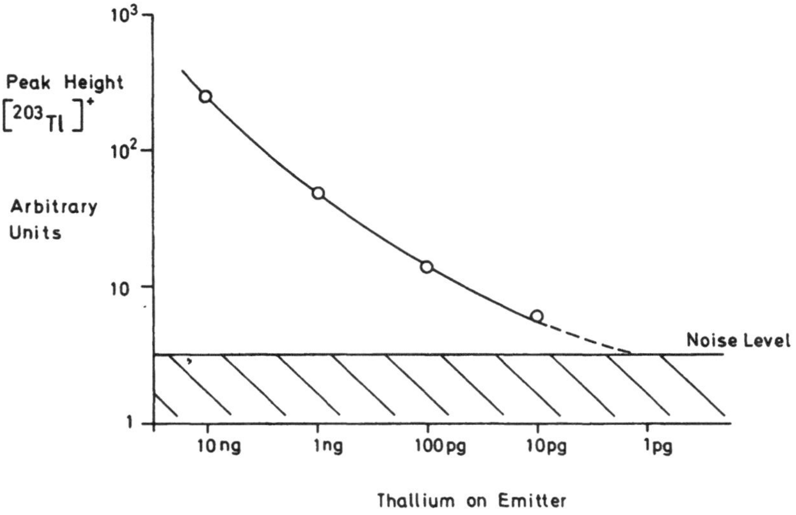

Fig. 18. Accumulated peak heights of the thallium isotope at m/z 203 (29.5% natural abundance) as a function of the total sample amount of thallium desorbed in one FD analysis[75]

certain the detection limit of FDMS for thallium, sample amounts between 10 ng and 10 pg thallium dissolved in distilled water have been applied to the FD emitter and completely desorbed. During the whole desorption the FD ion currents in the mass region m/z 200 — m/z 208 are accumulated by the use of the multichannel analyzer (Fig. 18).

About 10 pg thallium can be recorded at a signal-to-noise ratio of 3:1 which corresponds to approximately 50 fmol. Although these values are obtained from solutions of the heavy metal in distilled water and a considerably reduced sensitivity of the method is to be expected from biological samples, these pilot studies have prompted highly interesting pharmacological and pharmacokinetic investigations.

4.3.6.7 Quantitative Trace Analysis of Thallium in Biological Materials

The recent discovery of high-level thallium pollution in the environment has focused attention on the teratogenicity (fetus malformation). For detailed investigations in this field a method is required which enables the quantitative detection of thallium in extremely small tissue samples (embryos, placenta tissues etc.) thus permitting to establish a correlation between measured values and teratological findings. Regarding the pharmacokinetics of thallium in a test animal (mouse) the first results obtained by FDMS have been reported[76)].

In order to determine the distribution of thallium with time in an organism we administered orally 160 mg of thallium per kg body weight to mice. After fixed periods of time the acutely poisoned mice were killed and the thallium concentrations in the heart, liver, kidney and brain were determined by FDMS (Fig. 19).

According to the results it would appear that the brain possesses an inbuilt barrier for thallium, which however, breaks down as a function of dosage after loss of the excretory function of the kidney (see curves a and b in Fig. 19). In constrast, in the remaining organs a short-term enrichment of thallium takes place, followed by a washing-out process. High concentrations are again observed in the kidney[77)] only after ca. 12 h. After 24 h an increased concentration of about the same order of magnitude is found in all organs.

For the teratological investigations pregnant mice were given doses of 8 mg Tl/kg body weight. At this dosage 50% of the embryos were found to have serious malformations of the skeleton (Fig. 20).

The teratogenic dose 50% was lower than the corresponding lethal dose 50% by a factor of approximately 40. As an example, one mother proved to have 5.1×10^{-5} mol/l of thallium in the kidney, 1.5×10^{-6} mol/l in the brain, and 2.6×10^{-5} mol/l in the uterus together with the embryos. These values were found one hour after administration of the thallium. Furthermore, experiments with this line of test animals revealed that even one thousandth part of the lethal dose 50% still gave 12.5% of fetal malformations. If this were transformed to humans it would mean that an oral dosage of ca. 10 microgram of thallium (per kg body weight) at the time of formation of the extremities and organs in the embryo would result in a significant enhancement of malformations.

Consecutively, a quantitative measurement of the time dependent thallium distribution in organs of mice by FDMS[78,90)] was performed. The results of this recent investigation can be summarized as follows. The time dependent distribution of the

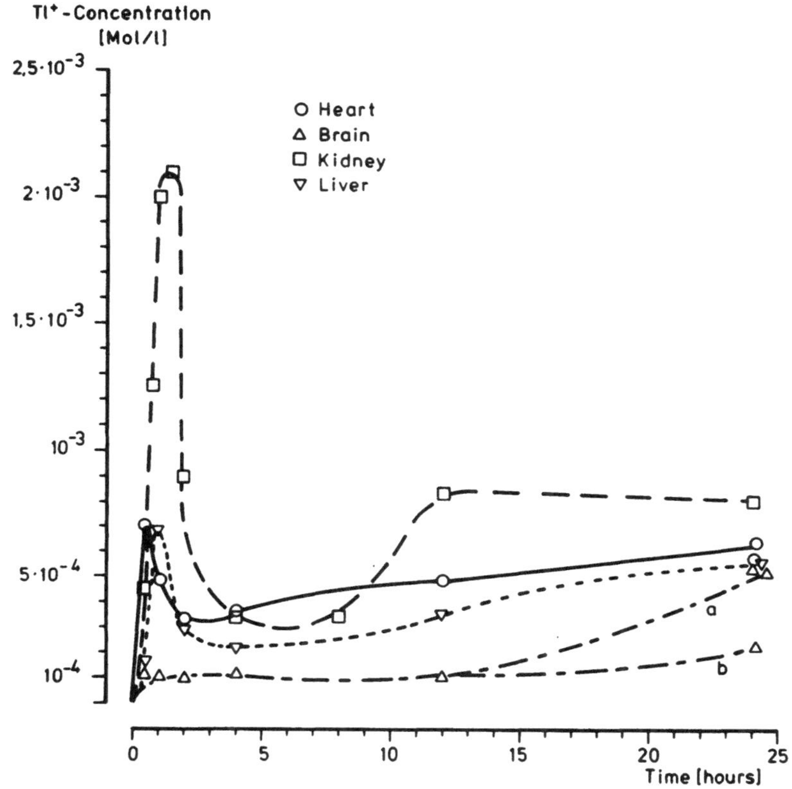

Fig. 19. Distribution of thallium with time in the heart ○, liver ▽, kidney □, and brain △ of mice after administration of 160 mg Tl/kg body weight. Curves **a** and **b** for the brain show the variation in increase of thallium concentrations according to doses of 80 and 130 mg/kg of the toxic heavy metal[76])

toxic heavy metal thallium in mouse organs was determined after feeding 80, 130 and 160 mg/kg of thallium. Quantitative measurements were performed by FDMS using stable-isotope dilution. No pretreatment of the tissue samples, other than homogenizing and centrifugation, was necessary. The precision of the data obtained was about $\pm 10\%$. The main results are:

a) Heart, liver, kidney and stomach show an organ specific initial uptake of thallium during the first 2–3 h;
b) this uptake is followed by a period of wash-out to relatively low thallium levels;
c) brain thallium uptake is comparatively low and constant during the first 12 h;
d) in the terminal stage (24 h) all organs, i.e. including the brain, contain increased thallium levels of the same order of magnitude.

4.3.6.8 Laser-Assisted Field Desorption Mass Spectrometry

Since the introduction of FD as new ionization technique in mass spectrometry, a number of methodological and technical improvements have been accomplished.

Fig. 20. Skeletons of mice embryos. Left: normally developed embryo; center and right: damage after a single dose of 8 mg Tl/kg body weight to the mother animal[76]

The focal points in this previous work have been an approach to the understanding of the basic principles of field ionization and field desorption processes, developments in the production and detection of FD ions and the utilization of the analytical capacity of the technique.

In order to supply the required thermal energy for the desorption of metal cations which desorb at temperatures higher than the alkali metal ions and to extend the technique to the area of high temperature chemistry, indirect heating of the FD emitter using a laser has been developed[79]. From both theoretical and practical considerations, one would expect laser heating to offer advantages over direct heating by: increasing the ionization efficiency and thus the sensitivity; facilitating high-resolution FD measurements; and giving access to very high emitter temperatures.

The experiments were carried out with a Varian MAT 731 double focusing mass spectrometer. The combined EI/FI/FD source commercially available from Varian and a home-made source for FD only were used. The mono FD source is superior in two respects: first, the adjustment of the FD emitter is fast and easily performed by means of the micromanipulator and second, the source is much less sensitive to contaminations because of its simple and open construction. The 514 nm line of a tunable argon ion laser, Spectra Physics model 166, was used for indirect heating of the emitter. Fig. 21 shows the experimental set-up.

A lens of 20 cm focal length is used to focus the laser beam on the emitter. With this the original laser beam diameter of 1.5 mm can be condensed to produce a hot

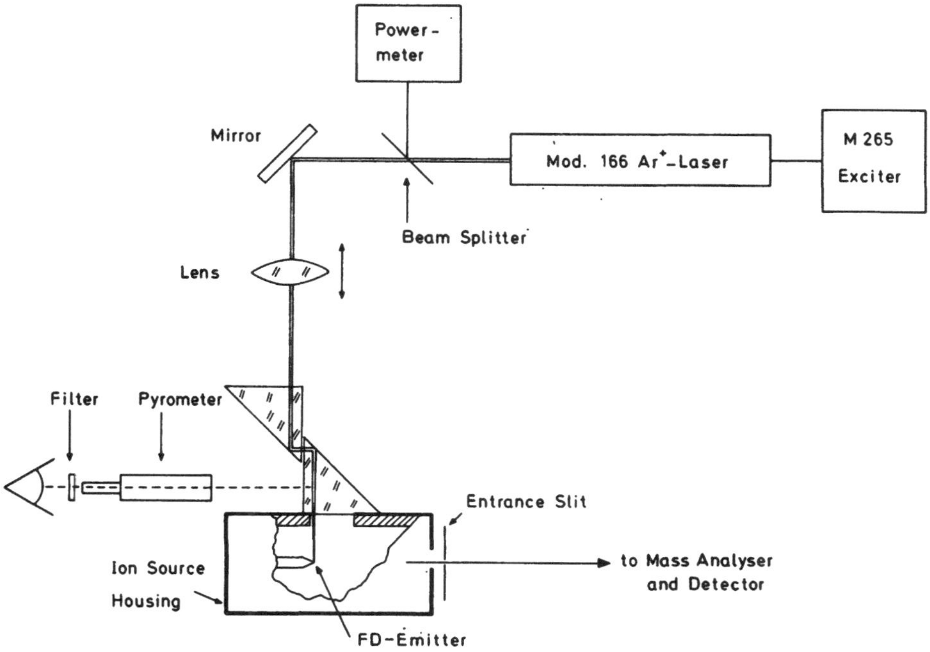

Fig. 21. Set-up of a mass spectrometer equipped with combined electron impact/FD ion source and laser for indirect heating of the FD emitter and the sample. The laser beam passes through a quartz window and strikes the emitter wire perpendicular to the direction of the ion beam produced. Simultaneously, observation of the emitter and measurement of the emitter temperature by a pyrometer are possible[84)]

spot 16 μm in diameter. However, because the emitter diameter is about 80 μm (corresponding to an average length of the carbon microneedles of 30–40 μm) the beam is deliberately defocused to generate a hot spot of the same size as the activated wire. With this arrangement a power density of 35 kW cm^{-2} on the FD emitter is obtained from a 1 W laser line. The laser power is measured with a pyroelectric power meter, type PR 200, from the Molectron Corp. For the relatively low temperatures required for the detection of organic ions (e.g. up to about 300 °C) the argon ion laser is adjusted to provide power ranging continuously from 1 to 200 mW. For high temperatures, however, the laser has to be adjusted optimally to make up to 2.2 W available at 514 nm. A mirror system movable in two dimensions (Fig. 21) enables any desired point of the emitter to be heated.

Indirect laser heating offers the advantage of producing high emitter temperatures without significant reduction of the emitter lifetime. This is because only the central part of the wire is heated and only the emitter surface, not the tungsten core of the wire, suffers the highest temperatures. In contrast, direct heating of emitters to temperatures above 1200 °C results in considerably shortened lifetimes, due to the fact that the unactivated sections of the emitter wire, having less surface area, are unable to dissipate the thermal energy sufficiently rapidly. Thus, laser heating offers a particular advantage in the analysis of metal cations that require higher emitter temperatures than alkali metal ions.

Among these are the alkaline earth metals and, for instance, such elements as Ba[79], Cd[80] and Zn. Fig. 22 shows the isotopic distribution of cadmium using the $[Cd]^+$ ion generated by laser-assisted FDMS. It has been found that integration of the order of 100 cyclic scans permits the determination of isotopic distributions of metals by FDMS up to a few tenths of a percent precision[2], which is comparable with that observed in the investigations of organic compounds[64,81,82].

Similar results of the investigation of isotope abundance ratios of Cu, Sn, Ag, Te, Cd and Sb have also been obtained using Si wiskers (instead of carbon micro-needles) as FD ion source[83]. However, as only single mass sweeps have been recorded the obtained accuracy is only a few percent.

In continuation of our efforts to analyze metals by laser-assisted FD a great number of metals, inorganic metal salts and metalorganic compounds have been

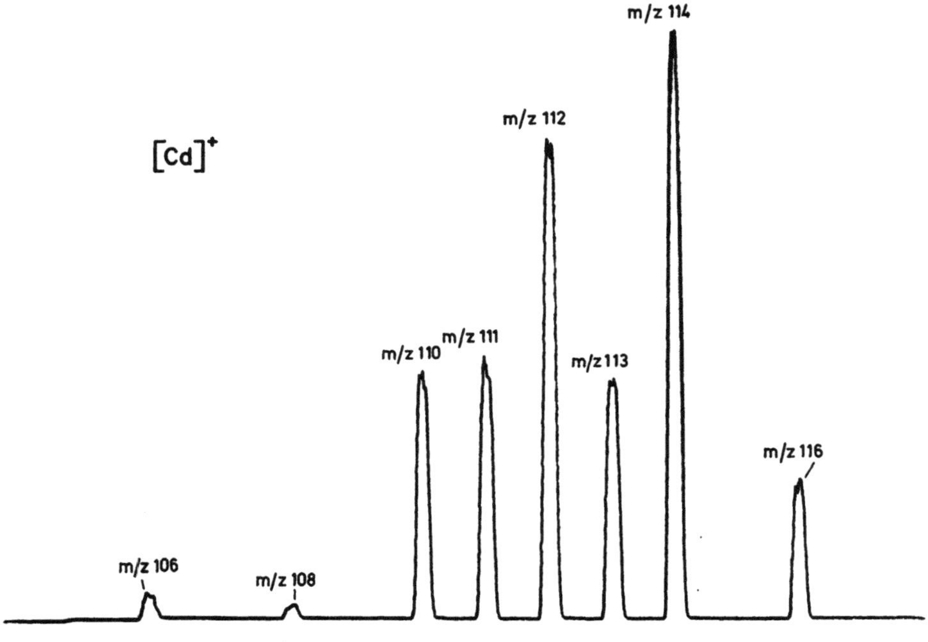

Fig. 22. Determination of the natural abundances of the eight stable cadmium isotopes by FDMS under laser-assisted desorption. The theoretical values are[87]: m/z 106 = 1.22% (found values in brackets, 1.2%), m/z 108 = 0.88% (0.86%), m/z 110 = 12.4% (12.4%), m/z 111 = 12.8% (12.8%), m/z 112 = 24.1% (24.2%), m/z 113 = 12.3% (12.1%), m/z 114 = 28.9% (29.1%) and m/z 116 = 7.6% (7.2%).
The $[Cd]^+$ ion is released from cadmium chloride and 28 scans are accumulated in a multichannel analyzer. Recently this toxic metal has also been determined from a biological matrix[86].

[2] Previously, it has been demonstrated that by use of a double detector and ion counting optimal precision and sensitivity in the quantitative determination of isotopic distributions can be achieved[88].

Table 9. Laser-assisted field desorption mass spectrometry of metals and alloys[85]

Metal	Metal cation (Intensity)	Intensity of metal impurities	e.h.c. (mA)	Laser (W)	Melting point (°C)	Emitter temperature (°C)
W	0.01	$[Rb]^+$ 300	70	5	3410	2250
Sb	0.3		42–45	—	630	700*
Fe	300		70	2	1535	
Hf 99%	500	$[Ba]^+$ 3000	70	4.5	2150	2200
Hf 95%	1000	$[Ba]^+$ 300; $[HfO]^+$ 0.1	70	4.4	2150	2200
Zn	24000		35	—	420	500*
Cu	30000		70	—	1083	1100
Mn	50000	$[Fe]^+$ 1000	70	0.4	1244	1260
Sn	100000		70	0.1	232	950
Ti	200000		70	1.2	1675	1840
Zr	400000		45	2.5	1852	1890
Ag	1000000		70	—	962	950*
Al	3000000		50	—	660	680*
Alloy	**Intensities of metal cations**					
Cr80/Al20	$[Cr]^+$ 100000; $[Al]^+$ 10000		70	0.2		1150
Cu70/Zn30	$[Cu]^+$ 50000; $[Zn]^+$ 2000		70	—		900
Fe71/Cr18/Ni8/Mo3	$[Fe]^+$ 10000; $[Cr]^+$ 20000 $[Ni]^+$ 100000; $[Mo]^+$ 0.01		70	0.3		1160

* The emitter temperatures were measured by a pyrometer or taken from a calibration curve[85].

studied. Here, it has become obvious that many high-melting metals do not yield any FD spectra using conventional, direct emitter heating but do so by laser assistance.

As shown in Table 9 metal powders with a particle size between 5 μm and 15 μm of tungsten, antimony, iron, hafnium (two qualities), zinc, copper, manganese, tin, titanium, zirconium, silver and aluminium can be analyzed by laser-assisted FDMS[84]. The intensities of the ion currents of the singly charged metal atoms increase from top to bottom. Whereas by direct heating of the 10 μm FD wire emitter with heating currents between 110 and 130 mA, corresponding to temperatures of approximately 1400 °C, the emitters are destroyed[85], laser heating allows temperatures up to 2300 °C. Thus, a new range in the application of FD in high temperature investigations is opened up. It is particularly noteworthy that the technique can be used for the identification of trace impurities in metal powders as well as for the qualitative and (if a calibration curve can be established) quantitative determination of the composition of alloys. From the comparison between the observed temperature of the emitter (and sample) at the outset of an *intense* ion current for the singly charged metal cations and the melting point of the metal, it can be derived that desorption occurs *after* melting of the metallic sample. In considering this point it is obvious why no cations are found for tungsten and molybdenum.

Table 10. Laser-assisted field desorption mass spectrometry of metalorganic and inorganic compounds[89)]

Compound	Metal cation (intensity)		Abundant FD ions (m/z)	e.h.c. (mA) + Laser (W)
BeO	$[Be]^+$	0.1	Be(9)	70 + 2
$MgCl_2$	$[Mg]^+$	3000	Mg(24); $MgCl_2$(94)	70 + 2
$BaTiO_3$	$[Ti]^+$	200000	^{138}Ba(138); ^{48}Ti(48)	70 + 0.6
$K_2Cr_2O_7$	$[Cr]^+$	3000	$K_3{}^{52}Cr_2O_7$(333); K_2Cl(113); $K_5{}^{52}Cr_4O_{14}$(627)	70 + 4
$C_{10}H_{14}FeO_{14}$	$[Fe]^+$	3000	^{56}Fe(56); $C_{10}H_{14}{}^{56}FeO_4$(254)	70 + 2
$Br_3Co(C_6H_5PF_2)_3$	$[Co]^+$	3000	^{138}Ba(138); CoBr(138); $Br_3Co(C_6H_5PF_2)_3$(734)	70 + 2
$CoCl_2$	$[Co]^+$	30	^{138}Ba(138); $CoCl_2$(129); Co(59)	70 + 2
$(C_5H_5)_2Ni$	$[Ni]^+$	3000	Ni(58)	70 + 5
$ZnSO_4$	$[Zn]^+$	30	Zn(64)	70 + 2
$SrTiO_3$	$[Sr]^+$	12000	^{88}Sr(88)	70 + 0.06
YCl_3	$[Y]^+$	300000	Y_2Cl_5(353); Y_3Cl_8(547); YCl_2(159); YCl_3(194)	70 + 2
Ag_2SO_4	$[Ag]^+$	300000	Ag_2Cl(249); ^{107}Ag(107); AgNaCl(165); Na_2Cl(81)	42 + 0
$CdCO_3$	$[Cd]^+$	6000	$^{114}CdCO_3$(174)	70 + 0
$BaTiO_3$	$[Ba]^+$	400000	^{138}Ba(138)	70 + 0.3
$HgCl_2$	$[Hg]^+$	—	$^{202}HgCl_2$(272)	0 + 0
C_5H_5Tl	$[Tl]^+$	100000	^{205}Tl(205)	30 + 0
$PbSO_4$	$[Pb]^+$	600	^{208}Pb(208)	70 + 1
$(CH_3COO)_2Pb$	$[Pb]^+$	300	^{208}Pb(208)	70 + 0
$UO_2(NO_3)_2$	$[UO_2]^+$	3000	$^{238}UO_2(NO_3)$(332); $(^{238}UO_2)_2(NO_3)_3$(726); $^{238}UO_2$(270)	70 + 1

The metal cations are listed with increasing atomic weight from top to bottom. Their intensities are given in arbitrary units. The abundances of the other FD ions drop from left to right. The emitter heating current (e.h.c.) indicates the applied direct heating; the indirect heating by an argon ion laser is given by the laser power in Watts. The experimental details are described in Ref.[84)].

Together with lanthan and other rare earth metals such as cerium, praseodymium and neodymium, more than 20 metals have been analyzed in inorganic and metal-organic compounds by FDMS[89]. Some results listed in Table 10 demonstrate the wide applicability of laser-assisted FDMS. Molecular ions, cluster ions and fragments can often be generated by indirect heating alone. In contrast, the optimum conditions for the desorption of the metal cations in most cases are met only when additional transfer of thermal energy by the laser is supplied.

In summarizing the results of FDMS in the analysis of metals, the following principal facts emerge. Although the area of metal trace analysis is covered by a number of well-established analytical techniques, such as the mass spectrometric variants described in this chapter but also spectroscopic, electrochemical and radiochemical methods, in a number of cases the use of FDMS has become attractive because of the following characteristics:

a) First, only minute sample amounts of the order of a few microliters are needed and many samples such as physiological fluids or tissue homogenizates can be analyzed without pretreatment;

b) second, in combination with stable-isotope enriched internal standards, the technique exhibits an unmatched reliability since matrix effects are effectively excluded. Thus, with regard to the accuracy of the results the alternative is either no result where no ions are detected or an accurate result if FD ions are detected. The intermediate situation, namely an incorrect result which looks accurate appears much less probable than with other techniques using an external standardization principle;

c) third, the same mass spectrometer with a combined EI/FD ion source can be utilized for an unequalled variety of analytical problems, e.g. identification of thermally labile drug metabolites, trace determinations of biocides, molecular weight determination of natural products, pyrolysis studies of polymers and microorganisms, etc. *and* metal assay *without any modification*. The FD technique offers the option to investigate organic components in the first step and, consecutively, inorganic traces in one and the same sample.

5 Valuation and Prospects

Regarding the ratios of the applied sample amount and the information obtained, mass spectrometry can be considered as one of the most efficient analytical procedures. One of its principal disadvantages, the destruction of the sample, can usually be neglected because only sample amounts between 10^{-6} and 10^{-12} g are consumed. The considerable instrumental effort and labor involved as well as the high demands on patience, ability and technical comprehension of the person who operates the instruments, might be the main arguments against a more rapid expansion of mass spectrometry as a routine procedure for the trace analysis of metals. On the other hand, the sensitivity, reliability and accuracy obtainable by mass spectrometric investigations are characteristics which can be used for the standardization and control of other analytical procedures which, on their part, supply comparable data more quickly and less expensive. Used as a definitive analytical technique in this manner, the outlook for the application of MS in the trace analysis of metals appears very promising and a rapid expansion of this field can be expected in the near future.

6 Acknowledgement

This work was supported by Deutsche Forschungsgemeinschaft (Schu 416/1-3) and Ministerium für Wissenschaft und Forschung des Landes Nordrhein-Westfalen. We are grateful to D. Haaks, University of Wuppertal, for his expert help with the laser experiments and to W. D. Lehmann, University of Hamburg, for his long-standing cooperation in metal analysis by FDMS.

7 References

1. Birkenfeld, H., Haase, G., Zahn, H. (eds.): Massenspektrometrische Isotopenanalyse. Berlin: Deutscher Verlag der Wissenschaften 1962
2. Brunnée, C., Voshage, H. (eds.): Massenspektrometrie. Weinheim: Verlag Chemie 1968
3. Hintenberger, H.: Ann. Rev. Nuc. Sci. *12*, 435 (1962)
4. Ahearn, A. J. (ed.): Trace analysis by mass spectrometry. London: Academic Press 1972
5. Iyengar, G. V., Kollmer, W. E., Bowen, H. J. H. (eds.): The elemental composition of human tissues and body fluids. Weinheim: Verlag Chemie 1978
6. Purves, D. (ed.): Trace element contamination of the environment. Amsterdam: Elsevier 1977
7. Frieberg, L., Nordberg, G. F., Vouk, V. (eds.): Handbook on the toxicology of metals. Amsterdam: Elsevier 1979
8. Ahearn, A. J. (ed.): Analysis of solids. Amsterdam: Elsevier 1966
9. Stefani, R.: Mass spectrometry: a versatile aid to inorganic analysis. In: Advances in mass spectrometry, 7A. Daly, N. R. (ed.). London: Heyden 1978, pp. 729–740
10. Hillenkamp, F., Unsöld, E., Kaufmann, R., Nietsche, R.: Appl. Phys. *8*, 341 (1975)
11. Gray, A. L.: Isotope ratio determination on solutions with a plasma ion source. In: Dynamic mass spectrometry. Price, D., Todd, J. F. J. (eds.). London: Heyden 1978, pp. 106–113
12. Gray, A. L.: Trace analysis of solutions using an atmospheric pressure ion source. In: Dynamic mass spectrometry. Price, D., Todd, J. F. J. (eds.). London: Heyden 1976, pp. 153–162
13. Mattson, W. A., Harrison, W. W.: 23th Annual Conference on Mass Spectrometry and Allied Topics, Houston, 1975
14. Beckey, H. D. (ed.): Principles of field ionisation and field desorption mass spectrometry. Oxford: Pergamon Press 1977
15. Beckey, H. D., Schulten, H.-R.: Angew. Chem. *87*, 425 (1975); Angew. Chem. Int. Ed. *14*, 403 (1975)
16. Lehmann, W. D., Schulten, H.-R.: Chem. unserer Zeit *10*, 147 (1976); *10*, 163 (1976)
17. Bahr, U., Schulten, H.-R.: GIT Fachz. Lab. *12*, 1049 (1978)
18. Beynon, J. H.: Pure Appl. Chem. *50*, 65 (1978)
19. Habfast, K., Aulinger, F.: Massenspektrometrische Apparate. In: Massenspektrometrie. Kienitz, H. (ed.). Weinheim: Verlag Chemie 1968, pp. 29–230
20. Webster, R. K.: Isotope dilution analysis. In: Advances in mass spectrometry. Waldron, J. D. (ed.). Oxford: Pergamon Press 1959, pp. 103–119
21. Lehmann, W. D., Schulten, H.-R.: Angew. Chem. *90*, 233 (1978); Angew. Chem. Int. Ed. *17*, 221 (1978)
22. Inghram, M. G., Chupka, W. A.: Rev. Sci. Instr. *24*, 518 (1953)
23. D'Ans-Lax: Taschenbuch für Chemiker und Physiker, Bd. I, 3. Auflage. Berlin, Heidelberg, New York: Springer 1967
24. Langmuir, I., Kingdon, K. M.: Proc. Roy, Sci. *107*, 61 (1925)
25. Heumann, K. G., Gindner, F., Klöppel, H.: Angew. Chem. *89*, 753 (1977); Heumann, K. G., Kubassek, E., Schwabenbauer, W., Stadler, I.: Fresenius Z. Anal. Chem. *297*, 35 (1979)
26. Heumann, K. G., Klöppel, H., Kubassek, E.: Mikrochim. Acta *1977*, 551

27. Moore, L. J., Machlan, J. A.: Anal. Chem. *44*, 2291 (1972)
28. Wasserburg, G. J., et al.: Rev. Sci. Instr. *40*, 288 (1969)
29. Fenner, N. C., et al.: Int. J. Mass Spectrom. Ion Phys. *14*, 245 (1974)
30. Brunnée, C., et al.: Int. Lab. *1978*, 78
31. Dempster, A. J.: Proc. Phil. Soc. *75*, 755 (1935)
32. Hintenberger, H.: Arch. Eisenhüttenwesen *33*, 355 (1962)
33. Capellen, J., Conzemius, R. J., Svec, H. J.: 13th Annual Conference on Mass Spectrometry and Allied Topics, St. Louis, 1965
34. Brown, R., Jacobs, M. L., Vossen, P. G. T.: 22nd Annual Pittsburgh Conference on Analytical Chemistry and Applied Spectroscopy, 1972
35. Taylor, C. E., Taylor, W. J.: E.P.A. 660-274-01 U.S. Government Research Report, 1976
36. Jacobs, E. H., Sweeney, S. L., Rogowski, A. F.: 27th Annual Pittsburgh Conference on Analytical Chemistry and Applied Spectroscopy, Cleveland, 1976
37. Ball, D. F., Barber, M., Vossen, P. G. T.: Biomed. Mass Spectrom. *1*, 365 (1974)
38. Brown, R., Richardson, W. J., Somerford, H. W.: Amer. Soc. Mass Spectrom. *1967*, 157
39. Fitchett, A. W., Buck, R. P., Mushak, P.: Anal. Chem. *46*, 710 (1974)
40. Radermacher, L., Breske, H. E.: Improvement of analysis in spark-source mass spectrometry without standards by complete use of photoplate information. In: Advances in mass spectrometry, 7A. Daly, N. R. (ed.). London: Heyden 1978, pp. 545–548
41. Charalambous, J. (ed.): Mass spectrometry of metal compounds. London & Boston: Butterworths 1975
42. Litzow, M. R., Spalding, T. R. (eds.): Mass spectrometry of inorganic and organometallic compounds. Amsterdam: Elsevier 1973
43. Benninghoven, A., Wiedmann, L. (eds.): Quantitative Bestimmung der Sekundärausbeute sauerstoffbedeckter Metalle. Opladen: Westdeutscher Verlag 1978
44. Benninghoven, A., Müller, K. H., Plog, C., Schemmer, M., Steffens, P., Surface Sci. *63*, 403 (1977)
45. Aston, F. W. (ed.): Mass spectra and isotope. London: Edward Arnold 1933
46. Colby, B. N., Evans, C. A., Jr.: Anal. Chem. *46*, 1236 (1974)
47. Mattson, W. A., Bentz, B. L., Harrison, W. W.: Anal. Chem. *48*, 489 (1976)
48. Harrison, W. W., Magee, C. W.: Anal. Chem. *46*, 461 (1974)
49. Heinen, H. J., Wechsung, R., Vogt, M., Hillenkamp, F., Kaufmann, R.: Biotech. Umschau *11*, 346 (1978)
50. Beckey, H. D., Schulten, H.-R.: Fresenius Z. Anal. Chem. *273*, 347 (1975)
51. Schulten, H.-R.: Field desorption mass spectrometry and its application in biochemical analysis. In: Methods of biochemical analysis, Vol. 24. Glick, D. (ed.). New York: Wiley Interscience, 1977, pp. 313–448
52. Beckey, H. D., Schulten, H.-R.: Field ionization and field desorption mass spectrometry in analytical chemistry. In: Practical spectroscopy series. Merritt, C., McEwen, C. N. (eds.). New York: Marcel Dekker 1979, pp. 145–264
53. Schulten, H.-R.: Int. J. Mass Spectrom. Ion Phys. *32*, 97 (1979) and references cited therein
54. Schulten, H.-R., Beckey, H. D.: Org. Mass Spectrom. *6*, 885 (1972)
55. Schulten, H.-R., Röllgen, F. W.: Org. Mass Spectrom. *10*, 49 (1975)
56. Schiebel, H. M., Schulten, H.-R.: Naturwissenschaften *65*, 223 (1978)
57. Lehmann, W. D., Schulten, H.-R.: Anal. Chem. *49*, 1744 (1977)
58. Schulten, H.-R., Schurath, U.: J. Phys. Chem. *79*, 51 (1975)
59. Schulten, H.-R., Schurath, U.: Atmos. Environ. *9*, 1107 (1975)
60. Schulten, H.-R., Beckey, H. D.: Org. Mass Spectrom. *7*, 861 (1973)
61. Bahr, U., et al.: Clin. Chim. Acta *103*, 183 (1980)
62. Schulten, H.-R., Ziskoven, R., Lehmann, W. D.: Z. Naturforsch. *33c*, 178 (1978)
63. Isenberg, G.: Pflügers Arch. *365*, 99 (1976)
64. Lehmann, W. D., Schulten, H.-R., Schiebel, H. M.: Fresenius Z. Anal. Chem. *289*, 11 (1978)
65. de Bièvre, P.: Commission of the European Communities, Central Bureau for Nuclear Measurements, Geel 1974
66. Lehmann, W. D., Schulten, H.-R.: Angew. Chem. *89*, 890 (1977); Angew. Chem. Int. Ed. *16*, 852 (1977)
67. Schulten, H.-R., Bahr, U., Lehmann, W. D.: Mikrochim. Acta (Wien) *1979* I, 191

68. Schulten, H.-R., Kümmler, D.: Anal. Chim. Acta *113*, 253 (1980)
69. Johnson, F. N. (ed.): Lithium research and therapy. London: Academic Press 1975
70. Duhm, J., Becker, B. F.: Pflügers Arch. *370*, 211 (1977)
71. Ebstein, R. P., Reches, A., Belmaker, R. H.: J. Pharm. Pharmacol. *30*, 122 (1978)
72. Lehmann, W. D., Bahr, U., Schulten, H.-R.: Biomed. Mass Spectrom. *5*, 536 (1978)
73. Hamilton, E. I., Minski, M. J., Clary, J. J.: Sci. Total Environ, *1*, 341 (1972)
74. Welz, B. (ed.): Atomabsorptions-Spektroskopie. Weinheim: Verlag Chemie 1975
75. Schulten, H.-R., Lehmann, W. D., Ziskoven, R.: Z. Naturforsch. *33c*, 484 (1978)
76. Achenbach, C., et al.: Angew. Chem. *91*, 994 (1979); Angew. Chem. Int. Ed. *18*, 882 (1979)
77. Lund, A.: Acta Pharmacol. Toxicol. *12*, 260 (1956)
78. Achenbach, C., et al.: J. Toxicol. Environ. Health *6*, 519 (1980)
79. Schulten, H.-R., Lehmann, W. D., Haaks, D.: Org. Mass Spectrom. *13*, 361 (1978)
80. Schulten, H.-R., Lehmann, W. D.: Quantitative field ionization and field desorption mass spectrometry in life sciences. In: Quantitative mass spectrometry in life sciences II. De Leenheer, A. P., Roncucci, R. R., van Peteghem, C. (eds.). Amsterdam: Elsevier 1978, pp. 63–82
81. Schiebel, H. M., Schulten, H.-R.: Naturwissenschaften *67*, 256 (1980)
82. Bahr, U., Schulten, H.-R.: J. Label. Comp. Radiopharm. in press (1981)
83. Katakuse, I., et al.: Int. J. Mass Spectrom. Ion Phys. *32*, 87 (1979)
84. Schulten, H.-R., Müller, R. and Haaks, D.: Fresenius Z. Anal. Chem. *304*, 15 (1980)
85. Schulten, H.-R., Kümmler, D.: Org. Mass Spectrom. *10*, 813 (1975)
86. Schulten, H.-R.: G-I-T, Zeitschr. Lab. *24*, 916 (1980)
87. Seelmann-Eggebert, W., Pfennig, G., Münzel, H.: Chart of Nuclides, 4th edition 1974, München: Gersbach Verlag 1974
88. Lehmann, W. D., Schulten, H.-R.: Biomed. Mass Spectrom. *5*, 208 (1978) — this article gives a thorough and comprehensive survey and discussion of methodology and examples of applications of quantitative field desorption mass spectrometry
89. Schulten, H.-R.: Int. J. Mass Spectrom. Ion Phys., in press (1981)
90. Ziskoven, R., et al.: Z. Naturforsch. *35c*, 902 (1980)

Practical Aspects and Trends in Analytical Organic Mass Spectrometry

Urs Peter Schlunegger

Institute of Organic Chemistry, University of Berne, Freiestrasse 3, CH-3012 Berne, Switzerland

Table of Contents

Taking into account all facets of mass spectrometry, we may conclude now that a mass spectrometer is not only a spectrometer. It is, in fact, a whole laboratory containing synthetic, separating, and spectrometric stages. Synthesis is performed in the ion source, especially in the chemical ionization chamber, and in collision gas cells. Crude ion mixtures of very different origins can be separated directly by a mass spectrometric analyzer system. And in a second analyzing stage spectroscopy proper may be realized giving information about the structure, quantity, and reactivity of selected ions. Combined in the hands of a skilled analyst, mass spectrometry becomes a powerful tool. Applied correctly, lower detection limits, reduced chemical noise, often drastically reduced analysis time — thus requiring less man-power — may result.

However, we must not forget one very important point of view: Mass spectrometry has not yet come to an end but is developing further very rapidly and often offers unexpected new ways of analysis. Therefore, it is worthwhile for an analyst to consider new aspects and to follow the trends in modern organic mass spectrometry.

1 Introduction

Today, mass spectrometry is a well established tool in analytical organic chemistry. Worldwide, many analytical data are collected daily by mass spectrometry. But at this point, two crucial questions have to be asked: (a) Is mass spectrometry really one single, well-defined method and (b) is mass spectrometry in fact a spectroscopic method as it is for instance infrared spectroscopy or nuclear magnetic resonance?

Answering the latter question, it is perhaps most likely to define what we are expecting of a spectroscopic method. IR and NMR spectroscopy clearly show that a spectroscopic method has to provide information on one selected type of qualities of the analyzed molecules. So, infrared spectroscopy yields e.g. information on rotations and vibrations of atom groups, NMR provides data about the neighbourhood of atoms in the molecule. In this way, we expect one special type of information from one type of spectroscopy. Coming back to our starting point, we may now ask the question whether mass spectrometry belongs to the same kind of spectroscopy. Most organic chemists will agree with such a statement[24)] reflecting upon how the analytical tool mass spectrometry is normally used in organic chemistry. Namely, it is a tool for the determination of the molecular weight, for the registration of a mass spectrum (in most cases, only very few peaks can be unterstood!) and sometimes for the determination of the elemental composition of ions by peak-matching. Very often, mass spectrometry is used as a detector only in combined gas chromatography/mass spectrometry or combined liquid chromatography/mass spectrometry due to its outstanding sensitivity and rapidity. All of these methods are well established and represent the conventional, "classical" mass spectrometry.

But yet this enumeration of different conventional applications of mass spectrometry demonstrates that organic mass spectrometry is neither a well-defined spectroscopy nor a uniform method. The diversification of mass spectrometry often leading to the creation of new names is both its great potential and its problematic disadvantage simultaneously. Problematic because only the specialist can be master of all the different mass spectrometries, not every laboratory has available the adequate machines for all methods, and because in some cases the routine application of one type of mass spectrometry becomes very expensive. On the other hand, mass spectrometry still offers a lot of new aspects and possibilities. The development of the art has not yet come to an end although this is believed by some organic chemists. It is quite obvious that conventional mass spectrometers must be improved. This can for instance be done by simplifying the operation of the apparatus or by a simpler access to analytical results using more sophisticated computer and microprocessor techniques. Due to such a development, mass spectrometry will surely find access to more analytical fields of science. But there is still a collection of newer mass spectrometric methods which has not yet found wide spread application. The intention of this survey is to show some more recent developments in comparison with conventional mass spectrometry. In order to understand these newer aspects, we have to recall some important fundamentals of mass spectrometry.

Urs Peter Schlunegger

2 The Vacuum

It is well-known that a conventional mass spectrometer consisting of an ion source, an ion accelerating field, an analyzer, and a detector must be pumped out to a high vacuum. But very often, we do not bring in mind why this is done and how it works. The following chapters illuminate the most important aspects. The aim of a mass spectrometer is to pick out one ion type and to transfer it without any loss to the detector, that means, without any interaction between these selected ions themselves, with related ions, or with foreign neutral particles present in the system. This is normally achieved by use of a high vaccum. Here, the question arises, how good the vacuum really must be. If no interactions between particles in the mass spectrometer are allowed to occur, the mean free path length must be longer than the dimensions of the apparatus. According to the kinetic gas theory, the mean free path length λ is

$$\lambda = \frac{1}{n(2r)^2 \, \pi \, 2} \,. \tag{1}$$

As the number of particles depends on the pressure p, the Boltzman constant k, and the temperature T according to

$$n = \frac{p}{kT} \,, \tag{2}$$

the mean free path length λ is mostly influenced in mass spectrometry by pressure p and diameter r of the ions. As in our case the temperature can be kept constant, Eqs. (1) and (2) may be combined and written in the form

$$\lambda = \frac{kT}{p(2r)^2 \, \pi 2} = \frac{1}{p(2r)^2} \cdot \frac{kT}{\pi 2} = \frac{K}{p(2r)^2} \,. \tag{3}$$

Or, in other words, if we regard one single type of particles the product

$$\lambda \times p = K' \tag{4}$$

remains constant as well. In Table 1 the products K′ of some gases and vapors are compiled[1]. As the average of K′ is about $5 \cdot 10^{-3}$ cm torr, a rule of thumb for the estimation of the mean free path may be deduced:

$$\lambda = \frac{5 \times 10^{-3}}{p\ (\text{torr})} (\text{cm}) \,. \tag{5}$$

In accordance with this rule the mean free path in a mass spectrometer pumped down to 10^{-6} torr is astonishingly long:

$$\lambda = \frac{5 \times 10^{-3}}{1 \times 10^{-6}} \text{cm} = 5 \times 10^3 \text{ cm} \,. \tag{6}$$

Since the dimensions of a common organic molecule are about ten times larger than those of the small molecules listed in Table 1, the mean free path is in fact much smaller for such species, namely up to 100 times shorter, taking into account the diameter as the square according to Eq. (2). Therefore, it is concluded that the vacuum in a mass spectrometer must be about 10^{-6} torr or better if collisions are to be avoided. In terms of analytical performance, one very important consequence of this high vacuum must be kept in mind here, namely that the first step of the separation of a compound has already been achieved. The ions present in a mass spectrometer have been isolated one from the other. Therefore, the behavior and fate of selected ion species may be observed and studied. In fact, a mass spectrometer represents a powerful tool for the separation of very complex mixtures or, in other words, for the elimination of any "chemical noise" from an ion of interest. This excellent analytical quality has rarely been utilized in conventional mass spectrometry. On the contrary, its range of application is actually still growing and will be discussed later. Coming back to our starting point, it can be concluded that the pressure should be at least 10^{-3} torr or higher if an interference between particles is desired. In practice, reactions between ions and neutral particles are now commonly induced using local relatively high pressures in chemical ionization source chambers and collisional activation cells. These features will be discussed in the following chapters.

Table 1. Values of the product K' of pressure and mean free path of common gases and vapors

	gas	$K' = \lambda p$ (cm × torr) × 10^{-3}		gas	$K' = \lambda p$ (cm × torr) × 10^{-3}
H_2	Hydrogen	9.0	CO_2	Carbon dioxide	3.0
He	Helium	13.6	H_2O	Water	3.0
Ar	Argon	4.8	NH_3	Ammonia	3.5
O_2	Oxygen	4.9	C_2H_5OH	Ethanol	1.6
N_2	Nitrogen	4.6	Cl	Chlorine	2.3
HCl	Hydrochloric acid	3.3			

3 Production of Ions in the Mass Spectrometer

Today, many ionization methods yielding different types of ions are available. Therefore, the organic analyst has preferably to ask first what type of information he expects from an analysis. Among the most important questions are:

1) Must the molecular weight only be determined?
2) Is the purpose of the analysis a quantitation of one or several compounds?
3) Has a structure to be elucidated?

Once these analytical questions have been answered, considerations concerning the volatility of the sample will follow. At the end of this questionnaire, the analyst has to choose the adequate ionization method. But very often, the procedure is getting more complicated, as mostly more than one single question should be answered at the same time. Fortunately, modern mass spectrometry has prepared a series of different ionization[33] and fragmentation methods. Therefore, more and more problems can be solved today sometimes by combination of different ion producing methods. The following fundamental aspects may illustrate the most important technical possibilities.

3.1 Ions Produced from Volatile Samples

Ionization and fragmentation of a molecule as well as its volatilization are energy-consuming processes. Since the energy ranges may sometimes be very similar, it is worthwile to recall the corresponding data.

In general, the ion source of a mass spectrometer is heated to 200–250 °C in order to avoid condensation of the sample on the ion source itself. In this connection, it must not be forgotten that thermal fragmentations may occur at these elevated temperatures, thus simulating mass spectrometric fragmentations. A well-known example is the elimination of water from alcohols. In all cases, the analyst has to pay attention to this problem, especially when a too intense fragmentation should be avoided. However, in most cases, a compromise between volatilization of samples, a contaminated ion source, and analysis time must be found. This problem has to be solved in any case and with all ionization methods.

3.1.1 Electron Impact Ionization (EI)
(Review[104])

Due to the historical development, electron impact ionization is by far the most frequently used technique for the production of ions in organic mass spectrometry. Undoubtedly, electron impact ionization offers many advantages like high sensitivity, simple operation of the ion source and quite good reproducibilities of the results. On the other hand, one well-known disadvantage is the very often low intensity of the molecular ion. In this connection, we should keep in mind some points which are of special interest in the following considerations. Astonishingly enough, the organic analyst very often forgets that the ionization energy of a molecule is only about 7–10 eV (170–230 kcal/mol). As the energy of the ionizing electron beam is usually about 70 eV, the generated ions may acquire additional internal energy. The type of this surplus energy may be estimated by a simple calculation. A 70 eV-electron is travelling at a velocity of about 5×10^8 cm/s. Since the average molecular diameter of an organic molecule is about 10^{-7} cm, the impacting electron passes through the sample molecule in ca. 2×10^{-16} s. Ionization occurs within this short period. In comparison with this time, the fastest molecular vibration, a C—H stretching vibration, has a period of about 10^{-14} s. Therefore, all atoms can be considered to remain in their actual state[2]. Thus, additional internal energy is stored in the form of electronic excitation by a Frank-Condon type process. The magnitude of this energy is not limited as in chemical ionization (see 3.1.2). Obviously, it is in the range of the bond energies of organic molecules, namely 1–10 eV[65]. These odd electron ions are therefore in a highly excited state and thus undergo extensive fragmentation. The energy needed for such a fragmentation can be evaluated from the energy of the bonds. In large molecules it is about 3–4 eV for a single bond (C—C: 3.6 eV; C—H: 4.3 eV; C—O: 3.7 eV; C—Cl: 3.5 eV; etc), about 6–8 eV for a double bond (C=C: 6.3 eV; C=O: 7.8 eV; etc.) and about 9 eV for a triple bond (C≡C: 8.7 eV; C≡N: 9.2 eV). The result of these fragmentations is then illustrated by the EI mass spectrum. Unfortunately, a mass spectrum does not only indicate simple cleavage products of the molecular ion. Very often, cleavage products ions are still sufficiently excited to undergo further fragmentation, thus complicating the interpretation of a spectrum. Additionally, in many cases, rearrangement reactions may occur, yielding energetically very stable structural subunits not present in the primary molecule.

In view of this situation we may conclude that in terms of the analytical potential, electron impact ionization offers a good fingerprint of a sample compound, but frequently gives rise to a very complex spectrum which cannot be fully understood. Although the sensitivity of electron impact ionization is high, the intensity of the molecular ion is often very low due to extensive fragmentation, thus hindering molecular weight determination as well as structure elucidation.

3.1.2 Chemical Ionization

(Reviews[19,18,34,15,22,81,104])

The technique of chemical ionization mass spectrometry (CIMS) was first described in 1966 by Munson and Field[3]. Today, this method is well established and widely applied as a versatile tool in many branches of analytical chemistry. Instead of more or less uncontrolled high-energy processes induced by electron impact, selected ion-molecule reactions with well-defined energy transfer are used in chemical ionization. The reacting ion species are generated through bombardment of the so-called reagent gas with a beam of high-energy electrons (typically, ~400 eV) at a relatively high pressure of ~1 torr. At this pressure, the mean free path — according to the rule of thumb (Eq. (5)) — is shortened to the range of about $^5/_{100}$ of a millimeter or less. Thus, the mean free path is much shorter than the dimensions of the ion source, the collision probability and the interactions between the particles being increased. For instance, gas-phase Brønsted acids (CH_5^+, H_3O^+, $C_4H_9^+$, NH_4^+ etc) can be generated within the ion source. If a sample M of low concentration is now introduced into this reagent gas, a proton may be transferred, providing that the proton affinity PA of M is greater than that of A:

$$AH^+ + M \rightarrow MH^+ + A + \Delta H\,. \tag{7}$$

This exothermic proton transfer produces the energy ΔH, depending on the difference of the proton affinities:

$$\Delta H = PA(A) - PA(M)\,. \tag{8}$$

In Table 2 the proton affinities of the most commonly used reagent ions and of some typical organic functional groups are listed.

Table 2. Proton affinities of commonly used reagent ions[19, 14)]

Reagent ion	Energy (eV)	Reagent ion	Energy (eV)
NH_3	8.9	N_2O	5.9
H_2O	7.4	C_2H_6	5.7
O_2	4.4	H_2	4.4
N_2	4.9	CH_3OH	7.9
CH_4	5.5	$i{-}C_4H_{10}$	8.4

A sample molecule protonated by such a Brønsted acid may acquire additional internal energy (similar electron impact ionization). However, this surplus energy cannot exceed ΔH of the protonation reaction. Therefore, the fragmentation of the protonated sample MH^+, in turn, depend on ΔH. By an appropriate choice of the reagent gas AH^+, the magnitude of ΔH can be controlled and thus the extent of the fragmentation of the sample ion MH^+.

This control of the internal energy (ΔH_{max}) and the fact that most of the commonly used reagent gases generate even electron ion species such as MH^+, $(M{-}H)^+$, or $(M{-}H)^-$ are both responsible for more simple fragmentation reactions than in the case of radical cations produced by electron impact ionization. But not only reagent gases transferring a charge or a proton are used in chemical ionization, even real chemical reactions may be induced. For instance, vinyl methyl ether in a mixture of nitrogen and carbon disulfide (5:75:20) may be employed in reaction with olefinic couble bonds. The corresponding reaction product induces a typical bond cleavage pattern at the former site of the double bond, thus enabling the location of olefinic bonds in an unsaturated compound[29)] (Fig. 1).

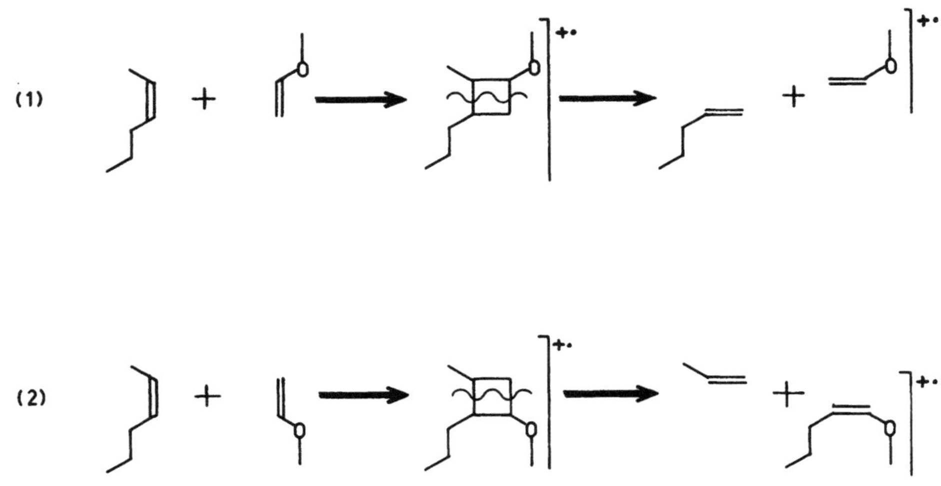

Fig. 1. Location of olefinic bonds in unsaturated compounds by chemical ionization reaction with methyl vinyl ether[29)]: generation of two pairs of fragments by two reactions, (1) and (2) respectively

Obviously, other types of reagent ions than Brønsted acids may be prepared and used for chemical ionization, namely charge transfer reagent ions (rare gases[4,5]), nitrogen[6]), N_2/NO mixture[7,8])), gases giving other positive reagent ions (tetramethylsilane[10]), amines[11,12,13])), and reagent ions producing negative ions (see 3.1.4).

Compared with electron impact ionization we may conclude that in chemical ionization the magnitude of the additional internal energy of the sample ions can be limited, thus diminishing the extent of fragmentation and increasing the intensity of the sample molecular ion, respectively.

3.1.3 Field Ionization
(Reviews:[32,28,26,36,104]))

In field ionization (FI) mode an electron is extracted from the sample molecule in the gas phase by a very high electric field of about 1 V/Å (10^7 to 5×10^8 V/cm). These high electric fields are generally generated by applying a high voltage on tips or edges of metal or organic polymers. This ionization is effected on non-excited molecules by means of a "tunneling" effect, and during ionization no additional energy is transferred to the ions. Therefore, field ionized molecules are commonly stable and tend to fragment to a very small extent only. This implies that in field ionization a molecular ion can very often be recognized but no fragment ions. Since fragment ions are representatives of structural subunits, field ionization spectra, frequently showing one or few peaks only, suffer from the lack of structure information.

Therefore, field ionization mass spectrometry is applied in analytical chemistry to molecular weight determinations only.

3.1.4 Generation of Negative Ions
(Reviews:[22,20,18,31,104]))

As early as in 1912[16]), Thomson detected the negative ions oxygen O^- and chlorine Cl^- in his first mass spectrometer. Then, about half a century passed until new attempts were made for the analytical application of negative ions. Using a normal electron impact ion source, spectra of negative ions were compared with those of positive ions in a comprehensive study[17]). The results obtained by this usual ionization technique (EI) (20–70 eV electron impact) were discouraging. With respect to molecular weight determination and structure elucidation the resulting spectra of the negative ions provided considerably less analytical information than those of the positive ions and were considered to be of limited value. Today, the reason of this failure is well understood. In a normal electron impact ionization chamber, negative ions may be generated mainly by three mechanisms: the resonance electron capture, the dissociative resonance electron capture and a non-resonant process.

1) the resonance electron capture process takes place with very low-energy electrons only:

$$M + e \rightarrow M^- . \tag{9}$$

These electrons must be in a very narrow energy range (thermal electrons) and may be generated in rather low concentration from higher energy electrons by collisions with the ion chamber walls. Therefore, the probability of negative ions to be produced by this process in a normal electron impact ion source is very low.

2) The dissociative resonance capture takes place when low energy electrons of up to about 15 eV collide at low pressure with sample molecules:

$$M + e \rightarrow (M - F)^{-} + F^{\cdot}\,. \tag{10}$$

The electron energy is still high enough to transfer a rather large amount of internal energy to the molecular ion. Therefore, cleavage of a bond is induced resulting in the loss of a radical fragment $F^{\cdot}$.

3) In a non-resonant process, the ionizing electron e is not attached to the sample molecule, but only transfers energy to it:

$$M + e \rightarrow (M - F)^{-} + F^{+} + e\,. \tag{11}$$

The resulting fragmentation of the molecule into two electron even species is usually induced by electrons with energies above 10 eV.

These three processes are not very abundant compared with normal electron impact ionization involving an electron loss of the sample molecule. Thus, under the conditions of low-pressure electron impact, many compounds give only few negative fragment ions and frequently no molecular ions. Consequently, the analytical efficiency of conventional negative ion mass spectrometry was rather low. In order to enhance the abundances of negative ions, methods producing more electrons of very low energy had to be developed. A practicable way to achieve this was found when ionization at relatively high pressures in chemical ionization chambers became possible. There again several ionization mechanisms may be distinguished:

4) Slowing down of ionizing electrons (three-body attachment):
Relatively high-energy electrons e* may be slowed down by an inert buffer gas B, thus generating a high concentration of thermal electrons:

$$M + e^{*} + B \rightarrow M^{-\cdot} + B^{*}\,. \tag{12}$$

Argon, for instance, has been shown to be a suitable buffer gas enhancing the negative ion abundance by several orders of magnitude[20,21]. Methane or isobutane is also a commonly used buffer gas.

5) Ion attachment:
Under chemical ionization, a rather high concentration of negative reactant ions R^{-} is produced; these undergo attachment to the sample molecule M:

$$M + R^{-} \rightarrow [MR]^{-}\,. \tag{13}$$

6) Charge Exchange:
Instead of an attachment the negative reactant ion may transfer its charge only to the sample:

$$M + R^{-} \rightarrow M^{-} + R\,. \tag{14}$$

Argon, nitrogen, carbon monoxide, for instance, have been reported to be suitable for charge exchange reactions producing spectra resembling conventional electron ionization spectra[15].

Once the abundance of negative ions was grasped the analytical applications of these reactions were tested. In terms of analytical power, there were recognized two main features. On the one hand, negative ion mass spectra very often tend to provide structural information complementary to that available from positive ion spectra[22]. On the other hand, the sensitivity of negative ion mass spectrometry of some compound classes is much higher than that of positive mass spectrometry. This especially applies to halogenated samples like pesticides. In order to make use of these findings, derivatization of non-halogenated compounds with pentafluorobenzaldehyde or pentafluorobenzoyl chloride may improve their detection limit. For instance, primary amines after such a derivatization may be detected at the femtogram (10^{-15} g) level by negative ion gas chromatography-mass spectrometry[22].

3.2 Ions Produced from Poorly Volatile Samples

(Reviews:[23, 104])

A sample attaining a vapor pressure of 10^{-6} torr or higher without thermal degradation may be analyzed by mass spectrometry using conventional sample inlet systems. If thermolysis occurs prior to adequate evaporation, the sample has to be derivatized in order to transform it into a thermally stable and evaporable form, or the sample must be converted into an ionized gas by special techniques. Chemical derivatization is well known and will not be discussed here. However, derivatization usually results in an increase in molecular weight and in view of the limited mass range of a mass spectrometer this technique may not be applied in every case. Therefore, dealing with samples of low volatility, the analyst is confronted mainly with two types of samples: (a) compounds containing thermally labile, mostly very polar groups like OH, COOH, NH_2, NRCO, etc, and (b) high molecular weight compounds (m/z 600 up to few thousands).

In both of these two cases, the heat of evaporation is greater than the energy of the thermal degradation of the molecules. Therefore, methods omitting evaporation prior to ionization had to be looked for. Several attempts were made to overcome this problem[23]. Today, the most promising methods using ionization of the sample in the solid state directly from a probe surface are field desorption (FD), desorption chemical ionization (DCI), ^{252}Cf-plasma desorption technique, and laser-induced desorption technique.

3.2.1 Field Desorption

(Reviews:[35, 27, 23, 104])

This ionization technique is extensively utilized in biomedical and environmental research because of its applicability to a wide range of samples from inorganic salts to polar metabolites. The sample is normally adsorbed on dendritic needles grown on a thin tungsten wire (the so-called emitter). When a high electric field is applied to this adsorbed sample layer, ionization will occur (~1 V/Å). Similar to field ionization (see 3.1.3), a rather small energy amount is transferred to the ionized molecule (~0.1 eV), thus increasing the probability of detecting intact molecular ions. As for structure elucidation not only the molecular weight must be known but a moderate fragmentation may additionally be induced by heating the probe emitter. However, there are some disadvantages facing these striking features. Thus, the ion currents produced by field desportion ionization often fluctuate and are normally less intense than after electron impact or chemical ionization. This not only limits both the sensitivity and the precision but very often prevents the application of field desorption itself. A possible way to overcome these shortcomings is the "emission-controlled desorption" by means of a computer-controlled heating of the emitter wire keeping constant the ion production[130]. Indeed, this technique is not very simple to perform and requires a very clean ion source (not always available at any time in an analytical routine laboratory), and the emitters are rather expensive. Hopefully, further developments will overcome these problems enabling a more frequent use of this very valuable technique also by less skilled people.

3.2.2 Desorption Chemical Ionization (DCI)

In view of the ionization of samples of low volatility, desorption chemical ionization (DCI) is one of the most promising new techniques. The sample is placed on a heatable probe tip[44] or on a field desorption emitter probe[42] and introduced directly into the plasma of a chemical ion source. It was shown that by such an exposure of the sample to the ion plasma, mass spectra can be obtained at much lower temperatures than usually required[43]. This extraordinarily simple sample handling and the apparently more intense and better reproducible ion beam than in field desorption ionization have obviously induced a rapidly growing field of applications of DCI. This development is also supported by a growing number of DCI probe devices available from different manufacturers at relatively reasonable prices. Although many applications, for instance to underivatized peptides[43], to cyclic adenosine monophosphate, guanosine, and thiophosphoric acid pesticides[42], as well to creatinine and arginine[44] have been reported, the analytical potential of DCI is not yet exhausted and will obviously result in many new possibilities in analytical research (for recent publications see[44]).

3.2.3 ^{252}Cf Plasma Desorption

Samples adsorbed on a solid probe surface are not only desorbed by a chemical ionization plasma but also by charged particles originating from an atom nucleus decay as well. This has been shown for the Californium isotope 252[37,38,39,40]. Samples like cystine, xanthinetyrosine, tetrodotoxin and others have been desorbed by the ^{252}Cf fission products and the corresponding mass spectra have been recorded by a special time-of-flight mass spectrometer. The major problem involved in this ionization technique is a low ion yield. Therefore, single ion counting, very high transmission of the mass spectrometer, and a low ion background are essential to obtain an interpretable mass spectrum. The fragmentation of the samples is normally much weaker than in electron impact ionization but more intense than in field desorption ionization[41]. Although samples with molecular weights over m/z 1000 have been analyzed and the technique seems to be very promising, the technical problems discussed above will probably hinder a worldwide routine application in analytical laboratories.

3.2.4 Laser Desorption

Laser desorption technique has recently been shown to be useful for the ionization of non-volatile biomolecules[84]. Quasimolecular ions are desorbed by submicrosecond laser pulses delivering about 10^6 Watt/cm^2 to the sample. Ionization occurs mainly by alkali attachment and, for some classes of molecules, by proton transfer as well. The internal energy of these ions is rather low giving rise to a moderate fragmentation only.

This interesting way of ionization is actually being extended to other fields of application[85], especially to the desorption of poorly volatile samples from a stainless steel belt transporting the effluents of a liquid chromatograph into the ion-source[86]. Successful attempts were also made to enhance the ionization probability by combined laser desorption/chemical ionization. Recording of mass spectra of thermally very labile molecules has been possible, for instance of the trisaccharide raffinose (MW 504)[87], of serveral steroid glucuronides and of bile acid conjugates[88]. Obviously, laser desorption ionization is still further developing and will yield further progress, especially in the analysis of biomolecules.

3.3 Ions Generated from Precursor Ions within the Mass Spectrometric Analyzer

Up to now, we have placed the origin of the ions exclusively into the ion source. The mean residence time of ions in the ion source has been shown to be about 10^{-6} s. That means, a fragment ion which is generated in a shorter period of time (10^{-7} s or less) from a precursor ion, due to excess internal energy, will be extracted out of the ion source together with all other ions. It is accelerated in the high-voltage field of the ion source to the standard kinetic energy and analyzed together with other ions yielding the conventional mass spectrum of the sample.

In fact, here we are doing the contrary of what should be performed by an analyst, namely a new mixture of ions with mostly unknown structures is synthesized. Even in the case of pure compounds, a very complex ion mixture is created instead of attempting to simplify the analytical task. However, the mass spectrometer has yet separated this new mixture in distinct components, thus repairing the primary damage. The only remaining disadvantage in a conventional mass spectrum is the fact that we very often do not know where a fragment ion originates from. In the case of pure compounds we only know that a fragment ion has been generated from the molecular ion, but we do not know whether this was done in one single or several fragmentation reactions. Or, in other words, we do not know the genetic relationship between the ions present in a conventional mass spectrum.

The consequence of this missing genetic information is far-reaching. Mainly, the interpretation of a conventional mass spectrum becomes rather difficult and must be based on experience, on the intuition of the specialized analyst, and on the knowledge of a plethora of wellknown fragmentation reactions. Mostly, an interpretation equals a puzzle which has to be solved and brought to a plausible whole. However, even this comparison is not absolutely correct, because in the puzzle the position of a fragment, compared with its neighbouring fragments, is unequivocally determined by its exterior form, the colors, and the drawing contours. Consequently, the origin of a fragment in the puzzle is always directly perceptible by different criteria. Unfortunately, a fragment in a conventional mass spectrum is not characterized very clearly. In most cases, it is assigned to one single criterion only, the m/z number. Therefore, a conventional mass spectrum contains a lot of hidden, "blocked up" information. Many attempts were made to gain these hidden informations (see Chapter 4). Two types of ions are generated after leaving the ion source and the acceleration field within the analyzer of the mass spectrometer, the metastable ions and the ions produced by collisional activation.

3.3.1 Metastable Ions

(Reviews:[2, 65, 50, 104, 59])

According to the length of the flight path through the analyzer and the velocity attained in the accelerating field behind the ion source, the flight time of the ions through the analyzer is in the range of 10^{-5} s, i.e. about then times longer than their mean residence time in the ion source. Therefore, ions with a mean lifetime of 10^{-5} s, the so-called metastable ions, may decompose within the analyzer of the mass spectrometer according to the equation

$$m_1^{+/-} \rightarrow m_2^{+/-} + m_3^0 . \qquad (15)$$

As every fragmentation reaction needs energy, only ions containing enough excess internal energy will undergo fragmentation. Eq. (15) must then be written in the form

$[m_1^{+/-}]^*$	$\rightarrow$	$m_2^{+/-}$	+	m_3^0	+	E,	(16)
excited precursor ion		product ion		neutral particle		energy	

according to the fact that metastable ions are excited, "hot" ions and are thus not only susceptible to bond cleavage but also to isomerization or rearrangements in order to release their surplus energy E.

Interpreting this situation, the following consequences for the analytical chemist can be derived from Eq. (16):

a) The structure of the product ion $m_2^{+/-}$ must not necessarily be considered as a copy of a part of its precursor ion $m_1^{+/-}$ since rearrangements may occur. Therefore, the knowledge of the structure of $m_2^{+/-}$ has to be interpreted with caution.
b) As the momentum (m_1v) and the kinetic energy ($^1/_2 m_1 v^2$) of the precursor ion picked up in the accelerating field are distributed between the products, $m_2^{+/-}$ cannot pass the analyzer at the settings for its precursor. Thus, special techniques must be applied (compare Chapter 4).

c) A fraction of the excess internal energy E may be released in the form of additional kinetic energy during the dissociation process of the products $m_2^{+/-}$ and m_3^0. In fact, a certain spread of the velocity of $m_2^{+/-}$ may be observed, as a small velocity component due to this energy release in any direction must appear. This dissociation velocity, in particular, can be opposed wholly or partially to the original direction of flight of $m_1^{+/-}$ (Fig. 2, case a). The result is a somewhat smaller final velocity of $m_2^{+/-}$ and, accordingly, a diminished kinetic energy of $m_2^{+/-}$. In case b (Fig. 2) the contrary occurs. Obviously, any energy amount between these two extremes is possible leading to a broadening and to a substructure of the peaks[49, 2, 59]. As the amount of internal energy transformed into kinetic energy depends on the dissociation reaction, the energy release is a very sensitive tool for the comparison of fragmentation reaction types (example in[47]) and thus an additional tool for the structure elucidation of ions.
Unfortunately, very often a small fraction of a distinct ion type only is metastable; thus, the corresponding product ions are of low abundance. It is quite natural that an enhancement of ion decomposition has been attempted. A possible way has been found in the so-called collisional activation.

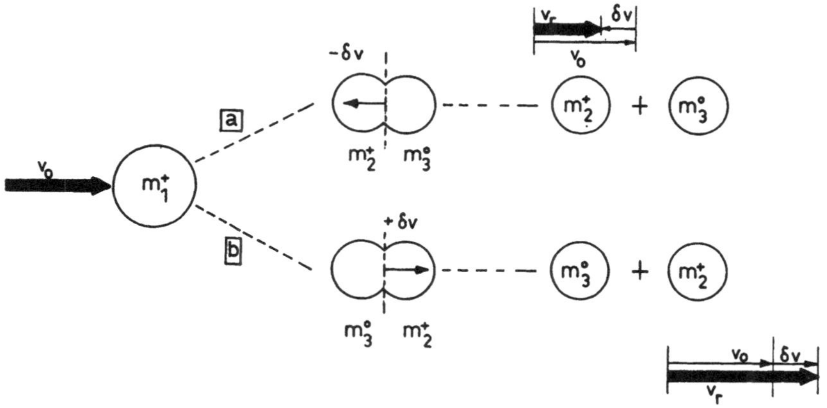

Fig. 2. Peak broading due to kinetic energy release upon dissociation of the product particles m_2^+ and m_3^0 (case a: diminution; case b: increase of primary kinetic energy)

3.3.2 Ions Produced by Collisional Activation (CA)

(Reviews:[69, 30, 2, 50, 70, 104])

The fragmentation rate of ions within the analyzer can be enhanced if additional energy is pumped into ions surviving the travel through the mass spectrometer, i.e. if ions with lifetimes longer than 10^{-5} s are decomposed. In other words, the fragmentation of stable ions must be induced by some sort of activation after they have left the ion source. In this connection, an old well-known observation has been helpful: It has been recognized that the abundance of ions decreases with increasing pressure in the mass spectrometer. In accordance with the rule of thumb (Eq. (5)), the mean free path already at a pressure of 10^{-4} torr is reduced to a smaller value than the dimensions of a mass spectrometer. Therefore, the collision probability of an organic molecule is increased leading to more frequent collision-induced decompositions. As the number of the ions is decreased by such decompositions, the sensitivity of the mass spectrometer is reduced accordingly. To avoid this loss of sensitivity many attempts were made to improve the vacuum in the mass spectrometer. However, systematic research performed during the last ten years reveals that such collision processes can provide valuable information on the structure and origin of ions[69,70]. Therefore, collisons of ions with neutral target gas molecules like helium or nitrogen molecules are allowed to occur within collision chambers introduced into the ion beam. This may be performed in the first field-free or in the second field-free region of a double focusing mass spectrometer (Fig. 3) or in a double[79,80] or triple[61,77,78] quadrupole system. If an organic ion impinge upon the collision gas — preferably helium — electronic excitation of the impact ion occurs. In the first approximation, this process may be regarded as an inelastic impact. In this event, a small fraction of the kinetic energy of the impinging ion is transformed to internal excitation energy. If the target gas is a small atom or molecule, and especially if it is inert (high ionization potential), then the energy transfered to the target gas may be neglected[96,97]. Therefore, helium is preferably used as target gas. In this case, the energy amount transformed to internal energy is approximately equal to the loss of kinetic energy of the ion before collision. This energy can be measured directly from the shift of the peak center toward lower energies in the mass spectrometer, thus permitting the determination of the internal energy fraction transformed to translational energy.

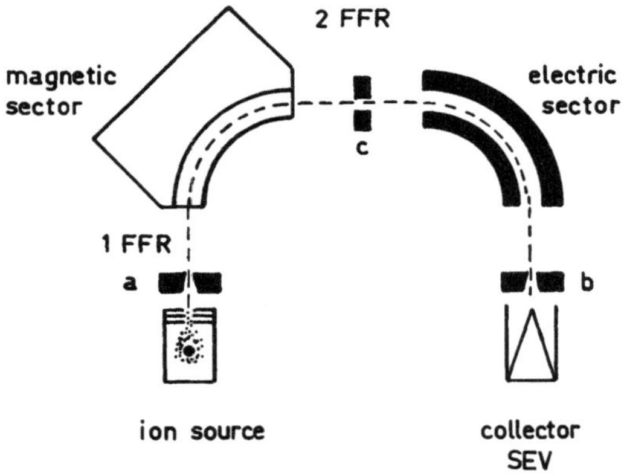

Fig. 3. Inverse Nier-Johnson geometry. 1 FFR: first field-free region, 2 FFR: second field-free region, a, b, e: slits. Observation windows are in 1 FFR and 2 FFR with or without collision gas cells

This additional internal energy of the impinged ion is converted within a few pico seconds into vibration energy giving rise to further fragmentation. The mechanism of this collisional activation corresponds, in principle, to electron impact ionization. Therefore, it is obvious that a collisional activation spectrum corresponds to an electron impact spectrum as well. As experience reveals, 70 eV spectra and collisional activation spectra of ions with 8—10 keV are almost similar as regards the main fragments and their relative intensitges[65,50,669].

In other words, collisional activation is a valuable tool for providing mass spectra generated from stable, "cold" ions. Thus, the analyst does not only have a very sensitive tool for the elucidation of ion structures but also a powerful instrument for structure elucidation.

4 Ions in the Analyzer of a Mass Spectrometer

Up to now, it has been shown that in many cases several ion types can be generated from one single compound: a) very excited ("hot") ions susceptible to fragmentation and isomerization, b) ions of low internal energy ("cold ions") without any fragmentation and c) different ion species containing various internal energy amounts inducing moderate decomposition of the parent ion.

In conventional mass spectrometry, these different ionization methods are usually applied to the generation of a suitable fingerprint type mass spectrum only. The points of interest are molecular weight and a fragmentation that permits to perform a reliable comparison of the spectrum of an unknown compound with those in a spectrum library. The corresponding methods are well known and well established in every mass spectrometric laboratory and will not be discussed further. Thus, the aim of this survey is a discussion of more recent mass spectrometric work dealing with ion structure elucidation and with reactivities of ions. But how can we look at the reactivity and structure of an ion? The logical way is at first to isolate the ion of interest and then in a second step to study the behavior of this ion. Especially important is to know the origin and the mode of fragmentation of the ion. In other words, we would like to know all the possible precursors of the ion under study as well as every reaction or fragment generated from it. Therefore the measuring procedures used for the elucidation of the structure and reactions of the ions will be discussed in the following sections.

4.1 Detection of the Fate of Ions

Review:[50])

Metastable ions decompose during their flight through the mass spectrometer (see 3.2.1). According to the reaction Eq. (15), the momentum as well as the kinetic energy is partitioned between the precursor $m_1^{(+/-)}$ and its products $m_2^{+/-}$ and m_3^0. As the magnetic analyzer represents a momentum filter and the electric field an energy filter, $m_2^{+/-}$ cannot reach the detector at the same settings as the precursor $m_1^{+/-}$. This has already been known in the case of the conventional "metastable peaks". However, the "metastables" in the conventional mass spectrum do not represent the metastables themselves but the product ions $m_2^{+/-}$ of fragmentations of metastable ions. The product ions may be associated with their precursors — the metastables — by the well known formula

$$m^* = \frac{(m_{product})^2}{m_{precursor}} . \qquad (17)$$

The broad ions m* can be recorded with single focusing and double focusing mass spectrometers embodying conventional Nier-Johnson or Herzog-Mattauch geometries. However, Eq. (17) involves a problem. Since m* is a quotient only, the mass of the precursor ion and that of the product ion is not exactly defined. Thus, an unequivocal assignement of m* to a precursor/product ion pair is not guaranteed. It is therefore not astonishing that attempts were made to overcome this shortcoming. Recalling Eq. (15), it can be stated that a product ion $m_2^{+/-}$ still travels with the same velocity as that of the precursor ion $m_1^{(+/-)}$. But the kinetic energy and the momentum are diminished according to the smaller mass of $m_2^{(+/-)}$. Therefore, a product ion $m_2^{(+/-)}$ can pass the analyzers at the settings for the precursor ion $m_1^{(+/-)}$ only if (a) the analyzer settings are reduced to the appropriate values of $m_2^{(+/-)}$, (b) the momentum and kinetic energy of the precursor ion $m_1^{+/-}$ are augmented by additional acceleration to $[m_1^{+/-}]^*$ in order to increase simultaneously the corresponding values of the product ion so that $[m_2^{+/-}]^*$ can pass the analyzer at the primary setting for $m_1^{+/-}$. The different technical possibilities will be discussed in the following, especially DADI/MIKE spectrometry.

4.1.1 DADI/MIKE Spectrometry
(Reviews:[49, 50, 51, 104])

This measuring procedure was developed simultaneously by two indenpendent teams and published as *D*irect *A*nalysis of *D*aughter *I*ons (DADI[45]) and the more physical denomination *M*ass analyzed *I*on *K*inetic *E*nergy *S*pectrometry (MIKES[46]). This technique may only be applied using a double focusing mass spectrometer embodying an inverse Nier-Johnson geometry (Fig. 3). In the first step, the ions are accelerated to an appropriate velocity so that they are travelling through the mass spectrometer with a kinetic energy W_1. In accordance with the kinetic energy W_1, the electric field (energy filter) is set to the value E_1, thus focusing the ions onto the detector D. Therefore, the ions which have passed the magnetic field M (mass analyzer, momentum analyzer) and the intermediate slit S_2 will reach the detector if they still contain the kinetic energy W_1. This is not the case if the kinetic energy has diminished to a value W_2 due to fragmentation of $m_1^{+/-}$ to $m_2^{+/-}$ in the second field-free region (2FFR). Only the product ion $m_2^{+/-}$ can reach the detector if the electric field E_1 has also been reduced to a value E_2, corresponding to the remaining fraction of the kinetic energy of $m_2^{+/-}$. This is accomplished according to Eq. (15) if

$$E_2 = \frac{m_2}{m_1} E_1 \,. \qquad (18)$$

Thus, it is possible to pick out an ion of interest by the magnetic field and to focus all its product ions, generated by fragmentation in the second field-free region (2FFR), onto the detector if the energy analyzer (electric field) is scanned from the precursor ion beam value E_1 downward. A DADI or MIKE spectrum will result representing a fragmentation spectrum of the ion selected by the magnet. An example is shown in Fig. 4. It is quite obvious that the number of product ions depends on the internal energy amount of the precursor ion. Very often, the internal energy is too small to induce further fragmentation. In this case, collisional activation may help, although this type of ion spectrum ("cold" ions, see 3.3.2) is physically different from the DADI/MIKE spectrum generated by unimolecular processes (excited, "hot" ions) (Fig. 4). But in therms of the analytical organic chemist, a collisional-activated spectrum can frequently be considered simply as an enhanced DADI/MIKE spectrum.

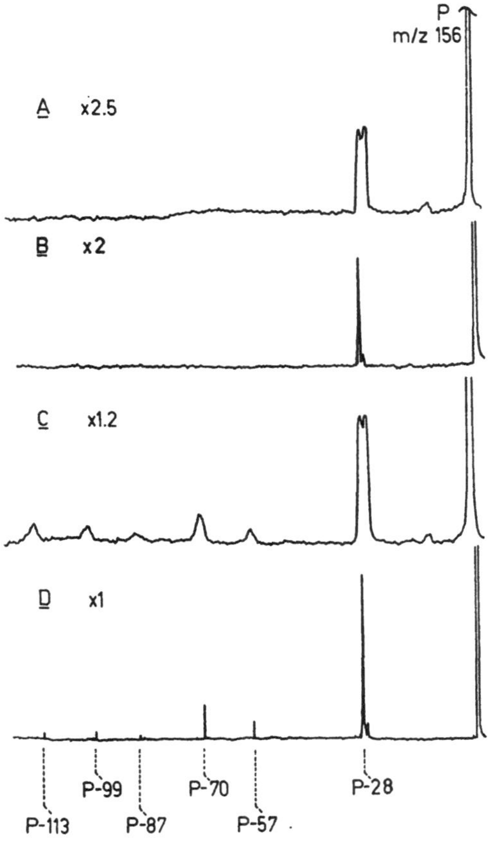

Fig. 4. Dissociation of the N-acetylleucyl ion P (m/z 156). A: DADI/MIKE spectrum (unimolecular process), B: linked scan B/E = const. (unimolecular process), C: DADI/MIKE spectrum (collisional activation), D: linked scan B/E = const. (collisional activation)

However, here we have to pay attention to another important point. The shapes of the different peaks resulting from unimolecular processes and from collision-induced fragmentations are normally rather different (see Fig. 4). The broadening of the peaks due to transformation of internal energy into kinetic energy[2] is a very sensitive indication of the type of reaction involved in a fragmentation step (see also 3.3.1). Therefore, this energy release may be used for the differentiation of reaction types[47,48].

4.1.2 Linked Scans
(Review:[104])

Using DADI/MIKE spectrometry, ion fragmentations are observed in the second field-free region of a double focusing mass spectrometer embodying the inverse Nier-Johnson geometry. This technique is not practicable in conventional mass spectrometers with the energy filter preceding the magnetic field. Product ions generated in the second field-free region of a conventional double focusing mass spectrometer give rise to the wellknown broad, "metastable" peaks according to Eq. (17). In order to overcome this problem attempts have been made to simulate DADI/MIKE spectra by observing ion fragmentations in the first field-free region (see Fig. 3). In accordance with reaction Eq. (16) it must be stated again that in this case a product ion generated in the first field-free region can pass the analyzer (a) only at reduced settings or (b) if its kinetic energy and momentum are increased.

1) It was shown that in the first case of constant kinetic energy of the precursor ion (constant accelerating voltage), both the mass and the energy filter settings must be diminished such that the ratio of the electric to the magnetic field strength remains constant[52, 53, 54].
In practice, first the precursor ion is focused onto the detector in the conventional mode. Then, its product ion spectrum is recorded by scanning the magnetic (B) as well as the electric (E) field simultaneously so that B/E remains constant.
In terms of analytical power, this measuring procedure has some advantages compared with the original DADI/MIKE spectrometry: Frequently, the linked scan peaks (B/E = constant) are more abundant than the corresponding DADI/MIKE signals, since the number of excited metastable ions susceptible to fragmentation is usually greater than that present in the second field-free region. Additionaly, the double focusing system in the linked scan mode is still working producing narrow and well resolved peaks. Therefore, assignment of the singals to the masses is normally readily which can sometimes be rather problematic in DADI/MIKE spectrometry, especially in the case of collisional activation spectra (see Fig. 4).
However, these advantages have to be paid by some disadvantages: a) An additional rather complicated electronic unit producing a linearized signal of the magnetic field probe (Hall probe which is used for the generation of the electric field strength) must be available. b) If no microprocessor-controlled unit or even a computer is available, the calculation of the appropriate mass units is rather time-consuming and complicated.
A further disadvantage is the loss of the very useful information about the energy release (transformation of internal energy to translational energy, see 3.3.1) due to the still working double focusing system.
2) The second possibility for the observation of fragmentations occurring in the first field-free region of a mass spectrometer involves an additional acceleration of the ions instead of a diminution of the analyzer field settings. This mode of operation, a linked scan keeping the ratio E^2/V constant (V = accelerating voltage) was developed prior to the E/B linked scan[57, 58]. Again, it simulates a DADI/MIKE spectrum. But the E^2/V-linked scan has some disadvantages: The scanning of the accelerating voltage leads to a defocusing of the ion source, thus providing non-constant sensitivity. In addition, the practical mass range is reduced by the

limited high-voltage stability of the mass spectrometer. As in this linked scan mode, the mass spectrometer is still double focusing, the peaks are narrow and well resolved. Resolving powers of some thousands (10% valley) are possible. Unfortunately, the information on the energy release is lost as in the B/E-linked scan procedure. Naturally, the E^2/V-linked scan may also be combined with collisional activation in the first field-free region[59].

4.1.3 Recording of Ion Fragmentations with Quadrupole Mass Filter Systems

In the normal scan mode of a quadrupole mass filter, no product ions of fragmentations occurring within the analyzer system can be recorded. Attempts to overcome this lack have led to the development of triple quadrupole mass spectrometers. The mass of interest is selected from the ion main beam by use of a first quadrupole mass filter. In a second "RF-only" quadrupole, producing a focusing but no mass filtering effect, collisional activation may be performed. The resulting product ions are then separated in a third quadrupole mass spectrometer and recorded[60, 61, 77, 78]. Analogous studies using double quadrupole systems[80] have been carried out. Resolving power readily providing unit mass resolution in the product ion spectra faces the disadvantageous loss of information of energy release. Additionally, the question arises if the collision efficiency of the relatively slow precursor ions is really adequate to the state of the art (see 3.3.2).

4.1.4 Consequences

Since DADI/MIKE spectrometry was developed first it has most widely been applied to the recording of ion spectra. Providing many advantages like simple principle, easy technical realization and additional information on the energy release, DADI/MIKE spectrometry is now used worldwide in many laboratories. All the other methods mentioned above offer minor advantages which can however not overcome the disadvantages. Probably, the most efficient way of recording ion spectra is to use a combination of methods according to the analytical problem. For instance, a DADI/MIKE-scan, with or without collisional activation, may be assisted by a B/E-linked scan for the assignment of masses of fragments, providing reliable analytical results. (This is especially important in view of the possible appearance of the so-called artefact peaks[55, 56] which may give rise to errors in the interpretation of ion spectra.)

Finally we should keep in mind one very important principle: The mass spectrometer is a separating system itself. Thus, a double focusing mass spectrometer is a double separating system; one may be used as mass separator and the other one as ion spectrometric device as it is realized in DADI/MIKE spectrometry. Trends for the improvement of this type of mass spectrometry ("MS/MS") by the addition of a third or even a fourth analyzer are going on: Many applications have shown its excellent analytical potential (see Chapter 6.)[66, 67, 68, 82, 83].

4.2 Detection of the Origins of the Ions

(Review:[50])

The uncritical observer will see the origin of all ions in a mass spectrum generated from the molecular ion of the analyzed compound. For the analyst, the situation is not so simple expecially in the case of mixtures, unknown compounds or rearrangement processes occurring in the mass spectrometer. All these points may lead to misinterpretations of a conventional mass spectrum. Thus, very early attempts were made to detect the origins of ions appearing in a mass spectrometer. As the information available from these methods is very valuable for the analyst — especially in connection with data concerning the fate of ions (see 4.1) — the different ways of the detection of ion origins will be discussed in the following sections.

4.2.1 Accelerating Voltage Scan (AVS)

This technique was already described in the middle of the sixties[62,63,64] and the principle is easily understood.

A product ion $m_2^{+/-}$ generated in the first field-free region of a double focusing mass spectrometer (see Fig. 3) is, in the first approximation, travelling with the velocity of its precursor ion. However, its kinetic energy makes up only a fraction of the main beam energy and therefore it cannot pass the energy analyzer at the settings for the precursor ion $m_1^{+/-}$. This is only possible if the product ion $m_2^{+/-}$ is additionally accelerated to $[m_2^{+/-}]^*$ to attain a value equal to the kinetic energy of the main ion beam.

In practice, the product ion $m_2^{+/-}$ of interest is firstly focused onto the detector in the conventional way. Then, the accelerating voltage is scanned upward keeping constant the settings of the analyzer at the initial values chosen for the detection of $m_2^{+/-}$. Thus, the kinetic energy of the precursor ions generating a product ion of mass m_2 is raised to a higher level so that the energy fraction of $[m_2^{+/-}]^*$ also increases to that of the main ion beam in the analyzer. By this way, all possible precursor ions can be detected successively according to their mass.

The technical realization of this scan mode is rather simple. Today, it is available in most double focusing mass spectrometers but very often unused.

One disadvantage of this method is that the scanning of the accelerating voltage gives rise to a defocusing and changing sensitivity. Nevertheless, the accelerating voltage scan should taken into account by the analyst.

4.2.2 Linked Scan

In the accelerating voltage-scan mode, the kinetic energy of both the precursor ion and accordingly of the product ion is increased while the settings of the analyzing field remain constant. On the other hand, it should be possible to lower the field strenghts of the analyzer keeping constant the kinetic energy in order to detect the precursors of an ion of interest. This type of scanning mode has been realized only recently[52]. It offers the advantage that the working conditions of the ion source remain constant and therefore no defocusing takes place. The precursor ions are succesively detected by a linked scan in such a way that the ratio of the square of the magnetic field strenght (B^2) to the voltage E at the energy analyzer is kept constant.

This procedure may only be applied by means of an additional relatively complex electronic unit of high accuracy. The mass resolving power is not superior to that of the accelerating voltage scan (AVS), and the information on the energy release is lost. Therefore, the more simple scan mode, the AVS, is normally preferred for practical purposes.

4.3 Detection of Selected Reactions of Ions

Up to now scan methods allowing (a) the detection of all possible precursors of an ion (constant product ion spectrum of a mixture) and (b) the detection of all product ions of a selected species (constant precursor-ion spectrum) have been discussed. Recalling process Eq. (15) it may be deduced that all these scan methods do not provide direct information on the neutral particle m_3^0. However, the analytical chemist usually wants to know all ions undergoing one special type of fragmentation or, in other words, he would like to look for all ions losing one special neutral species. It is obvious that such a scan may produce invaluable information (a constant neutral loss spectrum) about, for instance, a mixture of homologuous compounds.

Indeed, the concept of a constant neutral spectrum was developed more than ten years ago[89]. It has been applied to the analysis of various reactions involving a loss of hydrogen atoms and molecules from toluene ions. The spectra were obtained by scanning of the magnetic field with iterative adjustment of the electric field in a double focusing mass spectrometer. Only recently has this "by hand scan" been replaced by a fully automated computer-controlled scan[95,91,94,90]. The constant neutral spectrum ("functional group scan") is produced by controlling the magnetic (B) and electric (E) field strength of the mass spectrometer such that the ratio B/E $(1 - E)^{1/2}$ remains constant. Obviously, this scan type may be realized even more conveniently using quadrupole systems, e.g. in a combination of a magnetic analyzer with a double quadrupole system[92], in a triple quadrupole system[93], or in a double quadrupole analyzer[80].

5 General Considerations

Numerous ionization and scan methods used in modern mass spectrometry have now been discussed. This catalog does not reveal the picture of a conventional spectroscopic method but the idea that a mass spectrometer in fact represents a whole laboratory. Therefore, the analyst has to ask the question what his aim really is, which type of information he wants to know. In order to get an answer to this question some principal tasks have to be distinguished, namely

a) must a sample be characterized in the form of a fingerprint type spectrum, for instance in order to look for its possible structure by comparison with the spectra of a library;

Table 3. Localization of observation windows for metastable or collison-induced dissociation with corresponding scan modes

Instrument	Ion source + Acc. field	1 FFR	1st Analyzer	2 FFR	2nd Analyzer	Detector
Quadrupole	Ion source		Quadrupole Rf/DC mass filter			Detector
Single foc. sector field	Ion source	Products: $m^* = \frac{m_2^2}{m_1}$	Magnetic field			Detector
Triple quadrupole	Ion source		RF/DC mass filter quad	Products: Rf focusing only	RF/DC mass filter quad	Detector
Conventional double focusing Herzog-Mattauch, Nier-Johnson	Ion source	Precursors: AVS, B^2/E Products: E^2/V, B/E	Electric field Energy filter	Products: $m^* = \frac{m_2^2}{m_1}$	Magnetic field	Detector
Inverse Nier-Johnson double focussing	Ion source	Precursors: AVS, B^2/E Products: E^2/V, B/E	Magnetic field	Products: DADI/MIKE	Electric field	Detector

b) must the elementary composition of one or more ions be determined;
c) must a known compound be detected within a more or less complex mixture of other compounds,
d) has the structure of a selected ion to be elucidated and, in connection with this, is the reactivity of the ion our point of interest.

The first two problems can usually be solved by conventional mass spectrometry, combined gas chromatography/mass spectrometry (GC/MS) (see e.g.[73, 74]) or liquid chromatography/mass spectrometry (LC/MS) (e.g.[75]) and will not be discussed further.

The third task — the mixture analysis — may be performed by GC/MS or LC/MS. In this connection, gas chromatography and liquid chromatography are principally used for the isolation of the compound of interest or, in other words, for the elimination of the "chemical noise" from the interesting molecules. But here, the more recent mass spectrometric methods discussed before (Chap. 4) offer new possibilities. Thus, since the analyzer of a mass spectrometer is a separating device, it may be worthwile to examine whether the elimination of chemical contaminants or impurities may not be performed by the mass spectrometer itself in a more convenient, less time-consuming and less expensive way. Therefore, this feature will be discussed in more detail in Chap. 6. In the fourth case — structure and reactivity determination — conventional mass spectrometry may generally be useful only in combination with chemical derivatization, labelling experiments and intuition. In contrast, the more modern mass spectrometric methods offer different very effective ways of structure and reactivity elucidation. Selected examples will be described in the next chapter. Before discussing the corresponding application, the different techniques are recalled (Tab. 3). Although similar information may be acquired by different mass spectrometer types, it is obvious that an instrument embodying the inverse Nier-Johnson geometry is the most versatile one (magnetic sector preceeding the electric sector). Regarding all these methods, we must remember the fact that in many cases the best way to solve problem is by a combined application of different scan modes. The more information is obtained, the more easily a reaction or a structure may be understood.

6 Practice of Modern Mass Spectrometry: Selected Examples

In the introductory part of this survey, it has been stated that modern mass spectrometry is no more one single spectrometric method. In several chapters some of the most important actual techniques and possible trends in modern mass spectrometry have been discussed. The complexity of the numerous ionization techniques, scan modes and different mass spectrometer types — at least at first sight — may create a feeling of obscure diffuseness. However, this complexity of performing mass spectrometry clearly demonstrates what a mass spectrometer really can be, namely a complete laboratory in itself including synthetic and analytical parts.

Therefore, the modern mass spectrometrist at first will reflect upon the reactivity of the molecule to be analyzed. The corresponding findings combined with facts about the separation and isolation problems will consequently lead to the technical realization of an analysis. Obviously, this way of utilizing mass spectrometry has induced quite a plethora of new possibilities in analytical work. As it is impossible to report all more recent work in this field, selected examples of using the reactivity of ions and modern scan methods may illustrate trends of modern mass spectrometry.

6.1 Determination of Fragmentation Pathways, Rearrangement Reactions and Ion Structures

Recalling the possibility to detect the product ions generated from one single precursor (Chap. 4.1) or to look for the precursors of one distinct ion (Chap. 4.2), it is obvious that fragmentation pathways may be analyzed in a very convenient way. In contrast to conventional mass spectrometry, modern methods can directly elucidate genetic relationships between ions present in a mass spectrum. A relatively simple example[98)] is described in Fig. 5 (N-Tosylprolinylacetate).

It has been demonstrated by DADI/MIKE spectrometry (see 4.1.1) that the molecular ion at m/z 297 produces the tropylium ion (m/z 91) and the tosylium ion m/z 237 ($M^{+\cdot}$-60, loss of acetic acid), and m/z 224 (loss of the acetylated side chain). But yet in this first generation of product ions, a rearrangement has been detected: the McLafferty rearrangement related to the reaction step m/z 297 → 237.[1] The reaction m/z 237 → 173 which cannot be interpreted by conventional fragmentation rules, thus indicating a second rearrangement. The third generation of ions produced from the rearrangement ion at m/z 173 provides a set of information which is consistent with a sulfur-free species. These findings have been corroborated by peak matching and deuterium labelling experiments[99, 50)].

This example clearly demonstrates that not only fragmentation pathways but also rearrangements may be detected as well as preliminary information on ion structure. This information very often represents the basis of the interpretation of a conventional mass spectrum. It has been used for instance in the case of poly(oxo-steroids) found in biological material. They have been suggested to be androstanes containing four oxygen atoms. The question was how to localize the position of these atoms. In a comparative study several of these tetraoxocompounds were synthesized and the conventional mass spectra recorded. Some of them exhibit a prominent peak at m/z 122 (like 3,17-dihydroxy-5β-androstane-11,16-dione (Fig. 6). The elemental formula for this fragment was determined by peak matching to be $C_8H_{10}O$. The high abundance of this ion gave rise to the question if it could not be used as a diagnostic signal. Therefore, it was important to know where this intense ion originated from and which one of the four oxygen atoms remained in the fragment[100)]. The answer to these question was given by DADI/MIKE spectrometry (D 1a). It was shown that the ion at m/z 122 can be generated by two routes (Fig. 7). The first route involves a three-step process with consecutive loss of ring D, water from

---

[1] For nomenclature and results see[50)].

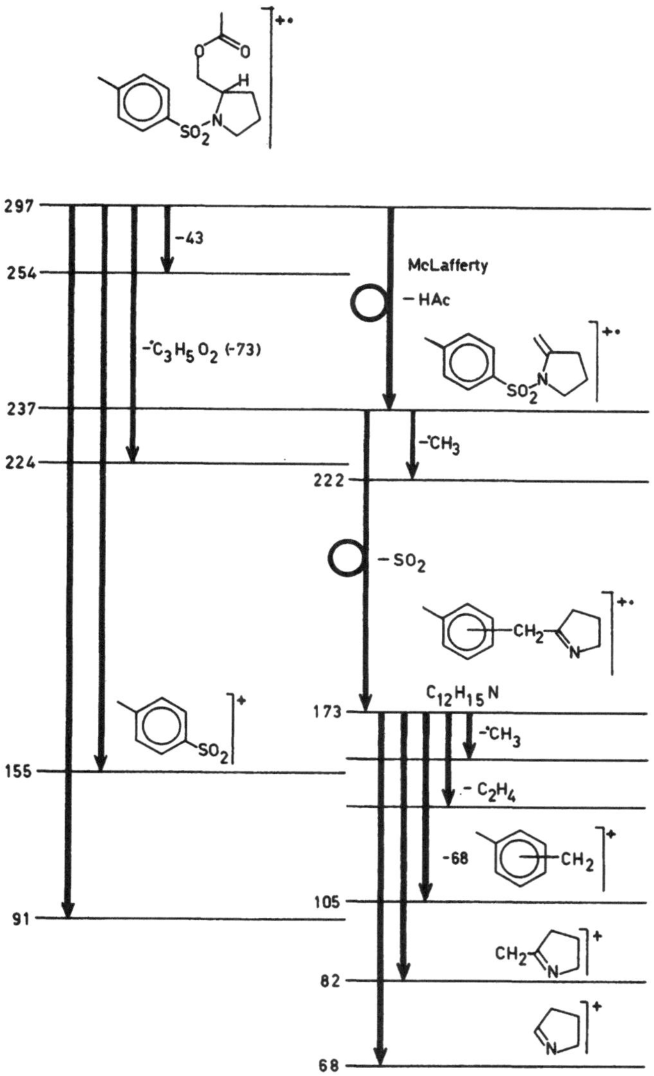

Fig. 5. Fragmentation pathways and rearragement reactions of N-tosylprolinyl acetate[98]

ring A, and finally of the AB ring system. In the second and simpler route a loss of the whole AB ring system and subsequently of ring D occurs. Thus, the detection of the origin of the fragment proved that the key ion at m/z 122 was the oxygen-containing ring C of the analyzed steroid.

Here again, principles of ion structure elucidation have been applied, although structure determination has not been the aim of the study. However, if an ion structure has to be elucidated, as many findings as possible about the ion in question must be collected and compared with one another. This has been accom-

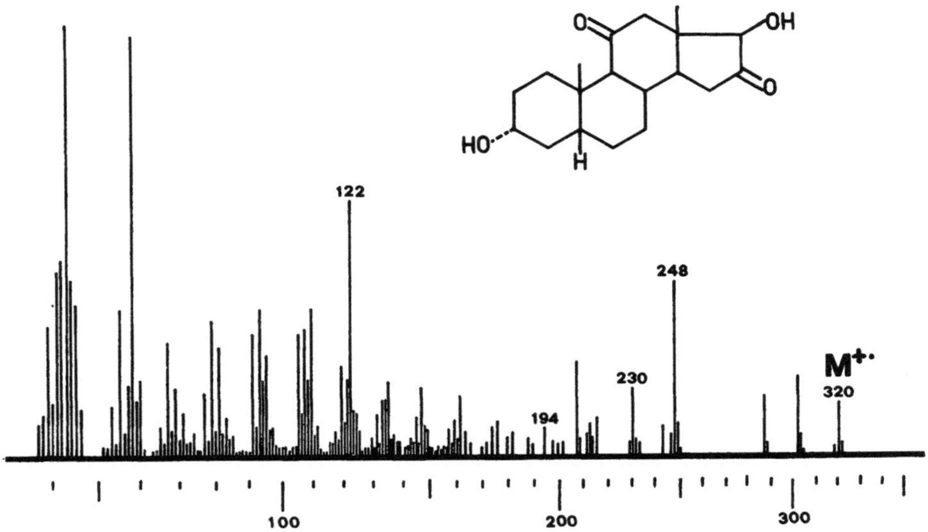

Fig. 6. Conventional mass spectrum of 3,17-dihydroxy-5-androstane-11,16-ione. Which of the four oxygen atoms is in the promininent ion at m/z 122 ($C_8H_{10}O$)?

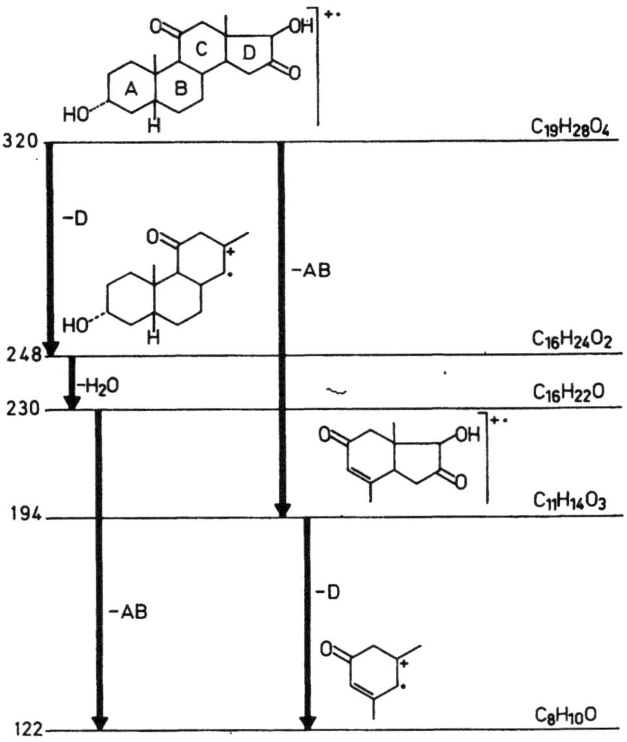

Fig. 7. Formation of the prominent ion at m/z 122 by two routes detected by DADI/MIKE spectrometry.
a m/z 320 → 248 → 230 → 122
b m/z 320 → 194 → 122

plished in the case of a key ion at m/z 178 of Bisamidin[101] — an intermediate in the synthesis of hexahydroporphines (Fig. 8). In the first step, all possible precursors of m/z 178 are looked for using accelerating voltage scan (Sect. 4.2.1). The second step involves the corroboration of all these detected relationships by DADI/MIKE spectrometry verifying the different precursor → m/z 178 transitions. To be sure, the

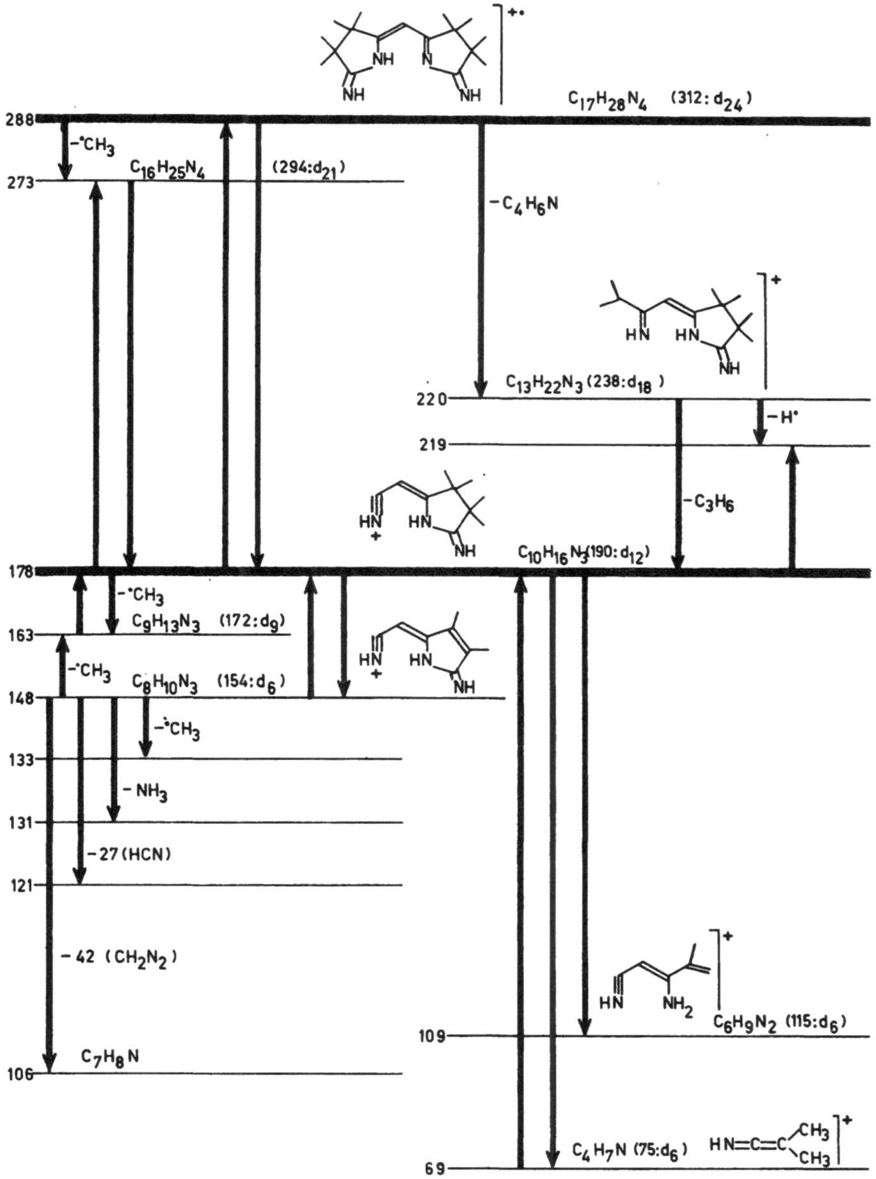

Fig. 8. Structure of the key ion at m/z 178 of bisamidin elucidated by DADI/MIKE spectrometry, accelerating voltage scan, accurate mass determination, and deuterium labelling[101]

whole procedure has been repeated with a deuteriated (d_{24}) homologous species (all methyl groups labelled). Yet, at this point, a rather clear idea of the structure of the m/z 178 has been obtained. The next step involves the study of the fate of m/z 178 using again DADI/MIKE spectrometry and, vice versa, accelerating voltage scan. Since all fragmentation reactions of the tested molecule and also the labelled bisamidin can be explained by conventional fragmentation rules, the suggested ion structure at m/z 178 can be considered as confirmed. There is only one main point

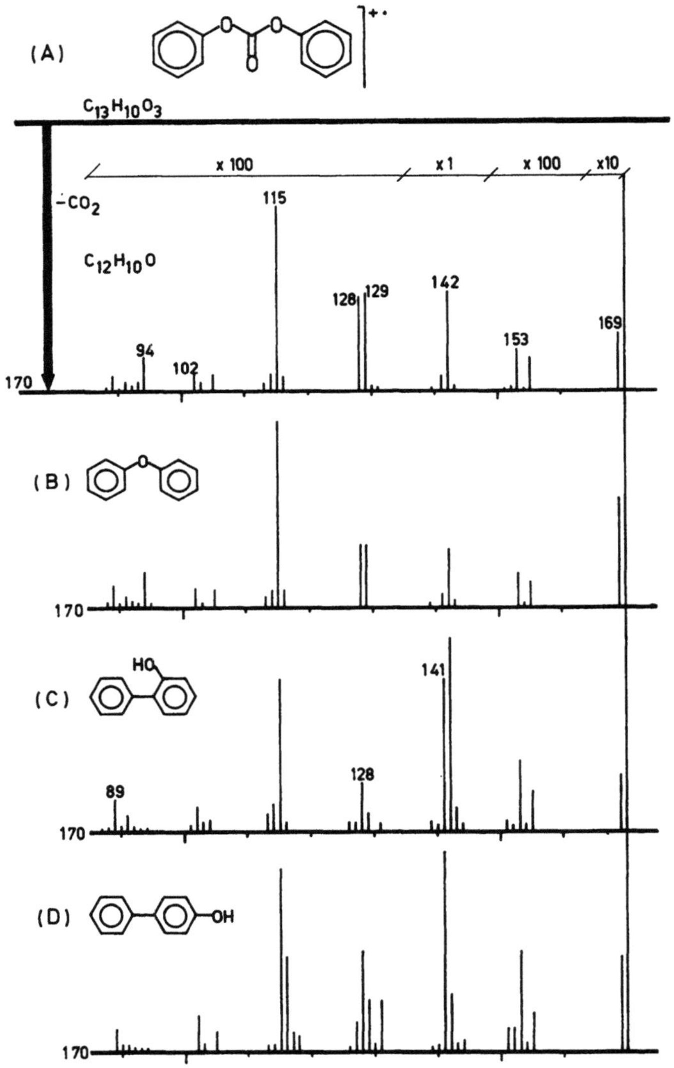

Fig. 9. Structure elucidation of the $(M\text{-}CO_2)^{+\cdot}$ ion at m/z 170, generated from diphenyl carbonate A, comparing diphenyl ether B, ortho phenyl phenol C, an para phenyl phenol, respectively, by DADI/MIKE Spectrometry and linked scan (E^2/V = const.) upon collisional activation[102, 103, 50)]

which must not be forgotten. The structure of the ion at m/z 178 was deduced according to its reactivity only or, in other words, all the observed transitions are based on unimolecular processes involving only excited, "hot" ions. Therefore, a certain ambiguity remains in this way of structure elucidation. According to more recent knowledge, an unambiguous determination of ion structures may be performed by collisional activation where stable, non-excited ions are observed (see 3.3.2). The determination of the structure of the $[M-CO_2]^{+\cdot}$ ion generated from diphenyl carbonate may serve as an example[102, 103, 50]. In this case, the collision-induced dissociation spectra of the ion in question ($(M-CO_2)^{+\cdot}$ at m/z 170), of ortho and paraphenylphenols and of diphenyl ether were compared directly (Fig. 9). They revealed the identity of the $(M-CO_2)^{+\cdot}$ ion with electron impact ionized diphenyl ether within experimental error. These examples of ion structure elucidation are picked out of a plethora of similar works being reported in accordance with the availability of the corresponding equipment in analytical laboratories (for reviews see[30, 50, 69, 104]).

6.2 Sequencing of Oligomers

By definition, a structural subunit is repeated periodically in an oligomer or in a polymer inducing a corresponding periodicity of fragmentation in the mass spectrometer. If a fragmentation series due to such a periodicity of structure is detectable, an analysis of the sequence of monomers in oligomers is possible. This may be discussed in the case of amino acid sequencing in peptides[105, 106, 107, 108, 76].

Upon electron impact ionization, peptides are cleaved on both sides of the carbonyl group (Fig. 10). Each of the resulting fragments X, Y, Z ... is composed of a different number of amine portions A, B, C ... and carbonyl groups. The amine portions A, B, C ... representing the different amino acids are composed of the repeating amide subunit and the amino acid characterizing side chains R^1, R^2, R^3 ... Thus, the amino acid sequence can be deduced from the fragmentation pathway $X \rightarrow (X-CO) \rightarrow Y \rightarrow (Y-CO) \rightarrow Z \ldots$, or $X \rightarrow (Y + A) \rightarrow Y \rightarrow (Z + B) \rightarrow Z \ldots$, respectively. Therefore, tracing the mass difference 28-A-28-B-28-C- ... by DADI/MIKE spectrometry, for instance, the sequence characterizing ions may be detected.

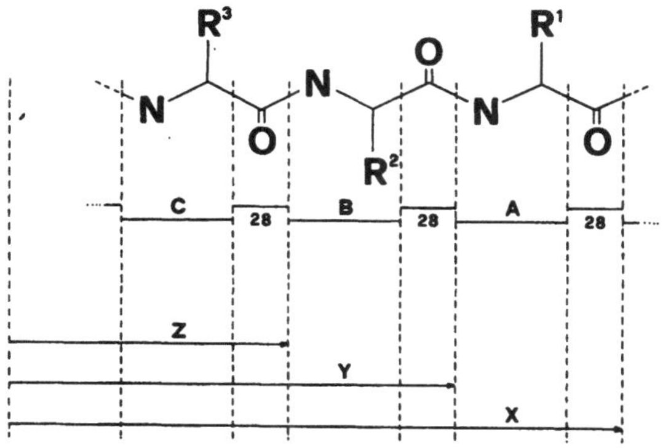

Fig. 10. Principle of the amino acid sequencing using DADI/MIKE spectrometry (upon electron impact ionization)

Thus, the following procedure successfully elucidates the sequence of amino acids in oligopeptides (Fig. 11).

1) Detection of the molecular ion, if necessary by field ionization.
2) Recording of a DADI/MIKE spectrum of the molecular ion. Amine portions and side chains of the more complex amino acid appear in the spectrum if the correct ion is analyzed.
3) DADI/MIKE analysis of the $(M-{}^{\cdot}OCH_3)^+$ ion must indicate the loss of CO and the whole first amino acid, if the correct ion is selected by the magnet settings.
4) The first amino acid can be characterized by analysis of the $(M\text{-}59)^+$ ion (loss of A).
5) In the next step, the ion (M-59-A) is set by the magnet and the corresponding product ion spectrum (DADI/MIKE spectrum) is recorded by a scan of the electric field of the energy analyzer. If the sequencing is still on the correct way, loss of CO (28 amu) occurs.
6) Consecutively, the generation of all ions may be traced by recording the product ion spectrum until a loss of 42 amu due to ketene elimination from the N-acetyl group finishes the sequencing.

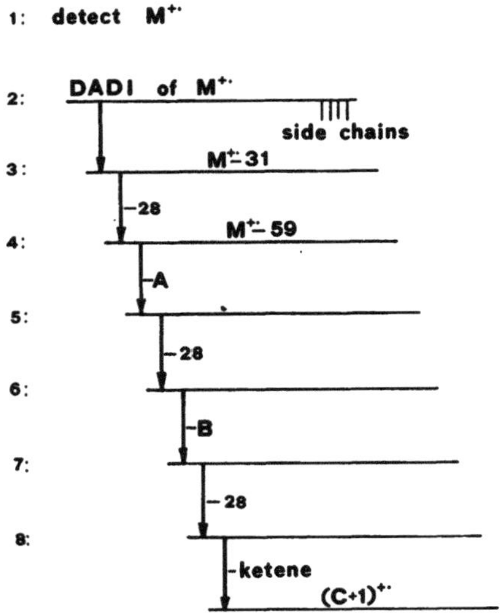

Fig. 11. DADI/MIKE sequencing procedure in an N-acetyltripeptidemethyl ester[106, 107, 108]

However, there is no need to record all these product ion spectra because the complete amino acid sequence may frequently be deduced directly from the DADI/MIKE spectrum of the molecular ion. This has been utilized for the sequencing of polypeptides. As it is possible to determine the sequence of amino acids in oligopeptides even in a peptide mixture by DADI/MIKE spectrometry[106, 76], the polypeptide is hydrolyzed to dipeptide subunits. The sequence of the different peptides is analyzed in the mixture and the data stored in a computer. In a second step, one single amino acid is hydrolytically split off from the original polypeptide. The remaining part is again analyzed in the same manner, yielding dipeptides which overlap the amino acid sequence of the first analysis. By combination of both dipeptide sequences, the amino acid sequence of the original peptide is deduced by a computer program[109]. Interestingly, this sequencing has been performed using negative chemical ionization in a triple quadrupole mass spectrometer. Although this method was applied to neuropeptides at the picomol level, an extension to the femtomol level appears to be feasible. The new techniques have been applied to other fields of analytical work. For instance, sequencing of nucleotides[110,111,134] and polysaccharides[112] have been studied using field desorption ionization and collisional activation. DADI/MIKE spectrometry is also helpful in the structure elucidation of natural lipids[124] and glycerophospholipids[123]. These examples clearly demonstrate the great analytical potential of modern mass spectrometry. It can be taken for sure that more and more applications will be developed.

6.3 Analysis of Complex Mixtures

The analysis of mixtures represents on of the most crucial tasks of the analyst and therefore emphasis has been laid on the development of mixture separating techniques. Unfortunately, conventional mass spectrometry complicates to a large extent the analysis of mixtures due to the creation of an additional mixture of fragments in the ion source. So far, it is not astonishing that mass spectrometry — after an initial success in the analysis of petrochemical mixtures — has lost its importance in this field with the introduction of gas chromatography. This set-back has been overcome by combination of mass spectrometry with gas chromatography.

At this point it is worthwhile to bring into mind what we are really doing in combined gas chromatography/mass spectrometry. There are two outstanding features to be recognized, namely the excellent separating power of gas chromatography and the extreme sensitivity of mass spectrometry enabling analysis in the nano-, pico- or even femto-gram region. Within this system, due to its separating power, gas chromatography has overtaken the task of eliminating the accompaning components or impurities from an selected compound. In terms of analytical chemistry, gas chromatography is responsible for the elimination of the "chemical noise" (with reference to the electronic noise, the well-known sensitivity-limiting feature of every spectroscopic method). Recalling the philosophy of modern methods in mass spectrometry (see Chapter 4) we may conclude now that in this connection a double focusing mass spectrometer or a dual- or triple-stage quadrupole mass filter represents an analogous system: a separating device combined with an analytical tool. In the past few years, many successful attempts have been made to eliminate the chemical noise by the mass spectrometer itself. Thus, some selected examples will be discussed in the following sections.

6.3.1 Analysis of Selected Components in Complex Mixtures

As shown before, ions of interest were isolated and analyzed by DADI/MIKE spectrometry for the detection of fragmentation pathways or structure elucidation. This means that even in chemically pure compounds, an analysis of the mixture must be performed. This principle was again applied to peptide mixtures for the determination of amino acid sequences[76]. The extreme case, the sequencing of oligopeptides with identical amino acid composition but different sequences of the latter has been shown to be also possible[106]. In fact, this is an analysis of isomers of identical molecular weight.

The great potential of these methods has been applied to different fields of analytical work. For instance, very complex mixtures of coal liquefaction products have been analyzed directly without prior treatment or fractionation of the sample[113]. The approximate molecular weight profile of the coal liquid has been determined by isobutane chemical ionization. Nitrogen-containing components have been recognized by using ammonia as chemical ionization reagent gas. Compounds of special interest have been analyzed directly by DADI/MIKE spectrometry and compared with authentic compounds for verification of their structure. For instance, tetrahydroquinoline has been detected and differentiated from tetrahydroisoquinoline directly in the crude coal liquid. This example demonstrates very well the excellent separating power of DADI/MIKE spectrometry. But not only the elimination of chemical noise is outstanding but also the extreme sensitivity of a DADI/MIKE spectrometer. The latter property is demonstrated by the specific determination of particular trace components in gasoline using electron impact and chemical ionization[114]. Thiophene, tetrahydropyran, and n-propylenzene may be quantified directly at levels of <25 ppm, <50 ppm, and <500 ppm, respectively. These new techniques may not only be applied to petrochemical mixtures but they are also very valuable in pharmaceutical chemistry. For instance, the fairly labile compound prostaglandine-dinoprostone may be determined directly in pharmoceutical preparations by a linked scan (B/E = constant) analysis after chemical ionization using ammonia reagent gas[116]. The specificity of the method is maintained for both prostaglandin and steroid product types with little interference from excipients such as suppository or ointment bases. So far, sensitivity is obviously influenced by the ionization method. In accordance with this, the logical next step consists in the testing of materials in the negative ion mode. As discussed before (see Sect. 3.1.4), the sensitivity of compounds with electronegative subunits may be enhanced by several orders of magnitude using negative ions. Simultaneously, more electropositive components are discriminated; thus, the chemical noise present in the mixture is further diminished. This procedure has been applied to different complex mixtures. For instance, hippuric acid ($\sim$65 μg) may be detected directly in 2 μl of urine[115] without prior treatment or purification. Similarly, about 100 ng of glucose in 1 μl of urine were detected by monitoring the loss of HCl from the $(M + Cl)^-$ ion generated by chemical ionization. Analogous methods involve the direct detection of the preservative benzoate in shampoo samples, salicylic acid as an impurity in aspirin, the antioxidant BHA (butylated hydroxyanisole) in dried yeast, and ascorbic acid in 3 μl of urine[117].

Surveying all these examples of direct mass spectrometric analysis of mixtures not only sensitivity and elimination of chemical noise are outstanding but there is an additional feature worthwhile to be mentioned, namely the possibility of analyzing directly very complex materials such as biological samples. Thus, time-consuming purification steps are avoided. In many cases, an analysis utilizing one of these new mass spectrometric techniques will be less expensive and carried out much more rapidly than a conventional analytical procedure. Typical examples are the detection of cocaine in coca leaves (detection limit < 1 ng, quantitative accuracy of about 30%) and in urine ($\sim$ few ng/μl), the detection of other drugs in 1 μl urine sample in the nanogram range (40 ng phenobarbital, 80 ng caffeine, 60 ng mescaline, 25 ng morphine, etc.)[118)], the determination of organophosphorus insecticides directly desorbed from soil samples[119)], and the quantification of N-methylsulfamethazine in swine tissues at the nanogram level[120)]. Also, the methodology has been applied to clinical chemistry, as e.g. in blood serum testing of traces of pyridine, dimethyl ether and urea, respectively (1–22 ng). The analysis frequency is reported to be up to 50 samples per hour[121)]. A simplification of analyzing polycyclic aromatic hydrocarbons in cancer research has also been published. The purification of metabolites produced in human or rodent cells can be greatly facilitaded. Additionally, a new, as yet unidentified metabolite was detected by the new mass spectrometric technique[122)].

Considering the ability of directly analyzing such complex mixtures, crude extracts or even whole biological samples, DADI/MIKE spectrometry and analogous methods are obviously very suitable for screening tests. This has been utilized for the direct analysis not only of the coca leaves of cocaine[118)] but also of the constituents in mushrooms (Helvella esculenta[125)]) of morphine, papaverine, coniine, and atropine in plant materials with a detection limit of about 1 to 10 ng of alkaloid[126)], and for the identification of other alkaloids linke ubine, mescaline, hordenine, and uberine in crude cacti extracts[127, 128, 129)].

In view of all these possibilities of simplifying analytical procedures, more applications especially in routine work can be expected.

6.3.2 Detection of Molecules Yielding a Selected Ion Type

One special ion type may be generated by different precursor species. This is especially true if a mixture of homologous compounds has to be analyzed. In this case, the analyst woud like to know where the ion of interest does originate from and the methods for the detection of fragment ion origins may be applied (see 4.2). The following examples may illustrate some possible applications.

For analytical purposes, amines especially biogenic amines, are frequently derivatized using N-dimethylnaphthalenesulfonylchloride to form the so-called dansyl amides. These derivatives generate the N-dimethylaminonaphthalene ion at m/z 171 upon electron impact ionization, especially in the case of low energy electrons[131)]. Thus, the transition m/z ($171 + SO_2 + \text{amine} - 1$) $\rightarrow$ 171 was applied to demonsfrate the presence of biogenic amines in a mixture. Sixteen different biogenic amines could be identified without preliminary separation by an acceleration voltage scan.

A similar type of analysis has been reported from environmental chemistry. Alkyl phthalates used as placticizers have become ubiquitous contaminants of our environment. In mass spectrometry, the prominent ion at m/z 149 generated from phthalic acid ester plasticizers is well known. It may be used for the detection of all possible precursors by accelerating voltage scan. This type of mixture analysis was realized for common plasticizers[132)]. Obviously, the time required for the analysis is much shorter than that needed for a conventional analytical procedure. But here the question arises if the direct mass spectrometric method is as accurate as the conventional one. A comparative study developed for the analysis of a mineral oil fraction may give the answer. Steranes and terpanes present in a shale extract were analyzed qualitatively and quantitatively by both methods, the gas chromatography-mass spectrometry as well as the accelerating voltage scan[132]. The values obtained (Table 4) impressively demonstrate the high efficiency of the direct mass spectrometric analysis without prior separation.

Table 4. Comparison of quantitative determination of terpanes and steranes in a shale extract by gas chromatography-mass spectrometry (GC-MS) and the direct mass spectrometric analyses of mixtures (acceleration-voltage scan, AVS)

Terpanes	Yield %		Steranes	Yield %	
	GC-MS	AVS		GC-MS	AVS
C_{31}	1.0	1.1	C_{29}	10.3	10.1
C_{30}	13.6	13.2	C_{28}	7.6	6.3
C_{29}	2.3	2.2	C_{27}	1.9	1.8
C_{21}	0.4	0.4	C_{22}	—	0.6
C_{20}	1.4	1.7			
	total: 18.7	total: 18.6		total: 19.8	total: 18.8

6.3.3 Detection of Molecules Undergoing a Specific Reaction

Up to now, two methods of analyzing mixtures have been discussed: (a) recording of the spectra (based on unimolecular processes or collision-induced dissociations) of selected ions and (b) the search of possible precursors of a selected ion type. In the first case, the analyst must have recognized the ion of interest within the mixture, in the second case he must be sure that the ion considered is a typical fragment ion unequivocally characterizing the interesting precursors. But very often the analyst neither knows which one of a homologous series of compounds is present in the mixture nor whether a typical product ion is generated by all possible precursors. In this case, the neutral loss scan (see Sect. 4.3) may be very suitable for the detection of all ions undergoing a specific fragmentation reaction. This optimization of chemical information has been utilized for the detection of the molecular weight profiles of special compound classes. For example, all negative ions, produced by chemical ionization of isobutane, which undergo loss of a neutral fragment of 44 mass units can be regarded as as carboxylic acids. Thus, in one single scan, the presence and the molecular weight of any carboxylic acid in a mixture are indicated[95]. An analogous experiment was used for the detection of pyrrolizidine alkaloids in senecio plant species[133], as well as of bromides and nitro compounds in a synthetic mixture[80]: The logical extension of this experiment consists in a combination of chemical and physical methods. This is performed by derivatizing the entire sample by a reagent which is both chemically selective for the compound class in question and which yields derivatives generating a characteristic neutral loss upon ionization. This combination of a chemical with a spectroscopic test effectively increases the selectivity of the analysis. For instance, this type of analysis has been applied to a coal liquefaction mixture containing alcohols and phenols. This mixture has been treated with an acetylating agent to form the acetyl derivatives of those compounds bearing hydroxy groups. The reaction mixture has been analyzed by a constant neutral loss scan for all ions which produce a neutral fragment of mass 42 — the well-known loss of ketene from acetylated compounds. By this way, the corresponding molecular weights have been recognized and a profile of the quantitative composition has been established[95,97].

The great analytical potential of this method facilitating screening and profiling of selected compound classes will undoubtedly find further applications in the near future although only few examples have hitherto been reported.

7 References

1. Leybold-Heraeus: Berechnungsgrundlagen für die Vakuumtechnik. HV 150, part H, p. B 68, 1973
2. Cooks, R. G., et al.: Metastable ions. Amsterdam, London, New York: Elsevier, Publ. Co. 1973
3. Munson, M. S. B., Field, F. H.: J. Am. Chem. Soc. *88*, 2621 (1966)
4. Field, F. H., Hamlett, P., Libby, W. F.: J. Am. Chem. Soc. *89*, 6035 (1967)
5. Ryan, P. W.: ASMS Meet., 25th Washington, D.C. Pap. WP-10, p. 23 (1977)
6. Whitney, T. A., Kleemann, L. P., Field, F. H.: Anal. Chem. *43*, 1084 (1971)
7. Jelns, B., Munson, M. S. B., Fenselau, C.: Anal. Chem. *46*, 729 (1974)
8. Hunt, D. F., McEwen, Ch. N., Harvey, T. M.: Anal. Chem. *47*, 1730 (1975)
9. Hunt, D. F., Harvey, T. M., Russell, J. W.: J.C.S. Chem. Commun. *1975*, 151
10. Odiorne, T. S., Harvey, D. J., Vouros, P.: J. Org. Chem. *38*, 4274 (1973)
11. Vouros, P., Carpino, L. A.: J. Org. Chem. *39*, 3777 (1974)
12. Wilson, J. M.: Mass Spectrom. *3*, 86 (1975)
13. Bowen, D. V., Field, F. H.: Org. Mass Spectrom. *9*, 195 (1974)
14. Aue, D. H., Bowers, M. T.: Gas phase ion chemistry, vol. 2, p. 1. New York: Academic Press 1979
15. Munson, B.: Anal. Chem. *49*, 772A (1977)
16. Thomson, J. J.: Rays of positive electricity, pp. 27, 70, 227. London: Longmans Green and Co. 1921
17. Aplin, R. T., Budzikiewicz, H., Djerassi, C.: J. Am. Chem. Soc. *87*, 3180 (1965)
18. Jennings, K. R.: Gas phase ion chemistry, vol. 2, p. 123. New York: Academic Press 1979
19. Richter, W. J., Schwarz, H.: Angew. Chem. *90*, 449 (1978)
20. von Ardenne, M., Steinfelder, K., Tümmler, R.: Elektronenanlagerungs-Massenspektrographie organischer Substanzen. Berlin, Heidelberg, New York: Springer Verlag 1971
21. Szulejko, J. E., et al.: Org. Mass Spectrom. *15*, 263 (1980)
22. Hunt, D. F., Sethi, S. K.: ACS Symp. Ser. High Perform. Mass Spectrom.: Chem. Appl. *70*, 150 (1978)
23. Daves, Jr., G. D.: Acc. Chem. Res. *12*, 359 (1979)
24. Beynon, J. H.: Appl. Spectrosc. *33*, 339 (1979)
25. McCormick, A.: Spec. Period. Rep. Mass Spectrom. *5*, 121 (1979)

26. Beckey, H. D., Schulten, H. R.: Pract. Spectrosc. Mass Spectrom. Part *A3*, 145 (1979)
27. Reynolds, W. D.: Anal. Chem. *51*, 283A (1979)
28. Beckey, H. D.: J. Phys. *E 12*, 72 (1979)
29. Greathead, R. J., Jennings, K. R.: 28th Ann. Conf. Mass Spectrom., New York, FAMOA 6 (1980), Org. Mass Spectrom. *15*, 431 (1980)
30. McLafferty, F. W.: ACS Symp. Ser. High Perform. Mass Spectrom.: Chem. Appl. *70*, 47 (1978)
31. Jennings, K. R.: Spec. Period. Rep. Mass Spectrom. *4*, 203 (1977)
32. Derrick, P. J.: Spec. Period. Rep. Mass Spectrom. *4*, 132 (1977)
33. Wilson, J. M.: Spec. Period. Rep. Mass Spectrom. *4*, 102 (1977)
34. Mathers, R. E., Todd, J. F. J.: Int. J. Mass Spectrom. Ion Phys. *30*, 1 (1979)
35. Schulten, H. R.: Int. J. Mass Spectrom. Ion Phys. *32*, 97 (1979)
36. Beckey, H. D.: Field ionization mass spectrometry. Oxford, New York: Pergamon Press 1971
37. Torgerson, D. F., Skowronski, R. P., Macfarlane, R. D.: Biochem. Biophys. Res. Commun. *60*, 616 (1974)
38. Macfarlane, R. D., Torgerson, D. F.: Science *191*, 920 (1976)
39. Macfarlane, R. D., Torgerson, D. F.: Int. J. Mass Spectrom. Ion Phys. *21*, 81 (1976)
40. Krueger, F. R.: Z. Naturforsch. *32a*, 1084 (1977)
41. Becker, O., et al.: Organ. Mass Spectrom. *12*, 461 (1977)
42. Hunt, D. F., et al.: Anal. Chem. *49*, 1160 (1977)
43. Baldwin, M. A., McLafferty, F. W.: Org. Mass Spectrom. *7*, 1353 (1973)
44. Hansen, G., Munson, B.: Anal. Chem. *52*, 245 (1980)
45. Maurer, K. H. et al.: 19th Ann. Conf. Mass Spectrom. Allied Topics, Atlanta 1971
46. Beynon, J. H., Cooks, R. G.: Res./Dev. *22*, 26 (1971)
47. Bowen, R. D., Williams, D. H., Schwarz, H.: Angew. Chem. *91*, 484 (1979)
48. Cooks, R. G.: High Perform. Mass Spectrom. *70*, 58 (1978)
49. Brenton, A. G., Beynon, J. H.: Europ. Spectrosc. News *29*, 39 (1980)
50. Schlunegger, U. P.: Adv. Mass Spectrom. Oxford, New York: Pergamon Press 1980
51. Schlunegger, U. P.: Angew. Chem. *87*, 731 (1975); Int. Ed. Engl. *14*, 679 (1975)
52. Boyd, R. K., Beynon, J. H.: Org. Mass Spectrom. *12*, 163 (1977)
53. Millington, D. S., Smith, J. A.: Org. Mass Spectrom. *12*, 264 (1977)
54. Bruins, A. P., Jennings, K. R., Evans, S.: Int. J. Mass Spectrom. Ion Phys. *26*, 395 (1978)
55. Morgan, R. P., Porter, C. J., Beynon, J. H.: Org. Mass Spectrom. *12*, 735 (1977)
56. Beilton, J. N., Kyriakidis, N., Waight, E. S.: Org. Mass Spectrom. *13*, 489 (1978)
57. Weston, A. F., et al.: Int. J. Mass Spectrom. Ion Phys. *20*, 317 (1976)
58. Kemp, D. L., Cooks, R. G., Beynon, J. H.: Int. J. Mass Spectrom. Ion Phys. *21*, 93 (1976)
59. Holmes, J. L., Terlow, J. K.: Org. Mass Spectrom. *15*, 383 (1980)
60. Yost, R. A., Enke, C. G.: J. Am. Chem. Soc. *100*, 2274 (1978)
61. Hunt, D. F., Shabanowitz, J., Giordani, A. B.: Anal. Chem. *52*, 386 (1980)
62. Barber, M., Elliott, R. M.: 12th Ann. Conf. Mass Spectrom. Allied Topics ASTM, Montreal 1964
63. Futrell, J. H., Ryan, K. R., Sieck, L. W.: J. Chem. Phys. *43*, 1832 (1965)
64. Jennings, K. R.: J. Chem. Phys. *43*, 4176 (1965)
65. Levsen, K.: Fundamental aspects of organic mass spectrometry. Weinheim: Verlag Chemie 1978
66. Maquestiau, A., et al.: Bull. Soc. Chim. Belg. *87*, 765 (1978)
67. McLafferty, F. W.: An automated analytical system for complex mixtures. In: Analytic pyrolysis. Jones, C. E. R., Cramers, C. A. (eds.), p. 39. Amsterdam. London, New York: Elsevier, Publ. Co. 1977
68. Vacuum Generators "MIKES PLUS" Europ. Spectrosc. News *29*, 43 (1980)
69. Levsen, K., Schwarz, H.: Angew. Chem. *88*, 589 (1976); Int. Ed. Engl. *15*, 509 (1976)
70. McLafferty, F. W.: Pure Appl. Chem. *50*, 831 (1978)
71. Boyd, R. K., Beynon, J. H.: Int. J. Mass Spectrom. Ion Phys. *23*, 163 (1977)
72. Cooks, R. G., Kruger, T. L.: J. Am. Chem. Soc. *99*, 1279 (1977)
73. McFadden, W. H.: Techniques of combined gas chromatography/mass spectrometry: applications in organic analysis. New York: Wiley Intersci. Publ. 1973

74. Middleditch, B. S. (ed.): Practical mass spectrometry. A contemporary introduction. New York: Plenum Press 1979
75. McFadden, W. H.: J. Chromatogr. Sci. *17*, 2 (1979)
76. Razakov, R. R., et al.: Bioorg. Khim. *3*, 600 (1977)
77. Boitnott, Ch. A., Steiner, U., Story, M. S.: 28th Ann. Conf. Mass Spectrom., New York, MPMOA 2 (1980)
78. Newcome, B., Enke, C. G.: 28th Ann. Conf. Mass Spectrom., New York, RAMOA 3 (1980)
79. Yost, R. A., Enke, C. G.: Anal. Chem. *51*, 1251A (1979)
80. Zakett, D., Hemberger, P. H., Cooks, R. G.: Anal. Chim. Acta 1980 (in press)
81. Hunt, D. F.: Adv. Mass Spectrom. *6*, 517 (1974)
82. Gross, M. L., Lyon, P. A., Crow, F. W.: 28th Ann. Conf. Mass Spectrom., New York, MPMOA 3 (1980)
83. Russell, D. H., McBay, E. H., Mueller, T. R.: 28th Ann. Conf. Mass Spectrom., New York, TPMP 2 (1980)
84. Posthumus, M. A., et al.: Anal. Chem. *50*, 985 (1978)
85. Kistemaker, P. G., et al.: 28th Ann. Conf. Mass Spectrom., New York, FAMOB 7 (1980)
86. Hardin, E. D., Vestal, M. L.: 28th Ann. Conf. Mass Spectrom., New York, RPMP 16 (1980)
87. Hunt, D. F., Bone, W., Shabanowitz, J.: 28th Ann. Conf. Mass Spectrom., New York, RPMP 18 (1980)
88. Cotter, R. J., Fenselau, C.: 28th Ann. Conf. Mass Spectrom., New York, RPMP 17 (1980)
89. Beynon, J. H., Baitinger, W. E., Amy, J. W.: Int. J. Mass Spectrom. Ion Phys. *3*, 55 (1969)
90. Lacey, M. J., Mcdonald, C. G.: Anal. Chem. *51*, 691 (1979)
91. Bill, J. C., et al.: 28th Ann. Conf. Mass Spectrom., New York, MPMP 23 (1980)
92. Glish, G. L., et al.: 28th Ann. Conf. Mass Spectrom., New York, TPMP 10 (1980)
93. Hunt, D. F., Shabanowitz, J., Giodani, A. B.: 28th Ann. Conf. Mass Spectrom., New York, RAMOA 8 (1980)
94. Haddon, W. F.: Org. Mass Spectrom. *15*, 539 (1980)
95. Zakett, D., et al.: J. Am. Chem. Soc. *101*, 6781 (1979)
96. Kim, M. S., McLafferty, F. W.: J. Am. Chem. Soc. *100*, 3279 (1978)
97. Zakett, D., Cooks, R. G.: 28th Ann. Conf. Mass Spectrom., New York, MAMOA 3, (1980)
98. Wiegrebe, W., Schlunegger, U. P., Herrmann, E. G.: Pharm. Acta Helv. *49*, 263 (1974)
99. Steinauer, R.: Diplomarbeit, Universität Bern 1977
100. Richter, H., Spiteller, G.: Monatsh. Chem. *107*, 459 (1976)
101. Schlunegger, U. P., et al.: Helv. Chim. Acta *58*, 65 (1975)
102. Levsen, K., McLafferty, F. W.: Org. Mass Spectrom. *8*, 353 (1974)
103. Robbiani, R., Kuster, Th., Seibl, J.: Angew. Chem. *89*, 115 (1977)
104. Burlingame, A. L., et al.: Anal. Chem. *50*, 346R (1978)
105. Levsen, K., Wipf, H. K., McLafferty, F. W.: Org. Mass Spectrom. *8*, 117 (1974)
106. Schlunegger, U. P., Hirter, P., von Felten, H.: Helv. Chim. Acta *59*, 406 (1976)
107. Schlunegger, U. P., Hirter, P.: Israel J. Chem. *17*, 168 (1978)
108. Steinauer, R., Walther, H. J., Schlunegger, U. P.: Helv. Chim. Acta *63*, 610 (1980)
109. Hunt, D. F., et al.: 28th Ann. Conf. Mass Spectrom., New York, WAMOB 4 (1980)
110. Levsen, K., Schulten, H. R.: Biomed. Mass Spectrom. *3*, 137 (1976)
111. Linscheid, M., Burlingame, A. L.: 28th Ann. Conf. Mass Spectrom., New York, RAMOA 4 (1980)
112. D'Angona, J., et al.: 28th Ann. Conf. Mass Spectrom., New York, RAMOB 7 (1980)
113. Zakett, D., Shaddock, V. M., Cooks, R. G.: Anal. Chem. *51*, 1849 (1979)
114. McLafferty, F. W., Bockhoff, F. M.: Anal. Chem. *50*, 69 (1978)
115. Kondrat, R. W., McClusky, G. A., Cooks, R. G.: Anal. Chem. *50*, 1223 (1978)
116. Duholke, W. H., Fox, L. E.: 28th Ann. Conf. Mass Spectrom., New York, TPMP 20 (1980)
117. McClusky, G. A., Kondrat, R. W., Cooks, R. G.: J. Anm. Chem. Soc. *100*, 6045 (1978)
118. Kondrat, R. W., McClusky, G. A., Cooks, R. G.: Anal. Chem. *50*, 2017 (1978)
119. Vincze, A., Bel, P., Gefen, L.: 28th Ann. Conf. Mass Spectrom., New York, WAMOA 8 (1980)

120. Hoffman, M. K., Harven, D. J., Hass, J. R.: 28th Ann. Conf. Mass Spectrom., New York, MPMP 14 (1980)
121. Glish, G. L., et al.: Anal. Chem. *52*, 165 (1980)
122. McClusky, G., Huang, S. S.: 28th Ann. Conf. Mass Spectrom., New York, ROMOA 5 (1980)
123. Batrakov, S. G., et al.: Bioorganicheskaya Khimiya *4*, 1390 (1978)
124. Batrakov, S. G., et al.: Bioorg. Khim. *4*, 1220 (1978)
125. McClusky, G. A., Cooks, R. G., Knevel, A. U.: Tetrahedron Lett. *46*, 4471 (1978)
126. Kondrat, R. W., Cooks, R. G., McLaughlin, J. L.: Science *199*, 978 (1978)
127. Kruger, T. L., et al.: J. Org. Chem. *42*, 4161 (1977)
128. Kondrat, K. W., Cooks, R. G.: Anal. Chem. *50*, 81A (1978)
129. Cooks, R. G.: Internat. Lab. Jan./Febr. 1979, pp. 79–94
130. Schulten, H. R., Nibbering, N. M. M.: Biomed. Mass Spectrom. *4*, 55 (1977)
131. Addeo, F., Malorni, A., Marino, G.: Anal. Biochem. *64*, 98 (1975)
132. Gallegos, E. J.: Anal. Chem. *48*, 1348 (1976)
133. Haddon, W. F., Molyneux, R. J.: 28th Ann. Conf. Mass Spectrom., New York, RAMOA 6 (1980)
134. Wiebers, J. L.: 8th Int. Mass Spectrom. Conf. Oslo 1979

Fourier Transform Nuclear Magnetic Resonance

Reinhart Geick

Physikalisches Institut der Universität, Röntgenring 8, D-8700 Würzburg,
Federal Republic of Germany

Table of Contents

This review starts with the basic principles of resonance phenomena in physical systems. Especially, the connection is shown between the properties of these systems and Fourier transforms. Next, we discuss the principles of nuclear magnetic resonance. Starting from the general properties of physical systems showing resonance phenomena and from the special properties of nuclear spin systems, the main part of this paper reviews pulse and Fourier methods in nuclear magnetic resonance. Among pulse methods, an introduction will be given to spin echoes, and, apart from the principle of Fourier transform nuclear magnetic resonance, an introduction to the technical problems of this method, e.g. resolution in the frequency domain, aliasing, phase and intensity errors, stationary state of the spin systems for repetitive measurements, proton decoupling, and application of Fourier methods to systems in a nonequilibrium state. The last section is devoted to special applications of Fourier methods and recent developments, e.g. measurement of relaxation times, solvent peak suppression, "rapid scan"-method, methods for suppressing the effects of dipolar coupling in solids, two-dimensional Fourier transform nuclear magnetic resonance, and spin mapping or zeugmatography.

1 Introduction

In the last three decades, nuclear magnetic resonance has become a powerful tool for investigating the structural and physical properties of matter. Today, nuclear magnetic resonance is the physical method most widely used in analytical chemistry. For special applications, e.g. relaxation time measurements, there is available a variety of modifications of the basic nuclear magnetic resonance experiments such as pulse and spin-echo methods. In the course of this development and when electronic computers were provided at a reasonable price, Fourier transform spectroscopy was applied to nuclear magnetic resonance in the middle of the sixties. At that time, Fourier methods were already used to a large extent in far infrared spectroscopy (see Refs.[23–27] and references cited therein).

When dealing with the Fourier transform method in infrared spectroscopy, the basic principles of optics have to be described. For nuclear magnetic resonance and especially for Fourier methods in this field, the basic principles are twofold and are found in two different chapters of standard textbooks of physics. First, most of the essential features of Fourier transform nuclear magnetic resonance (FTNMR) are exhibited already by simple vibrating systems which show resonance, free and forced vibrations. Secondly, we have to take account of the special properties of nuclear magnetism and of the quantum mechanics and thermodynamical statistics involved because a nuclear spin cannot be treated classically as a rotating top and because the measured signal in nuclear magnetic resonance arises from an ensemble of nuclear spins. As already pointed out in Ref.[26] (Vol. 58 of this series), Fourier transform methods are easily handled by modern commercial instruments well-equipped with computers, but the experimenter is recommended to gain some insight into the method which, in this case, is based on a mathematical formalism, the Fourier transform. In this review, the application of Fourier transform methods to nuclear magnetic resonance cannot be treated without the mathematical aspects. But it is hoped to be helpful to the reader that some of these aspects are introduced with an illustrative example, a simple oscillator. Of course, some mathematical formulae are unavoidable, but it is always attempted to explain the meaning of this mathematical "shorthand" in the text or by means of a figure. However, it will not be possible to derive in a rigorous way all the mathematical expressions used in this brief review. In this respect, the reader is referred to the literature[1].

2 Resonance Phenomena in Physics

As mentioned in the introduction, it seems useful to divide the discussion of the basic principles of nuclear magnetic resonance into two parts: the physical phenomenon of

[1] In the references, there are compiled a number of books and reviews dealing with nuclear magnetic resonance[1–15] and with pulse and Fourier methods in nuclear magnetic resonance[16–22].

resonance explained in context with a simple example and the basic properties of nuclear magnetism. Starting with the first part[2], let us consider the simple oscillator shown in Fig. 1. One end of the elastic spring with spring constant D is fixed, and at the other end, a magnet of mass m is mounted. By means of an electric current in coil L, a force F may be exerted on mass m. Including a friction term proportional to the velocity, the equation of motion (Newton's law) reads

$$m\frac{d^2s}{dt^2} + m\varrho\frac{ds}{dt} + Ds = F\,, \tag{1}$$

where s is a displacement from the equilibrium position small enough that Hook's law may be applied to the spring, i.e. the repulsive force to reduce the displacements is proportional to the displacement ($D \cdot s$). If an alternating current is applied to the coil, the force and the corresponding displacement will be periodic with the frequency ω of the alternating current ($\varrho < \omega_0$):

$$F(t) = F_0 \cos(\omega t)\,,$$
$$s(t) = A(\omega)\cos(\omega t - \varphi)\,, \tag{2}$$

where F_0 is the strength of the external force while $A(\omega)$ and φ are the amplitude of the displacement s and the phase shift between force and displacement, respectively. In order to determine the properties of the system experimentally, there is the possibility of applying the periodic force for a variety of frequencies ω and measuring the amplitude $A(\omega)$ and the phase shift $\varphi(\omega)$ as a function of frequency (see Fig. 1). The essential properties of the system to be determined are its eigenfrequency $\omega_0 = \sqrt{D/m}$ and its damping constant ϱ. For $\omega = \omega_0$, the system is at resonance with the external force. At this frequency, $A(\omega)$ exhibits the usual resonance maximum, the width of which is proportional to ϱ. The phase shift varies from $\varphi = 0$ to $\varphi = \pi$ for $\omega \to \infty$, passing through the value $\pi/2$ at resonance with a slope proportional to ϱ. Thus, the eigenfrequency ω_0 and the damping constant ϱ can be extracted from the experimental data $A(\omega)$ and $\varphi(\omega)$. Instead of these, one could also measure the two quantities $A\cos\varphi$ and $A\sin\varphi$. Note that

$$s(t) = A\cos(\omega t - \varphi) = (A\cos\varphi)\cos(\omega t) + A\sin\varphi)\sin(\omega t)\,. \tag{3}$$

After dividing $A\cos\varphi$ and $A\sin\varphi$ by the strength F_0 of the external force, we obtain the real part $A\cos\varphi/F_0$ and the imaginary part $A\sin\varphi/F_0$ of the complex response function

$$\frac{A}{F_0}e^{i\varphi} = \frac{A}{F_0}(\cos\varphi + i\sin\varphi)$$

which is independent of F_0 for the linear system under consideration (linear system means that the displacement is proportional to the applied force, see Eq. (1)). The real and imaginary part of such a complex response function contain the same information about the oscillating system, namely the value of the eigenfrequency ω_0 and

[2] For more details about resonance phenomena, the reader is referred to any of the standard textbooks in physics.

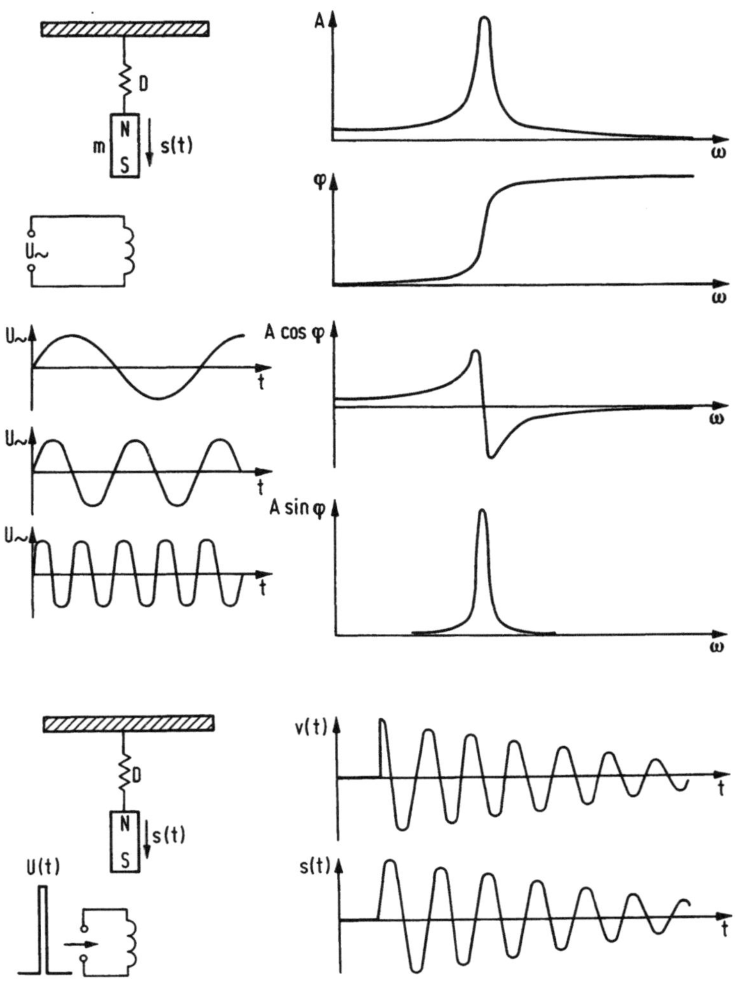

Fig. 1. Mechanical oscillator system and its dynamical properties: The measurement at various frequencies (upper part) yields the typical resonance curves, and the measurement as a function of time (lower part) yields typically damped oscillations

of the damping constant ϱ. The two parts are related with each other by the "Kramers-Kronig" integral relations[3]:

$$f'(\omega) - f'(\infty) = \frac{2}{\pi} \int_0^\infty \frac{\omega' f''(\omega')}{\omega'^2 - \omega^2} \, d\omega', \tag{4a}$$

$$f''(\omega) = -\frac{2\omega}{\pi} \int_0^\infty \frac{f'(\omega') - f'(\infty)}{\omega'^2 - \omega^2} \, d\omega', \tag{4b}$$

[3] See, for example, expecially with respect to nuclear magnetic resonance, Ref.[8].

where we have used the abbreviations $f' = A \cos \varphi/F_0$ and $f'' = A \sin \varphi/F_0$ for the real and imaginary part, respectively. Eq. (4) shows that $f'(\omega)$ can be calculated if $f''(\omega)$ has been measured for a sufficiently wide frequency range and vice versa. Note that in Eq. (4) ω is the frequency for which f' or f'' is to be calculated and that ω' is the frequency over which the integration is to be carried out.

Now let us return to more practical considerations. It would be very time consuming if the measurements mentioned in context with Eq. (2) were performed separately for a large number of frequencies waiting every time until the transient oscillations of the system have disappeared, and a steady state is reached. The more elegant way is to sweep the frequency of the force, i.e. of the current in the coil, from a value well below resonance to a value above and to obtain the required information in one measurement. Mostly, the frequency is swept in a linear way $\omega = a \cdot t$ where a denotes the frequency change per second. For small a and rather long time for one sweep (slow passage), the experimental results are equal to the expressions Eqs. (4a) and (4b) and represent the required information (see Fig. 2). For a rather high sweep rate a and corresponding small sweep time (rapid passage), deviations and wiggles will occur in the experimental data. If the sweep time becomes as short as the time for a few oscillations of the system, the rf-field acts more like a pulse as discussed in the next section and will excite a free damped oscillation of the system.

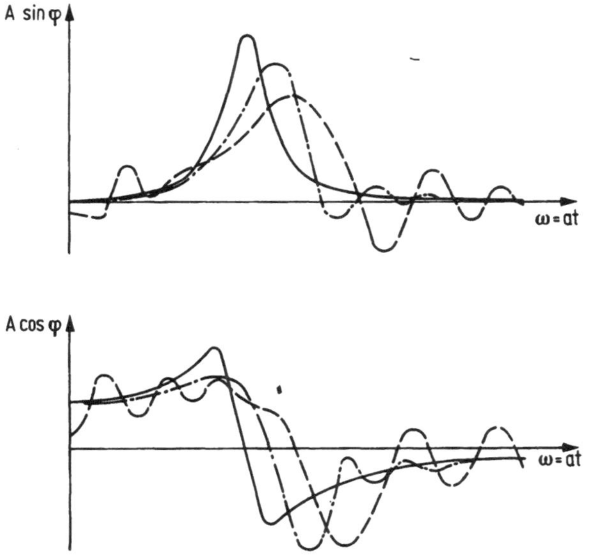

Fig. 2. Absorption mode signal A sin φ (upper part) and dispersion mode signal A cos φ (lower part) as a function of sweep rate a: (———) $a \leqq 0.16\frac{\varrho^2}{4}$; (—·—) $a = 1.6\frac{\varrho^2}{4}$; (---------) $a = 4\frac{\varrho^2}{4}$. Only for sweep rates a small compared to $\varrho^2/4$, the undistorted data are obtained (slow passage condition).

The other approach to the problem of determining the properties of the oscillating system (Fig. 1) is to apply a short and strong electric pulse to the coil. This means exerting a strong force F on the mass m during a short period Δt. Its reaction will be a damped free oscillation (see Fig. 1)

$$s(t) = \frac{P_0}{m\omega_0'} \sin(\omega_0' t)\, e^{-\frac{1}{2}\varrho t}, \qquad (5)$$

where $\omega_0' = \sqrt{\omega_0^2 - (\varrho/2)^2}$ and $P_0 = F \cdot \Delta t$ are the actual eigenfrequency in the case of damping and the momentum transferred to the mass by the pulse, respectively. From this so-called "impulse response function" (Eq. (5)), also the characteristic quantities ω_0 and ϱ can be derived. For a system with a single resonance or eigenfrequency, they are easily evaluated from the period of one oscillation and from the exponential decay of the vibration amplitude (see Fig. 1). Another important property of the impulse response function (Eq. (5)) is that it can be used to construct the response of the system to any external force even if this force acts not for a short time but for a longer period. In this case, the force may be divided into pulses of small duration for which the displacement s may be calculated by means of Eq. (5). The response of the system to an arbitrary external force can be calculated by a summation over all the short-pulse responses:

$$s(t) = \frac{1}{m\omega_0'} \int_0^\infty \sin(\omega_0'\tau)\, e^{-\frac{1}{2}\varrho\tau}\, F_{ext}(t - \tau)\, d\tau \tag{6}$$

where $F_{ext}(t)$ is the external force as a function of time. Eq. (6) is called a "convolution". For a linear sweep experiment, the dispersion and absorption mode signals are derived by means of Eq. (6) as follows (cf. Fig. 2):

$$\begin{aligned} A\cos\varphi &= \frac{F_0}{m\omega_0'} \int_0^\infty \sin(\omega_0'\tau)\, e^{-\frac{1}{2}\varrho\tau} \cos\left(at\tau - \frac{a}{2}\tau^2\right) d\tau \\ A\sin\varphi &= \frac{F_0}{m\omega_0'} \int_0^\infty \sin(\omega_0'\tau)\, e^{-\frac{1}{2}\varrho\tau} \sin\left(at\tau - \frac{a}{2}\tau^2\right) d\tau \end{aligned} \tag{7}$$

where a is the sweep rate and $\omega = at$ the frequency at time t during the sweep. The integration over τ means summing the contributions originating from the external force at different times τ. For rather small sweep rates a, we may neglect $\frac{a}{2}\tau^2$ in the argument of the cos- and sin-function, respectively, and may write $\cos(at\tau) = \cos(\omega t)$ and $\sin(at\tau) = \sin(\omega t)$. We shall see that this "slow passage" form of Eq. (7) is the Fourier transform of the impulse response function which is discussed below (see Eq. (8)).

If, instead of a single resonance frequency, the system has a number of resonance frequencies (with possibly different damping constants) as it is the case usually for a nuclear magnetic system, the question arises how to derive all the quantities ω_0 and ϱ from the damped free oscillation which is now the superposition of functions like that in Eq. (7). It should be noted that the application of a short pulse is experimentally the more elegant way than the frequency sweep method with a periodic force involving sweeping (rather slowly!) of a sufficiently wide range to cover all the resonance frequencies. But the interpretation of the experimental data is much easier in this case as there is a resonance maximum at each eigenfrequency with a width proportional to the corresponding damping constant. And we would like to convert the complicated impulse response function to the resonance curves as a function of frequency.

This problem can be solved by means of a mathematical procedure applied to the damped free oscillation data. This procedure is called a Fourier transform and can easily be performed with an electronic computer. For the mechanical example with on eigenfrequency, the basic equations of the Fourier transform read

$$A\cos\varphi = \int_0^\infty s(t)\cos(\omega t)\,dt = \frac{P_0}{m\omega_0'}\int_0^\infty \sin(\omega_0' t)\,e^{-\frac{1}{2}\varrho t}\cos(\omega t)\,dt$$

$$A\sin\varphi = \int_0^\infty s(t)\sin(\omega t)\,dt = \frac{P_0}{m\omega_0'}\int_0^\infty \sin(\omega_0' t)\,e^{-\frac{1}{2}\varrho t}\sin(\omega t)\,dt\,. \tag{8}$$

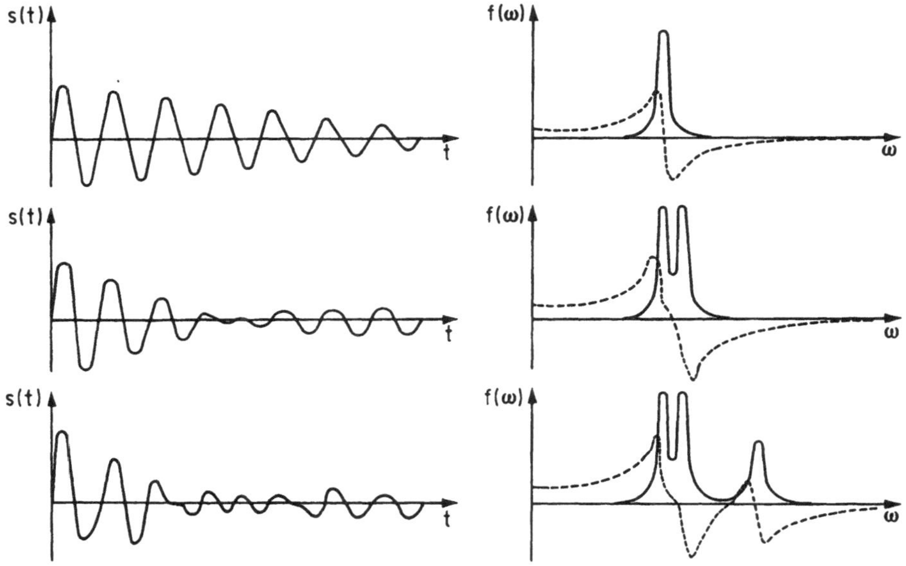

Fig. 3. Three examples of damped free oscillation curves s(t) and the corresponding absorption mode spectra $f(\omega) = A\sin\varphi$ (———) and dispersion mode spectra $f(\omega) = A\cos\varphi$ (··········) as obtained by the Fourier transform procedure

Fig. 3 shows some examples of free oscillation curves and the corresponding spectra $A\cos\varphi$ and $A\sin\varphi$ computed by means of Eq. (8). The main advantage of the Fourier method explained in this section is that it allows to deal with all resonance frequencies simultaneously in the experiment and to separate the data with respect to its frequency components later by means of the computer. This so-called "Fellgett" or "multiplex" advantage is the same as that mentioned in context with infrared Fourier transform spectroscopy[23–27] (Ref.[26] is Vol. 58 in this series). We have to realize, however, that the damped free oscillations s(t) can be studied only over a finite range ($0 \leqq t \leqq t_{max}$) and, therefore, the integration in Eq. (8) too, can be performed only over a finite range. If the free oscillations have decayed sufficiently, i.e. $e^{-\varrho t_{max}/2} \approx 0$ or $\frac{1}{2}\varrho t_{max} \gg 1$, no problems arise from the finite integration range. If this is not the case and, for example, the damping of the oscillation is very small, t_{max} will limit the resolution in the frequency domain ($\Delta\nu = 1/2t_{max}$ or $\Delta\omega = \pi/t_{max}$, the line shape function being of the type $\frac{\sin x}{x}$, cf. Vol. 58, Fig. 6, p. 86). And as in the case of infrared Fourier transform spectroscopy, an apodization can be applied to the experimental data in order to diminish the secondary extrema of the line shape function, at the expense of a reduced resolution ($\Delta\nu \approx 1/t_{max}$).

These considerations show how Fourier methods can be employed in analyzing systems with a number of resonance frequencies. As will be explained in the Section 3, nuclear magnetic systems are usually of this type, and the Fourier transform method discussed above is essentially that used in nuclear magnetic resonance. Therefore, the reader should bear in mind that a simple mechanical system was used to explain the basic principles but that all these considerations are already the first step of an introduction to Fourier transform nuclear magnetic resonance (FTNMR).

3 Basic Principles of Nuclear Magnetic Resonance

Nuclear magnetism arises from the magnetic moments μ of the nuclei[1–15)]

$$\mu = g\mu_N I\,, \tag{9}$$

which are connected with the nuclear spin I. In Eq. (9), g and $\mu_N = 6.347 \cdot 10^{-33}$ Vs m are the g-factor and the nuclear magneton. In Table 1, the values of g are compiled for a number of nuclei. Let us now consider the most simple nuclear spin system with one kind of non-interacting spins for the introduction of the basic properties of such a system. If a static magnetic field H_0 is applied, the energy is quantized

$$E_m = -g\mu_N H_0 m\,, \tag{10}$$

where m is the magnetic quantum number ($-I \leqq m \leqq +I$). At thermal equilibrium at temperature T, there will be a certain distribution of the nuclei over the (2I + 1) magnetic sublevels given by Eq. (10). The probability that a nucleus is in the state m is given by

$$p_m = \frac{1}{Z}\,e^{-E_m/kT} = \frac{1}{Z}\,e^{+mg\mu_N H_0/kT}\,, \tag{11}$$

Table 1. Nuclear spins and g-factors, natural abundancies and NMR resonance frequencies for a number of nuclei

Nuclens	Natural isotopic abundance (%)	Nuclear Spin I	Nuclear g-factor	NMR Resonance Frequency (MHz) at a field of		Electric Quadrupole Moment (10^{-24} cm^2)
				1.00 T	2.114 T	
^{1}n	—	$^1/_2$	−3.8261	29.165	61.65	—
^{1}H	99.98	$^1/_2$	5.5854	42.577	90.00	—
^{2}D	$1{,}56 \cdot 10^{-2}$	1	0.8574	6.536	13.82	$2.77 \cdot 10^{-3}$
^{3}He	10^{-5}–10^{-7}	$^1/_2$	−4.2549	32.434	68.56	—
^{6}Li	7.43	1	0.8219	6.265	13.24	$4{,}6 \cdot 10^{-4}$
^{7}Li	92.57	$^3/_2$	2.1707	16.547	34.98	$-4.2 \cdot 10^{-2}$
^{13}C	1.108	$^1/_2$	1.4044	10.705	22.63	—
^{14}N	99.64	1	0.4035	3.076	6.50	$2 \cdot 10^{-2}$
^{17}O	$3.7 \cdot 10^{-2}$	$^5/_2$	−0.7572	5.772	12.20	$-4.5 \cdot 10^{-3}$
^{19}F	100	$^1/_2$	5.2547	40.055	84.67	—
^{23}Na	100	$^3/_2$	1.4774	11.262	23.81	0.1
^{29}Si	4.70	$^1/_2$	−1.1098	8.460	17.88	—
^{31}P	100	$^1/_2$	2.2610	17.235	36.44	—
^{35}Cl	75.4	$^3/_2$	0.5473	4.172	8.82	$-8 \cdot 10^{-2}$
^{39}K	93.08	$^3/_2$	0.2607	1.987	4.20	$(0.7–1.4) \cdot 10^{-1}$
^{43}Ca	0.13	$^7/_2$	−0.3759	2.865	6.06	—
^{55}Mn	100	$^5/_2$	1.3844	10.553	22.31	0.5
^{57}Fe	2.245	$^1/_2$	0.1812	1.381	2.92	—
^{59}Co	100	$^7/_2$	1.3254	10.103	21.36	0.5

where k is Boltzmann's constant and

$$Z = \sum_{m=-I}^{+I} e^{-E_m/kT} = \frac{\sin h[(2I+1)\, g\mu_N H_0/kT]}{\sin h[g\mu_N H_0/kT]} .$$

As an example, let us consider protons with $I = 1/2$ ($m = \pm 1/2$) and $g = 5.5854$. Assuming a magnetic field of $H_0 = 7.96 \cdot 10^5$ A/m corresponding to a magnetic induction $B_0 = 1T$ (10 kG), we obtain for proton

$$g\mu_N H_0 = 2.82 \cdot 10^{-26}\ \mathrm{Ws} .$$

The average thermal energy, on the other hand, is for 300 K

$$kT = 4.14 \cdot 10^{-21}\ \mathrm{Ws} .$$

Thus, the essential factor $g\mu_N H_0/kT$ in Eq. (9) is much smaller than unity ($6.81 \cdot 10^{-6}$ for 300 K), even at low temperatures ($2.04 \cdot 10^{-5}$ for 100 K and $4.87 \cdot 10^{-4}$ for 4.2 K). Therefore, we are allowed to use the "high temperature approximation":

$$Z \approx 2I + 1$$

and

$$p_m \approx \frac{1}{2I+1}\,[1 + mg\mu_N H_0/kT]\,. \tag{12}$$

For protons at 4.2 K (liquid helium temperature), we obtain Z = 2,

$$p_{+1/2} = \frac{1}{2}\left[1 + \frac{1}{2}\cdot 4.87\cdot 10^{-4}\right] = 0.50012\,,$$

and

$$p_{-1/2} = \frac{1}{2}\left[1 - \frac{1}{2}\cdot 4.87\cdot 10^{-4}\right] = 0.49988\,.$$

If $p_{\pm 1/2}$ would be calculated by means of the exact Eq. (9), the difference between the two results would be insignificant.

Dividing the magnetic energy or Zeeman energy $g\mu_N H_0$ by Planck's constant $h = 6.626 \cdot 10^{-34}$ Js, a frequency results ($E = h\nu$!) which lies in the radiofrequency range, e.g. $\nu = 42.576$ MHz for protons in a magnetic field $H_0 = 7.96 \cdot 10^5$ A/m (= 10 kG). And if, in addition to the static field H_0, a radiofrequency field (rf-field) with the appropriate frequency is applied to the nuclear spin system, transitions between the magnetic sublevels may be induced with $\Delta m = \pm 1$ and $\Delta E = g\mu_N H_0$. These transitions and the interaction of the spin system with the rf-field should be treated quantummechanically. What we can observe experimentally, however, is not the reaction of one nuclear spin with respect to the rf-field, but that of the whole ensemble of the spins, which can be described as a time-dependent nuclear magnetization M(t). For M(t), on the other hand, we may use classical equations of motion which will be mostly done in the following considerations. A magnetic field will exert a torque on the magnetization and the corresponding equation of motion reads

$$\frac{d\mathbf{M}}{dt} = \mathbf{M} \times \gamma[\mathbf{H}_0 + \mathbf{H}_{rf}]\,,$$

with

$$\mathbf{H}_0 = [0, 0, H_0]\,,$$

$$\mathbf{H}_{rf} = [2H_1 \cos(\omega t), 0, 0]\,, \tag{13}$$

and where $\gamma = 2\pi g\mu_N/h$ is the gyromagnetic ratio. The components of $\mathbf{H}_0$ and $\mathbf{H}_{rf}$ show the coordinate system to be chosen in such a way that $\mathbf{H}_0$ and $\mathbf{H}_{rf}$ point along the z- and x-directions (cf. Fig. 4), respectively.

The effect of a magnetic field on the magnetization or, in other words, the

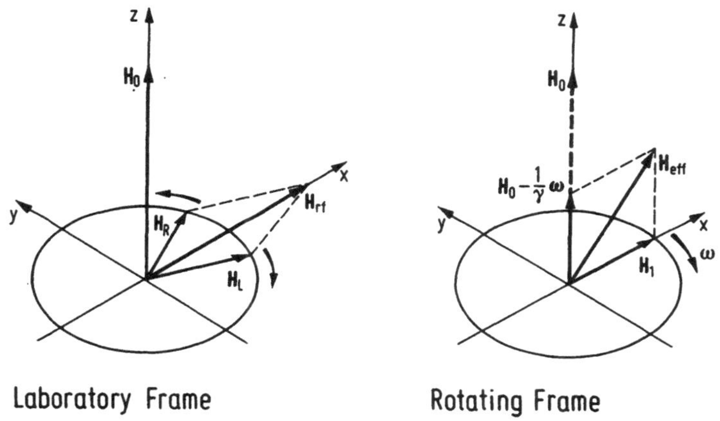

Fig. 4. Magnetic fields acting on the nuclear spins in the laboratory frame (to the left) and in the frame rotating with angular velocity ω (to the right). In the laboratory frame, we have time-dependent fields: $H_{rf} = (2H_1 \cos \omega t, 0,0)$, $H_L = (H_1 \cos \omega t, H_1 \sin \omega t, 0)$ and $H_R = (H_1 \cos \omega t, -H_1 \sin \omega t, 0)$

solution of the above equation of motion, is a precession about the magnetic field. The rf-field $\mathbf{H}_{rf}$ may be decomposed into two circularly polarized components

$$\mathbf{H}_R = [H_1 \cos(\omega t), H_1 \sin(\omega t), 0],$$

$$\mathbf{H}_L = [H_1 \cos(\omega t), -H_1 \sin(\omega t), 0], \tag{14}$$

where L and R denote a clockwise and counter-clockwise rotating field, respectively. For $\gamma > 0$, only the clockwise rotating field $\mathbf{H}_L$ will strongly interact with the magnetization, and we will neglect the other component $\mathbf{H}_R$ in our further considerations. In order to eliminate the time dependence of $\mathbf{H}_L$, we use now a coordinate system rotating also clockwise about the z-axis with frequency ω. In this "rotating frame", i.e. the rotating coordinate system, the rf-field H_1 will be static. The field H_0 will remain static as its direction coincides with the axis of rotation. Now, the equation of motion reads

$$\frac{d\mathbf{M}}{dt} = \mathbf{M} \times \gamma \mathbf{H}_{eff}, \tag{15}$$

with the effective magnetic field $\mathbf{H}_{eff} = [H_1, 0, H_0 - \omega/\gamma]$. The additional z-component $-\omega/\gamma$ originates from the time derivative of a rotating unit vector (rotating frame!) while H_1 and H_0 are the components of the applied fields.

At thermal equilibrium, the system will have a magnetization

$$\mathbf{M} = [0, 0, M_0] = [0, 0, \chi_0 H_0], \tag{16}$$

where the susceptibility χ_0 is in the high temperature approximation

$$\chi_0 = \frac{N(g\mu_N)^2\, I(I+1)}{3kT}. \tag{17}$$

N is the number of spins under consideration (per mol or per unit volume).

The solution of Eq. (15) is a precession of the magnetization **M** about the effective field $\mathbf{H}_{eff}$. In the laboratory frame, we have

$$\mathbf{M} = [M_x, M_y, M_z]$$

and in the rotating frame

$$\mathbf{M} = [u, v, M_z]$$

with

$$\begin{aligned} u &= M_x \cos(\omega t) - M_y \sin(\omega t) , \\ v &= M_x \sin(\omega t) + M_y \cos(\omega t) . \end{aligned} \tag{18}$$

The relation between u, v, and M_x, M is the transformation from the laboratory frame to the frame rotating with frequency ω about the z-axis. With the abbreviations $\omega_0 = \gamma H_0$ and $\omega_1 = \gamma H_1$, we obtain from Eq. (15) the equations of motion for the components of the magnetization in the rotating frame

$$\begin{aligned} \frac{du}{dt} &= (\omega_0 - \omega)\, v , \\ \frac{dv}{dt} &= -(\omega_0 - \omega)\, u + \omega_1 M_z , \\ \frac{dM_z}{dt} &= -\omega_1 v . \end{aligned} \tag{19}$$

The solution of Eq. (19), i.e. the precession of **M** with the precession frequency $\omega_p = \sqrt{(\omega_0 - \omega)^2 + \omega_1^2}$, is shown for a number of frequencies ω in Fig. 5. For these solutions, it was assumed that $\mathbf{M} = (0, 0, M_0)$ at $t = 0$. For the discussion of the results in Fig. 5, we have to distinguish the component $M_{\|}$ of **M** which is parallel to the effective field (static in the rotating frame) and the component $M_{\perp}$ of **M** which rotates with frequency ω_p about the effective field. The four cases shown in Fig. 5 are

a) $(\omega_0 - \omega) \gg \omega_1$ or $H_0 - \omega/\gamma \gg H_1$, where $M_{\|} \approx M_0$ and $M_{\perp}$ is rather small

b) $(\omega_0 - \omega) \approx \omega_1$ or $H_0 - \omega/\gamma \approx H_1$, where $M_{\|} \approx M_{\perp} \approx \frac{1}{\sqrt{2}} M_0$

c) $(\omega_0 - \omega) = 0$ or $\omega = \gamma H_0$, where $M_{\|} = 0$ and $M_{\perp} = M_0$

d) $+(\omega_0 - \omega) \approx -\omega_1$ or $\omega/\gamma - H_0 \approx H_1$, where $M_{\|}$ is negative (antiparallel to H_{eff}) and $|M_{\|}| \approx M_{\perp} \approx \frac{1}{\sqrt{2}} M_0$

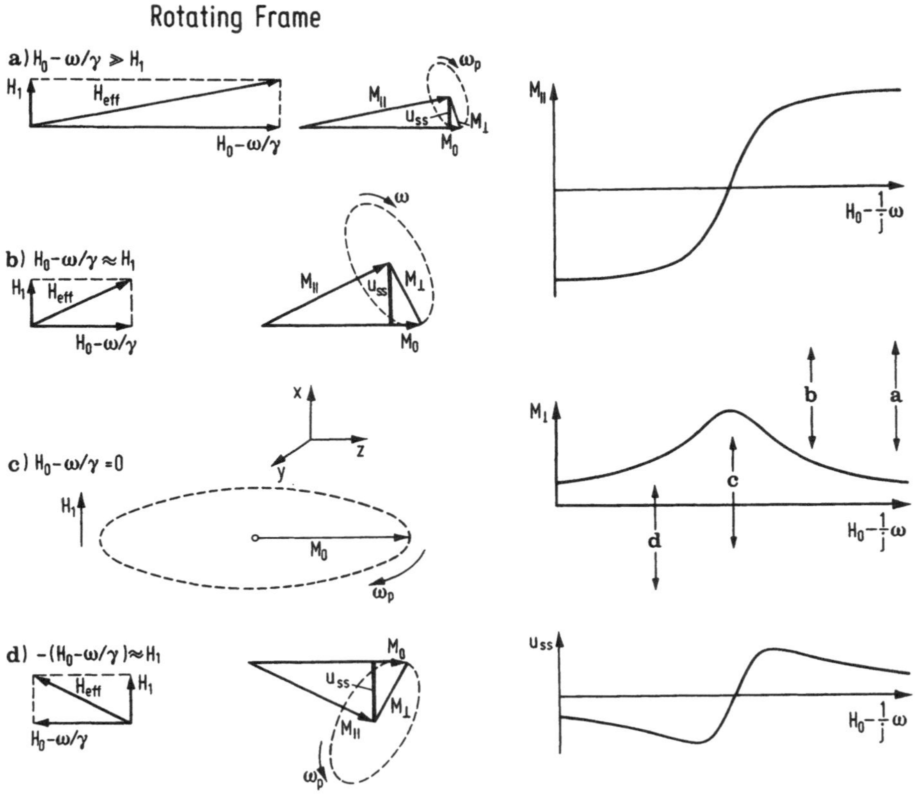

Fig. 5. Component $M_\parallel$ of the nuclear magnetization M parallel to the effective field H_{eff}, component M rotating with frequency ω_p and steady-state component u_{ss} of u: illustrating four particular cases (to the left) and as a function of $H_0 - \frac{1}{\gamma}\omega$ (to the right)

In Fig. 5 on the right hand side, $M_\parallel$, $M_\perp$ and also the part of u static in the rotating frame are plotted as a function of

$$H_0 - \frac{1}{\gamma}\omega = \frac{\omega_0 - \omega}{\gamma}.$$

The mathematical formulae for these quantities are as follows

$$\begin{aligned} M_\parallel &= \frac{\omega_0 - \omega}{\sqrt{(\omega_0 - \omega)^2 + \omega_1^2}} M_0 , \\ M_\perp &= \frac{\omega_1}{\sqrt{(\omega_0 - \omega)^2 + \omega_1^2}} M_0 , \\ u_{ss} &= \frac{\omega_1(\omega_0 - \omega)}{(\omega_0 - \omega)^2 + \omega_1^2} M_0 , \end{aligned} \qquad (20)$$

where u_{ss} means the steady-state component of u. It is clearly seen from Fig. 5 that these quantities (Eq. (20)) reveal a resonance behavior for ω near ω_0, and a comparison with Fig. 1 shows that the frequency dependence of $M_{\parallel}$, $M_{\perp}$ and u_{ss} is similar to that of the amplitude A (cf. Eq. (2)) of $A \sin \varphi$ and of $A \cos \varphi$ (cf. Eq. (3)), respectively. Due to this resonance behavior of the quantities under consideration, these phenomena are called *nuclear magnetic resonance*.

It should be noted that all our considerations up to now have been made for the rotating frame. For the experimental investigation of the nuclear magnetic resonance, we are interested in the component of the magnetization which rotates with the frequency ω in the laboratory frame and which is the response of the nuclear magnetic system to the rf-field at frequency ω. This component rotating with ω in the laboratory frame must be static in the rotating frame and must be perpendicular to the z-axis. Thus, the required response component is u_{ss} (cf. Eq. (20) and see Fig. 5).

Bearing in mind that the nuclear spin system is an ensemble perturbed by the rf-field, we have to consider the possibility that energy from the rf-field is transferred to the nuclear spins and dissipated further to the crystal lattice. These effects can be described by relaxation times that characterize the rates with which the system returns to thermal equilibrium after the perturbation has been switched off. There are the longitudinal or spin-lattice relaxation time T_1 and the transverse or spin-spin relaxation time T_2. Including the relaxation effects[31,37,38,46–51,55,60], the equations of motion in the rotating frame (cf. Eq. (19)) are

$$\frac{du}{dt} = (\omega_0 - \omega)\, v - \frac{1}{T_2}\, u\,,$$

$$\frac{dv}{dt} = -(\omega_0 - \omega)\, u + \omega_1 M_z - \frac{1}{T_2}\, v\,, \tag{21}$$

$$\frac{dM_z}{dt} = -\omega_1 v + \frac{1}{T_1}\,(M_0 - M_z)\,.$$

These are the famous "Bloch-Equations"[31] the solutions of which will be discussed in connection with a conventional nuclear magnetic resonance experiment[28–36, 38–44, 52, 65, 66]. "Conventional" in this context means probing the system by varying the frequency ω of the rf-field or by varying the magnetic field H_0. In both ways, the resonance condition $\omega = \omega_0 = \gamma H_0$ can be achieved (cf. Fig. 5). The experimental set-up for such a measurement is shown schematically in Fig. 6. The sample is placed in a magnet and in a coil which produces the rf-field of fixed frequency ω. By means of a sweep generator and of the modulating soils, the magnetic field can be swept through resonance. The reaction of the sample is picked up by the pick-up coil, amplified and detected by a lock-in system. The resonance signal can then be displayed as a function of the magnetic field on the screen of an oscilloscope. The variation of the magnetic field can also be achieved by a modulation technique[41,54, 57,62]. For our discussion, let us assume the magnetic field to be swept at a sufficiently low rate in order to avoid distortions and wiggles in the spectrum (see Fig. 2 for the mechanical example and Ref.[39] for these effects in nuclear magnetic resonance).

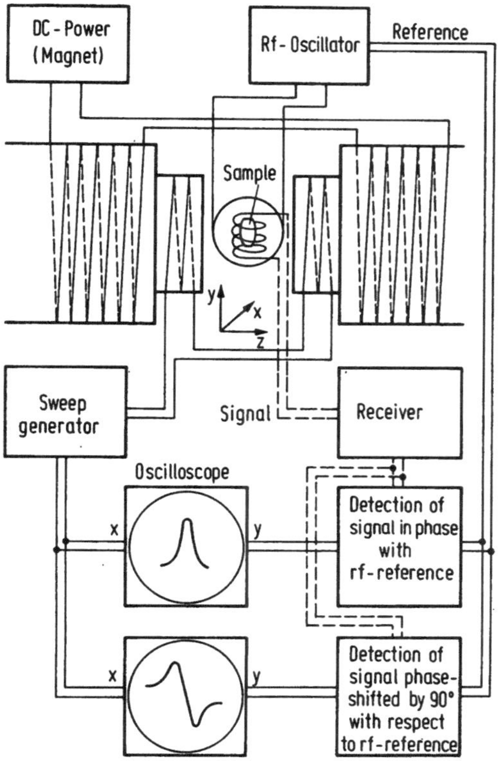

Fig. 6. Schematic diagram of a nuclear resonance spectrometer

Under these "slow passage" conditions, the solutions of the Bloch equations are (steady-state response to the rf-field):

$$u = \frac{\omega_1(\omega_0 - \omega)\, T_2^2 M_0}{1 + (\omega_0 - \omega)^2\, T_2^2 + \omega_1^2 T_1 T_2},$$

$$v = \frac{\omega_1 T_2 M_0}{1 + (\omega_0 - \omega)^2\, T_2^2 + \omega_1^2 T_1 T_2}, \tag{22}$$

$$M_z = \frac{1 + (\omega_0 - \omega)^2\, T_2^2 M_0}{1 + (\omega_0 - \omega)^2\, T_2^2 + \omega_1^2 T_1 T_2}.$$

Transformation to the laboratory frame yields

$$M_x = A \cos(\omega t - \varphi)$$

$$M_y = -A \sin(\omega t - \varphi) \tag{23}$$

where the amplitude is now

$$A = \frac{\omega_1 T_2 \sqrt{1 + (\omega_0 - \omega)^2 T_2^2} M_0}{1 + (\omega_0 - \omega)^2 T_2^2 + \omega_1^2 T_1 T_2}$$

and the phase shift

$$\varphi = \operatorname{arccot} (\omega_0 - \omega) T_2 .$$

Note that M_z is unaffected by the transformation. In the nuclear magnetic resonance spectrometer of Fig. 6, the pick-up coil is oriented in such a way that M_y is measured. If the lock-in amplifier is set to detect the signal in-phase with the exciting rf-field ($\sim \cos(\omega t)$, cf. Eq. (13)), we obtain the "absorption mode signal" (cf. Fig. 7):

$$A \sin \varphi = v = \frac{\omega_1 T_2 M_0}{1 + (\omega_0 - \omega)^2 T_2^2 + \omega_1^2 T_1 T_2} \tag{24}$$

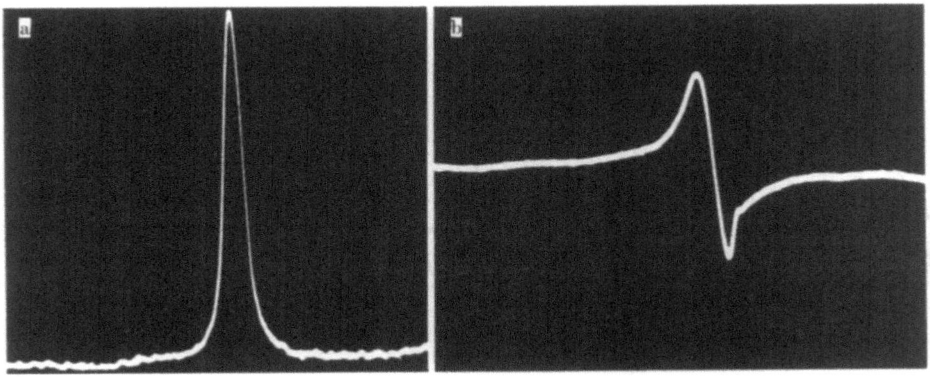

Fig. 7a. Proton resonance (absorption mode) in ferric nitrate solution (taken from Ref.[33]). **b** Proton resonance (dispersion mode) in ferric nitrate solution (taken from Ref.[33])

and if we set the lock-in amplifier to detect the signal which is phase-shifted by 90° with respect to the exciting rf-field, we obtain the "dispersion mode signal" (cf. Fig. 7):

$$A \cos \varphi = u = \frac{\omega_1 (\omega_0 - \omega) T_2^2 M_0}{1 + (\omega_0 - \omega)^2 T_2^2 + \omega_1^2 T_1 T_2} . \tag{25}$$

The dispersion mode and absorption mode signals (Eqs. (24) and (25)) are also the real and imaginary part of a complex response function $Ae^{i\varphi} = A \cos \varphi + iA \sin \varphi$ (cf. Eq. (3) and subsequent discussion). Since $\omega_1 = \gamma H_1$, $M_0 \doteq \chi_0 H_0$, and $\omega_0 = \gamma H_0$, we may rearrange the factors in Eqs. (24) and (25), divide by the strength H_1 of the rf-field and obtain the real and imaginary part χ' and χ'', respectively, of the dynamical susceptibility (cf. Fig. 7):

$$\chi'(\omega) = \frac{1}{H_1} A \cos\varphi = \frac{\chi_0\omega_0(\omega_0 - \omega) T_2^2}{1 + (\omega_0 - \omega)^2 T_2^2 + \omega_1^2 T_1 T_2},$$

$$\chi''(\omega) = \frac{1}{H_1} A \sin\varphi = \frac{\chi_0\omega_0 T_2}{1 + (\omega_0 - \omega)^2 T_2^2 + \omega_1^2 T_1 T_2}. \tag{26}$$

Eq. (26) shows that χ' and χ'' are independent of H_1 if we are allowed to neglect the term $\omega_1^2 T_1 T_2$ in the denominator. Only then, the nuclear spin system is a linear system and χ' and χ'' are related to each other by the Kramers Kronig relations (cf. Eq. (4)). For rather strong rf-fields, saturation effects[31,38,40,46,50] are observed, i.e. the resonance maximum of the amplitude A is diminished by the factor ($\omega = \omega_0$!)

$$\frac{1}{1 + \omega_1^2 T_1 T_2} = \frac{1}{1 + \gamma^2 H_1^2 T_1 T_2}. \tag{27}$$

4 Pulse Methods in Nuclear Magnetic Resonance

As in the case of the mechanical model system of section 1, a strong pulse of short duration can be used to investigate the nuclear spin system in an alternative way. In principle, the same magnetic resonance spectrometer as shown in Fig. 6 can be employed for this kind of experiment. Again, a static magnetic field is applied to the sample. But in contrast to slow passage experiments with small rf-field, and an rf-pulse with frequency ω and with rather large strength H_1 is applied during a short time τ such that

$$\omega_1 = \gamma H_1 \gg |\omega_0 - \omega|. \tag{28}$$

This means that the effective field acting on the nuclear magnetization of the sample is practically H_1 which is stationary in a frame rotating with frequency ω (cf. Fig. 5). The influence of $H_0 - \omega/\gamma$ can mostly be neglected. And there will be a precession of the sample about the effective field H_1. During the time τ, the magnetization will precess by an angle

$$\alpha = \omega_1\tau = \gamma H_1 \tau. \tag{29}$$

For nuclear magnetic resonance pulse experiments, H_1 and τ are usually chosen [67,68,77,78,80,84] in such a way that a precession angle $\alpha = \pi/2$ results.

Initially, the nuclear magnetization **M** is parallel to the static magnetic field **H** at thermal equilibrium. In the rotating frame, the effect of the pulse is then to rotate the magnetization by $\pi/2$ into the plane perpendicular to **H** (cf. Fig. 8). When the pulse is switched off, the magnetization will precess about the static field and will cause a large nuclear induction signal in the pick-up coil (cf. Figs. 5, 6 and 8).

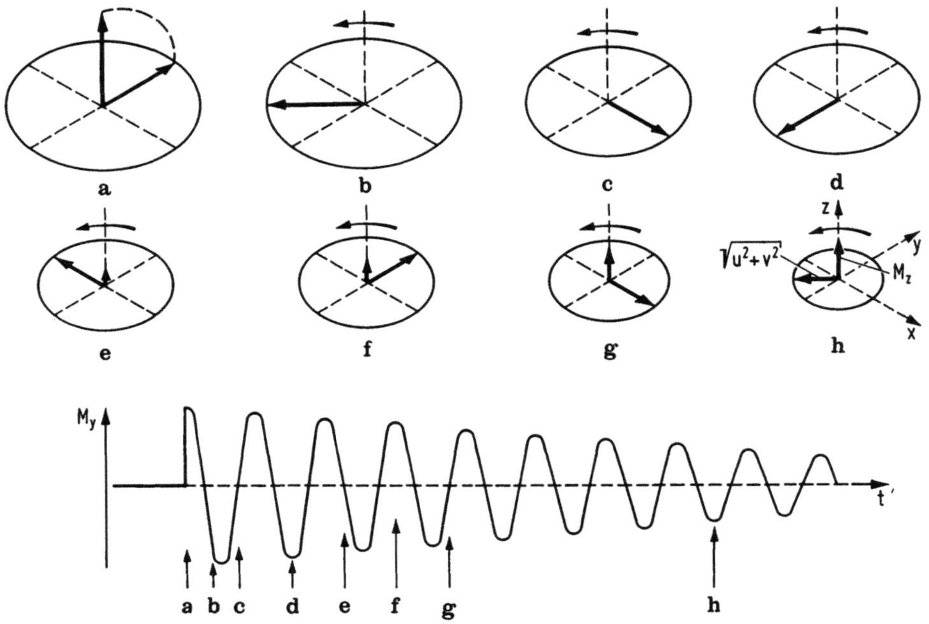

Fig. 8. Illustration of the precession of the nuclear magnetization M after application of a 90°-pulse (upper part) and free induction decay (lower part)

For the mathematical description of the behavior of **M** under the influence of the pulse, relaxation effects can safely be neglected because of $\tau \ll T_2, T_1$, and it is sufficient to use Eqs. (19) and its solutions in this case. For the precession of the magnetization about the static field on the other hand, relaxation effects have to be included. Thus, we have to consider the solutions of the Bloch equations (21) for $\omega_1 = \gamma H_1 = 0$. If the initial 90° pulse is applied along the x-direction in the rotating frame, the magnetization **M** will precess during the pulse from the equilibrium direction ($\| z$) into the y-direction. For this case, we obtain for the precessing M(t) at time t after the pulse has been switched off (cf. Eqs. (21) and Fig. 8) in the rotating frame

$$\begin{aligned} u &= M_0 \sin([\omega_0 - \omega]\, t)\, e^{-t/T_2} , \\ v &= M_0 \cos([\omega_0 - \omega]\, t)\, e^{-t/T_2} , \\ M_z &= M_0(1 - e^{-t/T_1}) , \end{aligned} \qquad (30)$$

and in the laboratory frame where the effects are actually observed (cf. Eqs. 22 and 23)

$$M_x = M_0 \sin(\omega_0 t)\, e^{-t/T_2},$$
$$M_y = M_0 \cos(\omega_0 t)\, e^{-t/T_2}, \qquad (31)$$
$$M_z = M_0(1 - e^{-t/T_1}).$$

The physical meaning of the results of Eqs. 30 and 31 is that the magnetization M precesses about the z-axis. Initially, the precession amplitude is M_0 which decays as time increases exponentially according to the relaxation time T_2. At times $t \gg T_2$, u and v (in the rotating frame) or M_x and M_y (in the laboratory frame) will have decayed practically to zero. On the other hand, the system will return to thermal equilibrium. That means the z-component M_z of the magnetization will return to its equilibrium value M_0 exponentially according to the relaxation T_1 (cf. Fig. 8). The decay of the transverse components of M (M_x and M_y) has been termed "free induction decay" (FID). It is the complete analogon to the damped free oscillation of the mechanical system (see Fig. 1 and Eq. (5) in Section 1). During the free and decaying precession (FID), the component M_y of the magnetization will induce an rf-signal in the pick-up coil (as will the component M_x in the other rf-coil, cf. Fig. 6). This signal will be an alternating current of frequency ω_0 decaying exponentially according to T_2. The properties of the FID signal are very similar to that of the impulse-response function of our mechanical example of Section 1. This will be considered in more detail in Section 5 when we discuss the Fourier transform of the FID signal which is the basis for the Fourier-transform nuclear magnetic resonance (FTNMR).

As already mentioned in context with the mechanical system, the advantage of the pulse methods is generally the easier handling of systems with more than one eigenfrequency. Let us consider as an example a system with two different kinds A and BX of nuclear spins $I = {}^1/_2$ which are coupled together. We assume that a $\pi/2$ pulse has been applied to the nuclear spins A. Then, the free induction decay of the magnetization M_A of the A system in the rotating frame can be written instead of Eq. (30) as follows[70–74,85,88,95]

$$M_{Ax} = \frac{1}{2} M_{A0} \left\{\sin\left(\left[\omega_A - \omega + \frac{1}{2} J\right] t\right) + \sin\left(\left[\omega_A - \omega - \frac{1}{2} J\right] t\right)\right\} e^{-t/T_{2A}},$$

$$M_{Ay} = \frac{1}{2} M_{A0} \left\{\cos\left(\left[\omega_A - \omega + \frac{1}{2} J\right] t\right) + \cos\left(\left[\omega_A - \omega - \frac{1}{2} J\right] t\right)\right\} e^{-t/T_{2A}}, \qquad (32)$$

$$M_{Az} = M_{A0}(1 - e^{-t/T_{1A}}),$$

where $\omega_A = \gamma_A H_0$, $M_{A0} = \chi_A H_0$ and J are the precession frequencies of the A spins, their equilibrium magnetization and the strength of their coupling to the X spins, respectively. In this rather simple system, we observe a splitting of the A spin NMR resonance line in a slow-passage experiment and, correspondingly, two components in the FID signal with the typical beat pattern (see Fig. 11, p. 112). In real systems of practical interest, the situation is much more complicated. Even nuclear spins of the same kind (^1H or ^{13}C) give rise to a number of nuclear magnetic resonance due to the so-called "chemical shift" which is different for like nuclei in non-equivalent positions.

For our, perhaps oversimplified, examples, we would be able to extract ω_0 and T_2 (in case of Eq. (30)) and ω_A, J and T_{2A} (in case of Eq. (31)) from the FID-signal without any complicated and sophisticated mathematical formalism. This is equivalent to the statements about the interferograms of one or two narrow laser lines in infrared spectroscopy (see Vol. 58 [26], p. 78 and 86). There are, however, some instrumental limitations which obscure the experimental results of FID. Due to technical imperfections, the magnetic field will not be perfectly homogeneous over the volume of the sample. The rather small, but finite field inhomogeneity will lead to a spread of resonance frequencies[68] in the sample and destructive interference effects between the free induction signals from different parts of the sample cause the observed signal to decay in a time T_2^* being much shorter than T_2. In slow-passage experiments, it is difficult to overcome the line broading due to field inhomogeneity. In pulse experiments, on the other hand, there are some ingenious concepts to obtain the true value of T_2 in spite of the inhomogeneity.

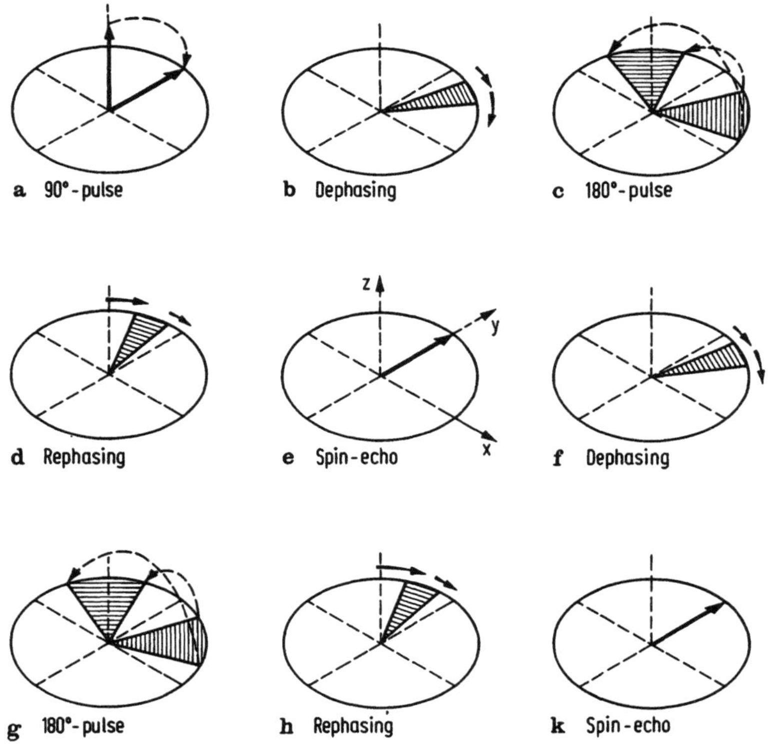

Fig. 9. Illustration of the formation of spin echoes obtained with the Maiboom-Gill modification[80] of the Carr-Purcell pulse sequence[76]

The technique for obtaining reliable values of T_2 involves the application of further short rf-pulses to the nuclear spin system such that spin echoes[67,68,76,80,84] are obtained. In this review, we shall discuss briefly the Carr-Purcell pulse sequence[78] for producing spin echoes with the modification introduced by Maiboom and Gill[80]. After the initial 90° pulse along the x-direction in the rotating frame (cf. first section of this chapter), pulses with $\alpha = \omega_1\tau = 180°$ are applied along the y-direction in the rotating frame at time $t = (2n + 1)\,T$ (cf. Fig. 9). In a short-hand notation, the pulse sequence can be written as follows

$$90^\circ_x - T - 180^\circ_y - 2T - 180^\circ_y - 2T - \ldots . \qquad (33)$$

As can be seen from Fig. 9, the 90°_x-pulse rotates the magnetization M_0 from the equilibrium orientation ($\|z$) about the x-axis into the y-direction. Then the FID develops during the time T, and due to the above mentioned field inhomogeneity, there is a spread of resonance frequencies ω_0, and thus a spread of precession phases ($[\omega_0 - \omega]\,t$) (cf. Eq. (30))[4] as indicated in Fig. 9. At time T, the 180°_y-pulse rotates all parts of M by 180° about the y-axis. The essential point is now that the reflection of the various precession components about the y-axis does not change the sense of their precession and, after another time T (altogether $t = 2T$)[5], all these components with different angular velocities $[\omega_0 - \omega]$ have returned to the y-direction and add up to a large signal. This effect is called a spin echo. For $t \geqq 2T$, the free precession continues, and the above mentioned spread occurs again. At $t = 3T$, another 180°_y-pulse is applied to the system causing another spin echo at time $t = 4T$. Repeating this procedure several times, we obtain a train of spin echoes. Solving the Bloch equations for the pulse sequence Eq. (33) and the free precession between pulses, we obtain (in the rotating frame!)

$$u(2nT) = 0\,,$$
$$v(2nT) = M_0\, e^{-2nT/T_2}\,,$$
$$M_z(2nT) = M_0 \frac{(1 - e^{-T/T_1})^2}{1 + e^{-2T/T_1}} \left[1 - (-1)^n e^{-2nT/T_1}\right] \qquad (34)$$

for $n = 1, 2, 3, \ldots$. The second line of Eq. (34) means that the transverse component v of the magnetization which is proportional to the observed signal decays exponentially according to T_2, i.e. to the true spin-spin-relaxation time, and not according to T_2^*.

Another important property of the spin echoes is that the envelope of the spin-echo signal shows not only an exponential decay but also a sinusoidal modulation for systems with more than one nuclear spin[69-74,79,85,88,95,99]. For the rather simple AX system with two $I = 1/2$ nuclear spins, the spin-echo envelope observed for the A system will be modulated as follows (cf. Eq. (32)):

$$v_A(2nT) = M_{A0} \cos(nJT)\, e^{-2nT/T_{2A}}\,. \qquad (35)$$

[4] Please note that even a small field inhomogeneity and a small spread of ω_0 may influence the difference $\omega_0 - \omega$ drastically since the rf-frequency ω is mostly chosen close to ω_0.

[5] Please note that in counting the time after the initial pulse the duration times τ of the 180°-pulses can safely be neglected.

It should be noted that this echo envelope modulation occurs only if the 180°_y-pulse (not necessarily the 90°_x-pulse!) is effective for both, the A- and also for the X nuclear spins[150,165]. Fig. 10 illustrates how the envelope modulation arises. In a frame rotating with angular velocity $\omega = \omega_A$ (cf. Eq. (32)), the free induction decay consists of two main components both rotating with $\omega = {}^1/_2$ J but with opposite sense, i.e. one clockwise and the other one counter-clockwise. In addition, both show the usual spread due to field inhomogeneity. If now the 180°_y-pulse at time T is effective for both kinds of nuclear spins, the two main components are not reflected at the y-axis and thus interchanged. Only the spread components are interchanged with respect to the center of each main component rotating exactly with $\omega = \pm {}^1/_2 J$. As illustrated in Fig. 10, the spin echo at time 2T means for this case that the spread components return to the center of their main component and add up for a large signal. The projection of the two main components on the y-axis (the observed signal is proportional to v_A!) yields then cos (JT) (cf. Eq. (35) for n = 1).

The modulation of the spin-echo envelope can be used to obtain information about the coupling constant J[150]. The spin-echo envelope is also influenced if chemical exchange between the two nuclei occurs[75,86,89–94]. Returning now to our main objective, i.e. the application of Fourier methods in nuclear magnetic resonance, we realize that the pulse methods lead to a decaying free-induction signal or a

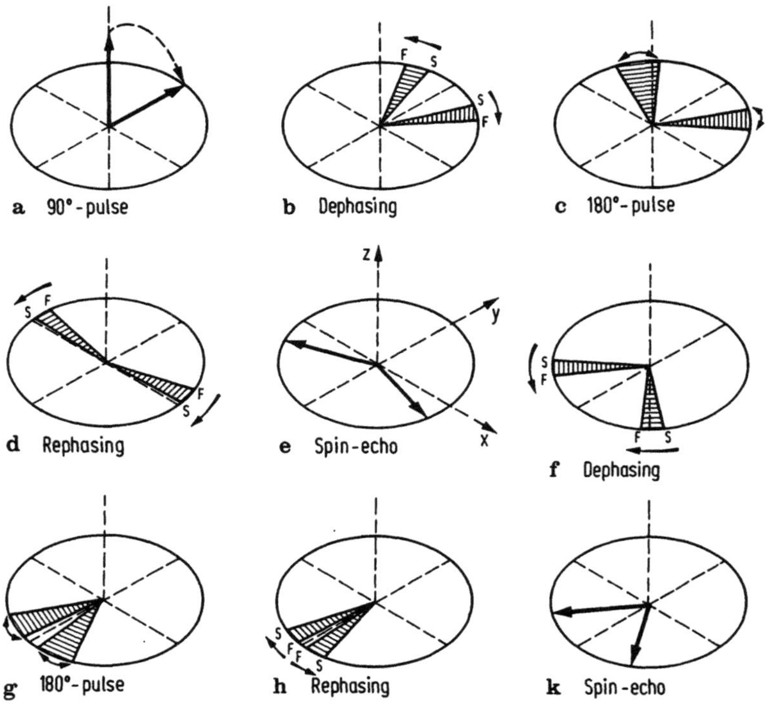

Fig. 10. Illustration of the modulation of the spin-echo envelope if the 180°-pulses are effective for both kinds of coupled spins (J-modulation)

decaying spin-echo envelope. What we would like to know on the other hand are the NMR resonance frequencies and their line widths (inverse of relaxation times!). From a slow-passage conventional NMR esperiment, we would obtain these data directly. But how can they be extracted from the recorded FID signal? As already mentioned, the interpretation is easy for exceptionally simple systems (cf. the two upper traces in Fig. 11). Here, we are able to gather the frequencies from the FID oscillations and from the beat pattern in the case of two frequencies. The exponential decay envelope yields the inverse of the relaxation time (T_2 or T_2^*). A glance at the lower trace in Fig. 11 reveals that such a procedure is not possible for a more complicated system. Unfortunately, most cases of practical interest belong to the latter type. In order to solve the problem for the more complicated cases, we remember the mechanical example in Section 1 that the results of frequency sweep experiments (Eq. 2)) and the results of pulse methods (Eq. 5)) are connected by a mathematical operation called Fourier transform (Eq. (8)). In the next section, these results will be adapted to nuclear magnetic resonance, and it will be shown that a Fourier transform of the FID signal will yield the required results equivalent to those of a slow-passage experiment.

5 Fourier Transform Nuclear Magnetic Resonance

It will be discussed in more detail later (p. 117) that pulse methods in nuclear magnetic resonance have some advantage in comparison to conventional experiments where the magnetic field is swept. But, as already mentioned, the latter type yields directly the wanted information, i.e. the various NMR resonance frequencies and their line-widths of the sample under investigation. The pulse methods on the other hand generally yield the free induction decay of FID signal. But the two types of data are equivalent as was shown in Section 1 for a simple mechanical system and may be converted into each other by a Fourier transform. This is generally true in physics for linear systems with a number of resonance or eigenfrequencies. And it were R. R. Ernst and W.-A. Anderson who applied these relations to NMR[102]. After the initial 90°_x-pulse, the FID signal is recorded. At equally spaced time intervals Δt, samples are taken from the analogue signal and digitized by means of a digital volt meter. The data are then prepared to be fed into a digital electronic computer which is an essential part of the Fourier transform method. In the computer, the resonance frequencies and line-widths are computed from the FID-data by means of the following mathematical relation (cos-Fourier transform)

$$C(\omega) = \int_0^\infty M(t) \cos(\omega t)\, dt\,, \tag{36}$$

where M(t) is the FID signal as a function of time t and ω the frequency for which we want to compute $C(\omega)$, the signal we would have observed as absorption mode at frequency ω in a conventional NMR experiment.

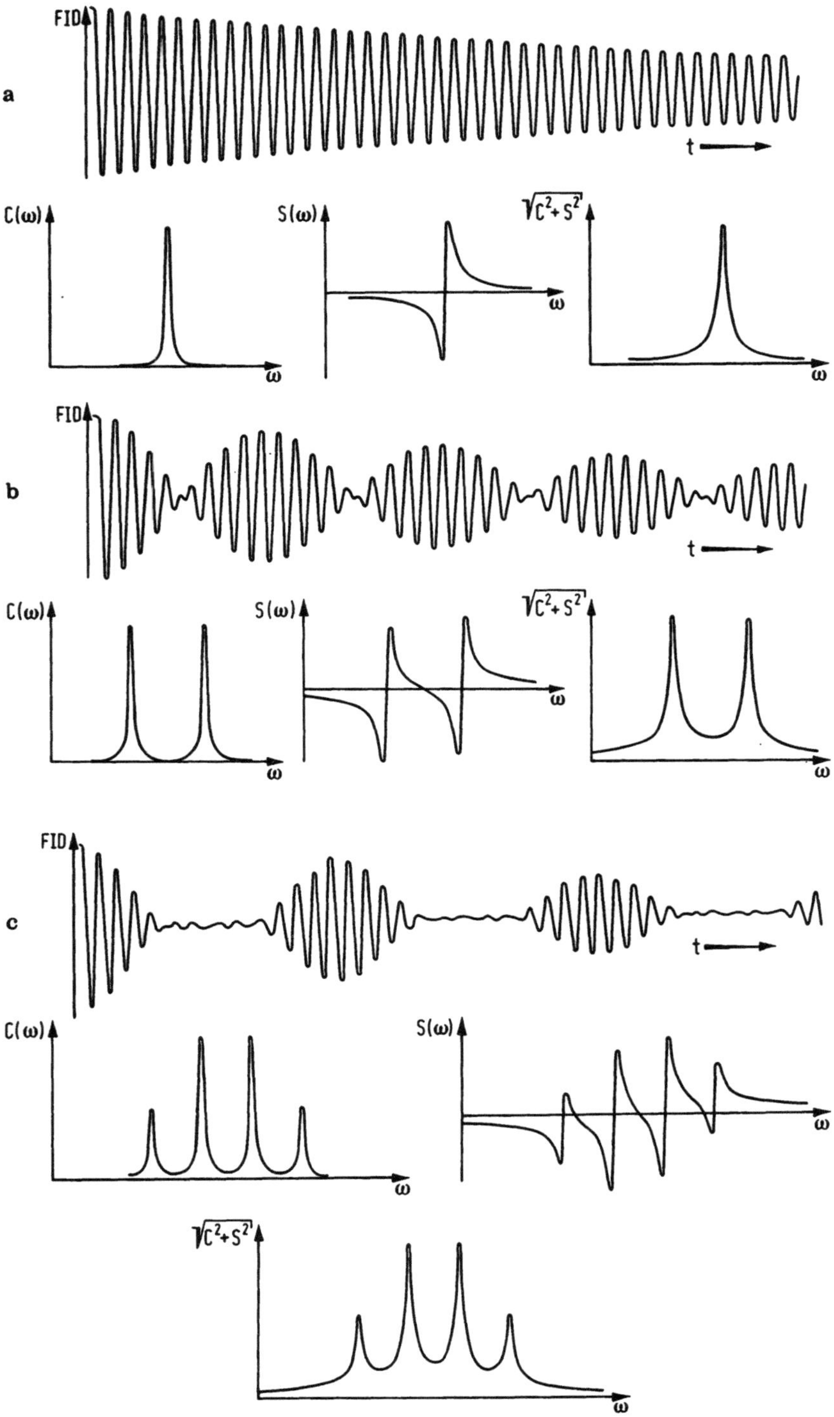
a
FID
t
C(ω)
S(ω)
√(C²+S²)
ω
b
FID
t
C(ω)
S(ω)
√(C²+S²)
ω
c
FID
t
C(ω)
S(ω)
√(C²+S²)
ω

For a simple system with a single NMR line, we have (cf. Eq. (31))

$$M(t) = M_0 \cos(\omega_0 t)\, e^{-t/T_2} \tag{37}$$

and the computation of Eq. (36) yields (cf. Fig. 11)

$$C(\omega) = \frac{1}{2}\frac{M_0 T_2}{1 + (\omega_0 - \omega)^2 T_2^2} \tag{38}$$

which is equal to

$$\frac{1}{2\omega_1} A \sin\varphi = \frac{1}{2\omega_1} v \qquad \text{(cf. Eqs. (22) and (24))}$$

and to $\chi''/2\gamma$ (cf. Eq. (26)), i.e. equal to the response function of the nuclear system, apart from some factors. Essentially the same result would have been obtained in a conventional experiment (cf. Fig. 6) with a sufficiently small sweep rate (wiggles, cf. Fig. 2) and a sufficiently small rf-field H_1 (no saturation $\gamma^2 H_1^2 T_1 T_2 \ll 1$, cf. Eqs. (26) and (27)). If the computer were programmed to evaluate the sine Fourier transform of M(t)

$$S(\omega) = \int_0^\infty M(t) \sin(\omega t)\, dt \tag{39}$$

instead of the cosine transform (Eq. (36)), we would obtain for the simple model system under consideration (cf. Fig. 11)

$$S(\omega) = -\frac{1}{2}\frac{M_0(\omega_0 - \omega) T_2^2}{1 + (\omega_0 - \omega)^2 T_2^2}, \tag{40}$$

which is equal to

$$-\frac{1}{2\omega_1} A \cos\varphi = -\frac{1}{2\omega_1} u \qquad \text{(cf. Eqs. (22) and (24))}$$

and to $\chi'/2\gamma$ (cf. Eq. (26)) and which could have been obtained in a conventional experiment under the same conditions as listed above. Under actual experimental conditions, there may arise phase errors in the FID signal. Then it is of advantage to compute both, the sine and the cosine transform, and to evaluate the absolute-value-spectrum or amplitude spectrum (cf. Fig. 11).

$$\sqrt{C^2(\omega) + S^2(\omega)} = \frac{1}{2}\frac{M_0 T_2}{\sqrt{1 + (\omega_0 - \omega)^2 T_2^2}} \tag{41}$$

◀ **Fig. 11.** Free induction decay (FID) for a singlet **a**, a doublet **b** and a quadruplet **c** and corresponding spectra $C(\omega)$, $S(\omega)$ and $\sqrt{C^2 + S^2}$ (absolute value spectra) which is equal to

$$\frac{1}{2\omega_1} A = \frac{1}{2\omega_1} \sqrt{u^2 + v^2} \qquad \text{(cf. Eqs. (22) and (24))} .$$

In addition to the example of a single NMR line, the spectra $C(\omega)$, $S(\omega)$ and the absolute-value-spectrum are shown for two more complicated systems (doublet and quartet) in Fig. 11.

These considerations serve the purpose to introduce the principles of applying Fourier methods to nuclear magnetic resonance. And it is this type of experiment (pulse methods, recording of an FID signal combined with a Fourier transformation in a computer) which is usually called Fourier transform nuclear magnetic resonance (FTNMR).

After explaining the principle of FTNMR, we shall discuss the problems arising in the practical application of Fourier transform methods[102,104–112,114–119,122–124,130–134]. Some of the problems generally connected with the application of Fourier transformations have already been mentioned in Section 1.

The first problem is that the integration cannot be performed for $0 \leqq t < \infty$ but only for a finite range $0 \leqq t \leqq T_0$ for which the FID signal has been recorded (T_0 = data acquisition time). This truncation of the FID signal leads to a finite resolution $\Delta\nu \approx 1/2T_0$ (cf. Vol. 58[26], Fig. 6, p. 86). The instrumental line shape function is of the type

$$\frac{\sin [(\omega - \omega_0) T_0]}{[(\omega - \omega_0) T_0]}$$

In many cases of practical interest therefore, it is advisable to multiply the signal by an appropriately chosen function (apodization or mathematical filtering) before performing the Fourier transform in order to obtain an optimum with respect to resolution and instrumental line shape function [102,116,118,124,131–133].

The second problem is that of aliasing. The sampling of the FID at equally spaced time intervals Δt causes replicas of the true spectrum $C(\omega)$ at regular intervals $\Delta\omega = m \frac{2\pi}{\Delta t}$ ($m = \pm 1, \pm 2$ etc., cf. Fig. 12). We realize that escaping the problem

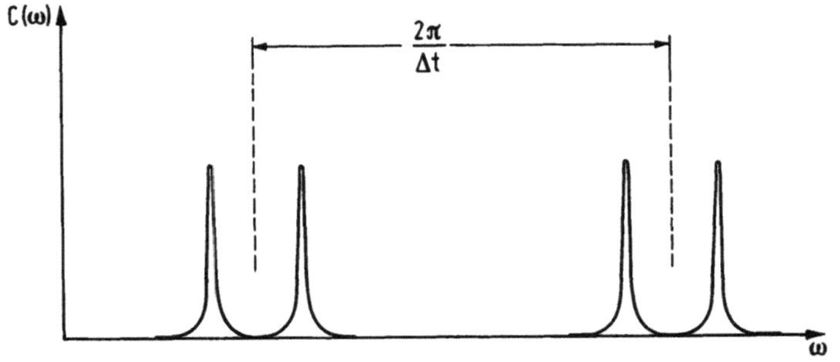

Fig. 12. Illustration of the repetition of spectra due to aliasing

of aliasing means a sufficiently small Δt for a certain frequency range under consideration and that both, decreasing of Δt (aliasing!) and increasing of T_0 (higher resolution), imply an increase of the number $N = T_0/\Delta t$ of data points to be handled by the computer.

While the two problems mentioned so far occur also in infrared Fourier transform spectroscopy[26], we have now to consider problems that are specific of FTNMR. Fig. 13 schematically describes a spectrometer for FTNMR. One coil is used to apply the 90°_x-pulse from the rf-generator (frequency ω_R) and the power amplifier to the sample and to pick up the FID signal from the latter. After amplification, this rf-signal is mixed with the reference frequency ω_R to obtain, after filtering the audio signal

$$M^c(t) = M_0 \cos [(\omega_0 - \omega_R) t] e^{-t/T_2} , \tag{42}$$

which has the same time dependence as the FID signal in a frame rotating with frequency ω_R but is obtained here in the laboratory frame by electronic means. This technique causes the problem of imaging which means that the Fourier transform consists of the true line at $\omega_R + (\omega_0 - \omega_R) = \omega_0$ and of an image at

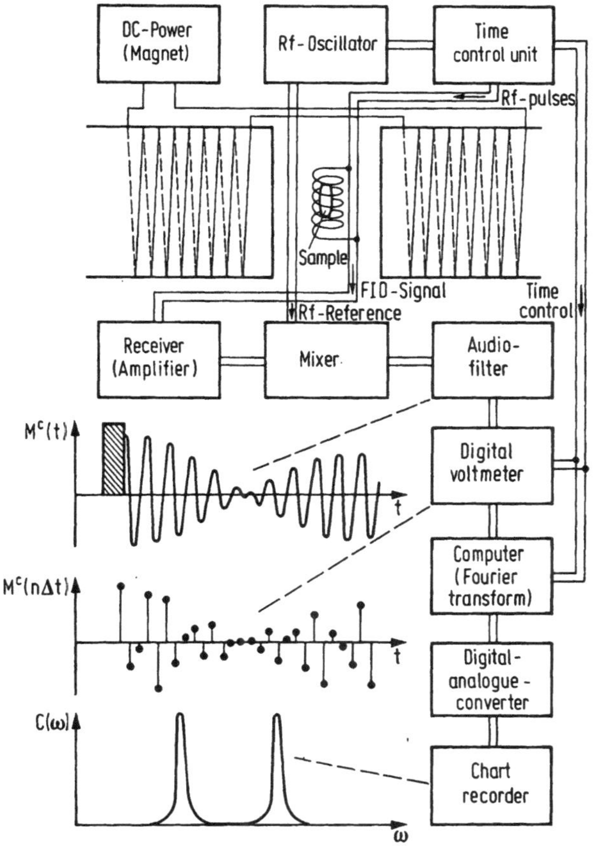

Fig. 13. Schematic diagram of a Fourier transform nuclear magnetic resonance spectrometer

$\omega_R - (\omega_0 - \omega_R) = 2\omega_R - \omega_0$. One remedy is to set the rf-frequency ω_R outside the frequency range of interest and to filter the spectrum appropriately. The frequency ω_R, however, may be fixed in the center of the range of interest if quadrature detection[115,117,122,123] is used. In this method (see Fig. 13), a second audio-signal is produced by mixing the rf-signal (Eq. (37)) with a rf-signal phase-shifted by 90°:

$$M^s(t) = M_0 \sin [(\omega_0 - \omega_R)\, t]\, e^{-t/T_2} . \tag{43}$$

The two signals (Eqs. (42) and (43)) are then considered as real and imaginary parts of a complex function, and a complex Fourier transform is performed in the computer. A further technical detail of the NMR spectrometer sketched in Fig. 13 is the so-called field-frequency lock. This implies that the rf-frequency is controlled in relation to the applied static magnetic field by monitoring the NMR signal of ^2H or ^{19}F nuclei.

A further problem special for FTNMR is a consequence of the repeated recording of the FID signal which will decay to zero at times of the order of T_2^* (field inhomogeneity) while the transverse magnetization relaxation time T_2 can be much larger. Moreover, thermal equilibrium ($\mathbf{M} = (0, 0, M_0)$) will be re-established after times longer than the longest spin-lattice relaxation time T_1. Therefore, a waiting period of the order of the longest T_1 is necessary to obtain repeatedly a free induction signal according to Eqs. (30), (31) and (37). For long relaxation times, this waiting period can mean a useless dead time of the instrument too long under practical aspects. If the nuclear spin system does not return to thermal equilibrium between pulses, a sequence of 90°-pulses will lead to a steady state with a modified FID signal[102,107,108,158]:

$$\tilde{M}(t) = \frac{(1 - E_1)\, M_0 \sin\alpha\, [(1 - E_2\cos\vartheta)\cos(\omega_0 t) - E_2 \sin\vartheta \sin(\omega_0 t)]}{(1 - E_1\cos\alpha)(1 - E_2\cos\vartheta) - E_2(E_1 - \cos\alpha)(E_2 - \cos\vartheta)}\, e^{-t/T_2} , \tag{44}$$

where α, ϑ, E_1 and E_2 are the flip angle (cf. Eq. (29)) of the initial pulse, the precession phase $\vartheta = (\omega_R - \omega_0)\, T$ within time T between two pulses, the spin-lattice relaxation rate $E_1 = e^{-T/T_1}$ and the spin-spin relaxation rate $E_2 = e^{-T/T_2}$, respectively. Clearly, Eq. (44) reduces to Eq. (37) if $T \gg T_1$, $T \gg T_2$ and $\alpha = 90°$. For smaller times T, there exist optimum flip angles α different from 90° [102,107,108,158]. Furthermore, there have been developed special pulse methods (DEFT and SEFT, i.e. driven equilibrium Fourier transform and spin-echo Fourier transform method) for extremely slowly relaxing systems[109,138,140–143,145,146,173]. The cosine Fourier transform (see Eq. (36)) of $\tilde{M}(t)$ (Eq. (44)) yields with no apodization and with the data acquisition time approximately equal to T

$$\tilde{C}(\omega) = \frac{(1 - E_1)\, M_0 \sin\alpha}{(1 - E_1\cos\alpha)(1 - E_2\cos\vartheta) - E_2(E_1 - \cos\alpha)(E_2 - \cos\vartheta)} \times \tag{45}$$

$$\times \frac{1}{2}\left\{\frac{T_2}{1 + (\omega - \omega_0)^2 T_2^2}\,[(1 - E_2\cos\vartheta)^2 - E_2^2 \sin^2\vartheta] + \right.$$

$$\left. + \frac{(\omega - \omega_0)\, T_2^2}{1 + (\omega - \omega_0)^2 T_2^2}\,[2E_2 \sin\vartheta (1 - E_2\cos\vartheta)]\right\} .$$

Eq. (45) means that $\tilde{C}(\omega)$ is a mixture of the absorption and of the dispersion mode signal multiplied by a factor dependent on α, E_1, E_2, and ϑ. In other words, the repetitive pulse sequence in FTNMR may give rise to phase and intensity errors which have to be taken into account for the interpretation of the results.

Most of the commercial NMR spectrometers (see also Fig. 13) provide the possibility of proton decoupling. This is a very useful tool in the NMR investigation of organic substances (e.g. ^{13}C-NMR). Decoupling is a special form of nuclear magnetic double resonance about which exists a vast literature[174–218] which cannot be reviewed here in detail. In principle, double resonance is a nuclear magnetic resonance experiment where a second rf-field (cw) is applied to the sample. And the effect of a sufficiently strong rf-field with a frequency near the proton NMR frequency is to remove the splitting of the ^{13}C-NMR lines due to coupling to the protons (see Fig. 14) such that a single line is observed for each inequivalent carbon site. Since the resonance frequency varies for different protons according to the chemical shift, it is advisable to use noise-proton decoupling[189,200] or coherent broad-band decoupling[215] instead of coherent single-frequency decoupling[184].

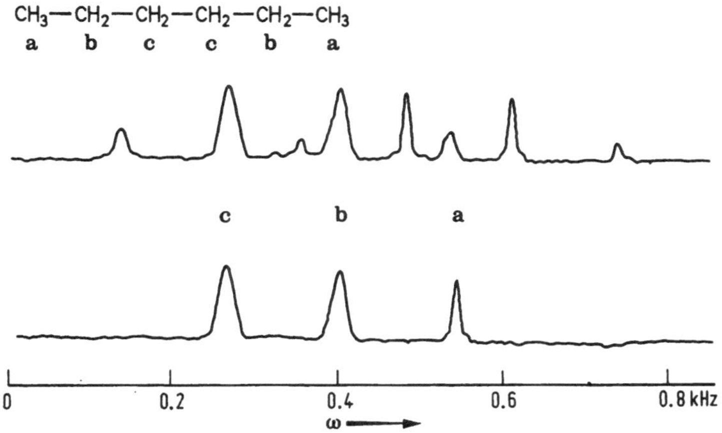

Fig. 14. Effect of proton decoupling on the NMR spectrum of *n*-hexane: ^{13}C spectrum without decoupling (upper trace) and with decoupling (lower trace), data taken from Ref. [282]

At last, it should be mentioned that, as always applies to Fourier methods[26], the major advantage of FTNMR is the multiplex advantage (see also Chapter 1). Ernst and Anderson have shown that the gain in the signal-to-noise ratio between FTNMR and conventional NMR is proportional to the square root of the number of spectral elements[102]. This result is the same as that obtained for infrared Fourier spectroscopy. In this context, it should be noted that a complete analogon to infrared Fourier spectroscopy is the nuclear magnetic Fourier-transform resonance with an incoherent rf-field (stochastic resonance)[103,104]. Of course, Fourier methods depend on electronic computers to perform the Fourier transform of the measured data and were widely used when sufficiently cheap computers became available. The use of the computer and of the mathematical treatment of the experimental data may be considered as a disadvantage. However, it must not be forgotten that the digital computer does not only perform the Fourier transform (mostly, fast Fourier transform = Cooley Tukey algorithm, see[26]) but can also be used for averaging, for mathematical filtering, for performing experiments of difference FTNMR[106,128,129] and even for comparison of the results with a computer library. At last, it is also worth mentioning that the Fourier transform is sufficiently fast to observe chemical reactions by NMR[135].

When discussing the general aspects of FTNMR, we have to remember that all principal statements about Fourier methods have been introduced for a strictly linear system (mechanical oscillator) in Chapter 1. In Chapter 2, on the other hand, we have seen that the nuclear spin system is not strictly linear (with Kramer-Kronig-relations between absorption mode and dispersion mode signal[114]). Moreover, the spin system has to be treated quantummechanically, e.g. by a density matrix formalism. Thus, the question arises what are the conditions under which the Fourier transform of the FID is actually equivalent to the result of a low-field slow-passage experiment[110-112,119]? Generally, these conditions are obeyed for systems which are at thermal equilibrium just before the initial pulse but are mostly violated for systems in a non-equilibrium state[219-254] (Oberhauser effect, chemically induced dynamic nuclear polarization, double resonance experiments etc.).

6 Special Applications of and Recent Developments in FTNMR

In the last section of this review, we will discuss some of the special applications and special recent developments of Fourier transform nuclear magnetic resonance. For example, the measurements of relaxation times T_1 or T_2 require specific pulse methods (e.g. inversion recovery for T_1)[100,136,137,139,144,147,153,159,163,167,224] and spin-echo methods [149-151,155-157,162], usually in combination with the Fourier transform method. In Fourier transform spin-echo spectroscopy[149,150], it is the spin-echo envelope which is Fourier transformed instead of the free induction decay.

When samples can only be investigated in aqueous solutions, one has always to overcome the problem of the rather strong NMR signal from the protons of H_2O which may obscure the signal from the sample. Solutions to this problem have been found in several ways[148,152,154,160,161,164,172] based upon selective excitation of the sample (flip angle $\alpha_{\text{sample}} = 90°$, $\alpha_{H_2O} = 360°$ [148]) or on the different relaxation times of the nuclei in the sample and of the protons (WEFT = = water eliminated Fourier transform spectroscopy[152]).

For some NMR investigations, it may be desirable not to employ the usual pulse method in FTNMR. At first, the high peak rf-power in the initial pulse can cause technical problems. Secondly, it could be necessary to scan only a limited portion of the spectrum in order to avoid recording large peaks of H_2O or to study the relaxation of some spins while not perturbing others. All these requirements can be met in a conventional NMR experiment (see Fig. 6) with linear sweep under rapid passage conditions. Modifying Eq. (7) (mechanical system in the first section) for nuclear magnetic resonance, we obtain for the absorption mode signal

$$\hat{C}(\omega_t) = M_0 \int_0^{\infty} \cos(\omega_0 \tau)\, e^{-\tau/T_2} \cos\left(at\tau - \frac{a}{2}\tau^2\right) d\tau \tag{46a}$$

and for the dispersion mode signal

$$\hat{S}(\omega_t) = M_0 \int_0^{\infty} \cos(\omega_0 \tau)\, e^{-\tau/T_2} \sin\left(at\tau - \frac{a}{2}\tau^2\right) d\tau \tag{46b}$$

where a is the sweep rate ($w_t = at$) and the other notation the same as in former sections (e.g. in Eq. (37)). For small sweep rates ($a/2\tau^2$ can be neglected), Eqs. (46a) and (46b) reduce to Eqs. (36) and (39), i.e. to the results obtained for slow passage. From the rapid scan signals $\hat{C}(\omega_t)$ and $\hat{S}(\omega_t)$, the wanted slow-passage information $C(\omega)$ and $S(\omega)$ can be derived only by means of a mathematical procedure with a computer, involving two Fourier transforms. Therefore, this method is called rapid scan FTNMR[120,121,125]. The first Fourier transform is the sum of the inverse cosine transform of $C(\omega_t)$ and the inverse sine transform of $S(\omega_t)$ is

$$R(T) = \int_{-\infty}^{+\infty} [\hat{C}(\omega_t)\cos(\omega_t T) + S(\omega_t)\sin(\omega_t T)]\, d\omega_t = M_0 \cos(\omega_0 T)\, e^{-T/T_2} \cos\left(\frac{a}{2}T^2\right) \tag{47}$$

where T is a new (artificial) time variable. After dividing by $\cos\left(\frac{a}{2}T^2\right)$, R(T) equals the usual FID signal M(T) (see Eq. (37)) and by means of the second Fourier transform (see Eqs. (36) and (39)), $C(\omega)$ and/or $S(\omega)$ are evaluated as in ordinary FTNMR.

In contrast to far infrared spectroscopy[26,27] operating at rather low levels of intensity of the source, high rf-field levels can easily be produced in NMR spectroscopy. These offer the possibility of observing double quantum transitions [53,56,61] as they have been observed also with high-power laser pulses in the visible range. Recently, there have been reported experiments of double-quantum FTNMR [126] and of double-quantum transitions in NMR double resonance[188]. As already indicated above, there is an analogy between pulse methods in NMR and optical laser spectroscopy. For example, the optical analogue of pulse FTNMR has been demonstrated with a CO_2 laser at $\lambda = 9.66\ \mu m$[127].

For chemically or isotopically dilute spins, e.g. ^{13}C, the signal from the dilute species can be enhanced by transferring nuclear polarization from a species of high abundance, e.g. protons, to the dilute species[239,243,245]. This requires that the two species are coupled to each other. The technique used for this polarization transfer is based on spin locking of the abundant species and on the spin temperature concept.

These effects together with other double resonance and "rotating frame" experiments[81,82,96,101,183,193,204,208-212,220-222,233-237,247,248] cannot be discussed and explained in more detail here. For an introduction, the reader is referred to Ref.[8].

Special problems arise in the NMR investigation of solids since the dipolar coupling of the nuclear spins causes a considerable broadening of the NMR lines as pointed out by van Fleck[37]. One method of partly removing the effect of the dipolar broadening is to rotate the sample, especially at the magic angle[45,54,58,59,63,64]. The Hamiltonian for the magnetic dipolar interaction is [37,38]

$$H = \sum_{i>j} \frac{\gamma^2}{r_{ij}^3} \left\{ (\mathbf{I}_i, \mathbf{I}_j) - 3 \frac{(\mathbf{r}_{ij}, \mathbf{I}_i)(\mathbf{r}_{ij}, \mathbf{I}_j)}{r_{ij}^2} \right\} \tag{48}$$

where I_i, I_j, r_{ij} and γ are the nuclear spin operator for the nuclei at lattice sites i and j, the vector connecting the two lattice sites i and j, and the gyromagnetic ratio, respectively. Retaining only those terms of Eq. (48) which have diagonal matrix elements (truncated Hamiltonian), we obtain[37,38]

$$H = \sum_{i>j} \frac{\gamma^2}{r_{ij}^3} \left\{ (1 - 3\cos^2 \vartheta_{ij}) \left[I_i^z I_j^z - \frac{1}{4}(I_i^+ I_j^- + I_i^- I_j^+) \right] \right\} \tag{49}$$

where ϑ_{ij} is the angle between r_{ij} and the z-axis (direction of the magnetic field) and where the spin operators I^+, I^- and I^z are defined in the usual way[6]. If now the sample is rotated about a direction inclined at an angle θ with the external magnetic field at rotational velocity Ω, the Hamiltonian becomes time-dependent. On the average, the time-dependent part vanishes, and only the time-independent part needs to be considered

$$H' = -\frac{1}{2}(1 - 3\cos^2 \Theta) \sum_{i>j} \frac{\gamma^2}{r_{ij}^3} \left\{ (1 - 3\cos^2 \vartheta_{ij}) \left[I_i^z I_j^z - \frac{1}{4}(I_i^+ I_j^- + I_i^- I_j^+) \right] \right\}. \tag{50}$$

If now the angle θ is chosen to be 54.74° ($\cos^2 \theta = 1/3$, magic angle), the time-averaged part of the dipolar interaction vanishes. Thus, rotation of the sample at the magic angle offers the possibility to suppress the unwanted dipolar interaction effects in solids. These are observed not only in conventional sweep NMR experiments but also when using pulse methods[77,87] and have been bypassed here also by rotation at the magic angle[97,98]. Another approach in dealing with the dipolar interaction was to perturb one of the interacting species, e.g. ^{19}F in NaF when observing the Na NMR signal[180]. Recently, the problem of suppressing the effect of dipolar interaction in solids has been attacked by means of special multiple pulse sequences[155-157,255-275,277-279]. In cyclic pulse sequences with an at least four-pulse cycle, the 90°-pulses can be chosen in such a way that the dipolar interaction (Eq. (49)) drops out in first order[258,260-263,265,267,271-273]. This method called "coherent averaging" is more efficient than the rotation of the sample at the magic angle. It should be noted that there exists also a chemical shift

[6] See for example Ref.[8].

anisotropy in solids, and a combination of sample spinning at the magic angle with cyclic pulse sequences was used to obtain the isotropic average for the chemical shift in solids and to suppress the dipolar effects[168–171].

As already mentioned above, there is usually the problem in the investigation of organic materials, e.g. by ^{13}C NMR, of a considerable overlap of the NMR lines originating from the various chemical shifts in a large molecule due to the splitting of these lines caused by the coupling to the protons. And it is difficult to interpret such complicated NMR spectra (see Fig. 14, upper trace). When proton decoupling is used[184,189,200,215], only a few lines appear in the spectrum (see Fig. 14, lower trace), but the information of the coupling-multiplet-structure is lost which could be useful in assigning the lines to the inequivalent carbon sites. In order to obtain spectra sufficiently simple to be interpreted without losing information, more sophisticated methods than proton decoupling are necessary. It is obvious that all the information mentioned above cannot be obtained in one measurement. The aim is therefore to repeat the measurement of the NMR spectrum with a well-defined variation of the conditions under which each of the measurements is performed. One possibility is to limit the excitation of the NMR lines by pulses selectively to one of the lines. This can be done by Fourier-synthesized excitation of nuclear magnetic resonance[133] where the exciting pulse is generated in such a way that its Fourier transform is a single line with a certain band width. More easily to realize with a commercial NMR spectrometer is the selective excitation method as developed by R. Freeman and coworkers[276,280]. Here, the selective excitation is achieved by a regular sequence of short identical radiofrequency pulses the Fourier transform of which has a maximum at the frequency of the line to be excited. More involved double resonance methods than simple proton decoupling, such as selective population transfer, can be used to retain all the information necessary for the interpretation of the NMR spectra[240,241]. When considering and reflecting the development of experimental technique in NMR, we realize that nuclear magnetic double resonance was at first a two-frequency experiment[184–187]. While sweeping the spectrum, a second rf-frequency is applied to the sample. With the development of Fourier transform and pulse methods, double resonance became a mixed frequency-

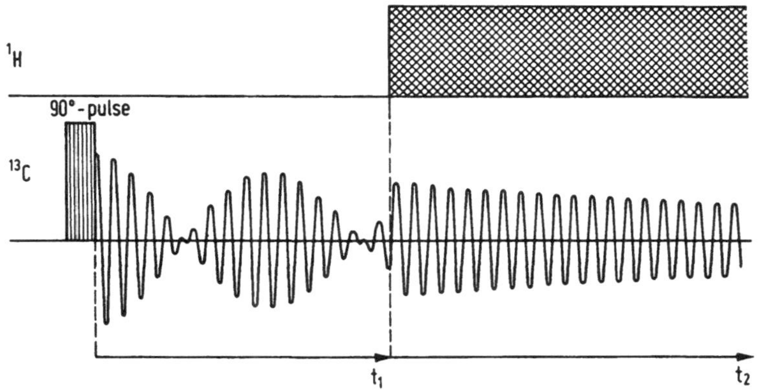

Fig. 15. Illustration of one possibility of 2D-resolved ^{13}C-NMR spectroscopy

time experiment[205,214]. After the initial pulse, the perturbing rf-field with frequency ω (e.g. $\omega \approx \omega_{proton}$) is applied while the free induction decay (e.g. of ^{13}C) is observed as a function of time. By means of the Fourier transform of the FID signal, an information is obtained which is similar to that of the two-frequency experiment. Clearly, the next step in the application of Fourier transform methods is to perform a two-time experiment and to obtain the corresponding spectra by a two-dimensional Fourier transform. In ^{13}C-NMR spectroscopy of organic materials, such a two-time experiment would be observing the ^{13}C-FID signal for a time t_1 without decoupling and for a second time t_2 with proton decoupling (see Fig. 15). The signal $s(t_1, t_2)$ is recorded for various times t_1 as a function of t_2 and is thus a function of t_1 and t_2. The two-dimensional spectra (functions of ω_1 complementary to t_1 and of ω_2 complementary to t_2) are then computed by a two-dimensional Fourier transform[281–283,290–292]

$$S^{CC}(\omega_1, \omega_2) = \int_0^\infty \int_0^\infty dt_1\, dt_2 \cos(\omega_1 t_1) \cos(\omega_2 t_2)\, s(t_1, t_2). \tag{51}$$

An example of such spectra is shown in Fig. 16 (*n*-hexane). The traces plotted for various values of ω_2 show that parallel to the ω_1-axis, the full multiplet structure is retained whereas in the ω_2 direction the completely decoupled spectrum results. The undecoupled spectrum is to be considered as a projection of the spectra for various values of ω_2 onto the ω_1-axis. This rather involved technique is less sensitive than ordinary FTNMR. It has been used mainly in ^{13}C-NMR spectroscopy. A number of applications as well as the solution to problems connected with this method have been reported[281–307].

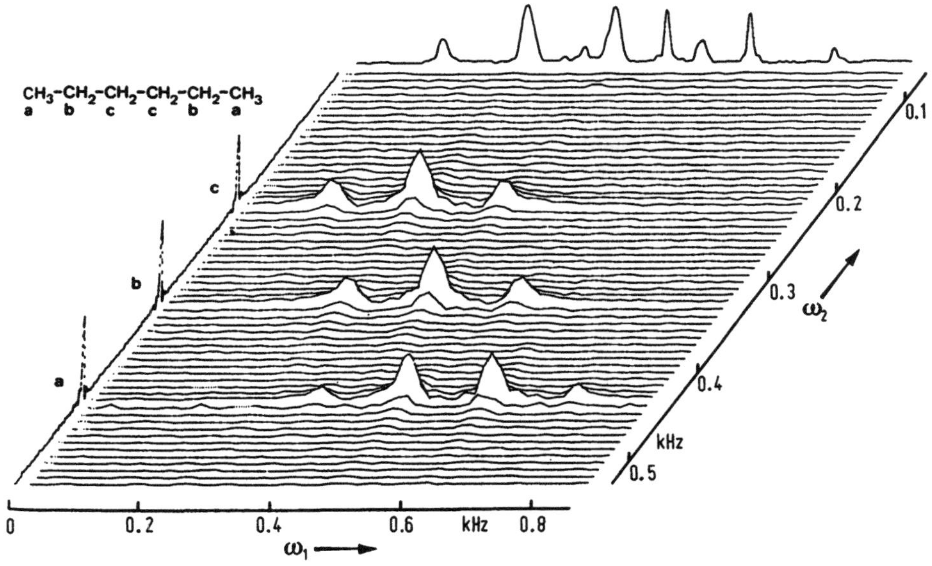

Fig. 16. 2D-resolved ^{13}C spectrum of *n*-hexane recorded with the technique illustrated in Fig. 15 and described in the text. Resolution is limited by the 64 × 64 matrix used to represent the 2D Fourier transform. The spectra are absolute value spectra. The undecoupled 1D system is indicated along the ω_1 axis and the proton-decoupled spectrum is shown along the ω_2 axis (taken from Ref. [282])

At last, we shall discuss NMR imaging or spin mapping or zeugmatography[308-337]. For this purpose, several techniques have been developed. The information obtained in such kind of experiments is the spatial distribution of spins and their properties, e.g. spin-lattice relaxation times. These techniques can be used also for the investigation of living biological objects in a non-destructive manner, and they could become a valuable research tool in medicine with a broad range of potential applications[308, 330-333]. One important fact in this context is that the spin-lattice relaxation time T_1 of protons is longer by a factor of 1.5 to 2.0 in cancerous tissues than in healthy tissues. Moreover, cancerous tissues contain more water and have therefore a higher proton nuclear spin density[309, 313, 321]. The first technique suitable for NMR imaging was proposed by Lauterbur et al.[310, 314, 320] in which the image is reconstructed from a number of projections of the nuclear spin density in the sample. A projection of the three-dimensional spin density onto a straight line is obtained by applying a magnetic field gradient along the chosen direction, and the nuclear spins in a plane perpendicular to this direction will all contribute to the resonance signal at the same frequency. Secondly, there have been introduced selective excitation techniques by Mansfield and coworkers[315, 322, 325, 327-329, 332, 336, 337]. For a three-dimensional or multi-planar NMR imaging[328, 329], a set of parallel regularly spaced planar slices perpendicular to a chosen direction is selected by means of saturating the NMR signal from the entire sample except the above mentioned slices, in the presence of a field gradient along the chosen direction, e.g. the x-direction. Next, a field gradient is applied along a direction perpendicular to the first one, e.g. along the y-axis, and a second set of parallel regularly spaced narrow slices (this time perpendicular to the second chosen direction) is excited by a comb of excitation frequencies. Finally, the FID proceeds in the presence of field gradients along all three directions, i.e. along the x-, y- and z-direction. By Fourier analysis and by sorting the responses of the various volume elements, an image of the entire sample is obtained. A further technique for scanning the nuclear spin density of a three-dimensional sample is the sensitive point method as proposed by Hinshaw et al.[312, 318, 326, 330]. In this case again, field gradients along three directions perpendicular to each other are applied to the sample. Each field gradient is modulated with a different frequency and, thus, it is possible to select a single point in the sample to produce an unmodulated response. By moving the center of the field gradients, the "sensitive point" can be moved through the sample, and the spin density can be scanned as a function of the location within the sample. The last technique for NMR imaging to be discussed is of particular interest within the scope of this review since it is based solely on a two- or three-dimensional Fourier transform. This method called "Fourier imaging" was developed by Ernst and his coworkers[316, 319]. It is very similar to the two-dimensional FTNMR discussed above. The experiment starts at $t = 0$ when transverse magnetization is created by an rf-pulse. Then a field gradient is applied along the x-axis for a time t_x. After that, a field gradient along the y-axis is applied for a time t_y. Finally, a field gradient is applied along the z-axis. Simultaneously, the FID signal is observed as a function of time (t_z). Varying the times t_x and t_y in a systematic way, the signal $s(t_x, t_y, t_z)$ is obtained as a function of all three times t_x, t_y and t_z. The three-dimensional spin density is then computed by means of a three-dimensional Fourier transform. All these methods for NMR imaging are still in a state of development and further improvement. Hopefully, its performance will be increased in the near future with respect to obtaining an image in a minimum of time with a maximum of sensitivity. Then, it seems that these techniques will become a useful diagnostic tool for clinical applications.

7 References

A. Books and Reviews

a) Nuclear magnetic resonance in general (selected bibliography)

1. Adrew, E. R.: Nuclear magnetic resonance. Cambridge: Cambridge University Press 1955
2. Roberts, J. D.: Nuclear magnetic resonance. New York: McGraw-Hill Book Co. 1959
3. Pople, J. A., Schneider, W. G., Bernstein, H. J.: High resolution nuclear magnetic resonance. New York: McGraw-Hill Book Co. 1959
4. Abragam, A.: The principles of magnetic resonance. Oxford: Clarendon Press 1961
5. Carrington, A., Mc Lachlan, A. D.: Introduction to magnetic resonance. New York: Harper and Row 1967
6. Mathieson, D. W.: Nuclear magnetic resonance for organic chemists. New York: Academic Press 1967
7. Bovey, F. A.: Nuclear magnetic resonance spectroscopy. New York: Academic Press 1969
8. Slichter, C. P., Principles of magnetic resonance (2nd edit.). Heidelberg: Springer 1978
9. Ernst, R. R.: Advan. Magn. Reson. *2*, 1 (1966)
10. Hall, G. E.: NMR Spectrosc. *1*, 227 (1968)
11. Nageswara Rao, B. D.: Advan. Magn. Reson. *4*, 271 (1970)
12. Redfield, A. G., Gupta, R. K.: Advan. Magn. Res. *5*, 81 (1971)
13. Jackman, L. M., Cotton, F. A. (eds.): Dynamic nuclear magnetic resonance spectroscopy. New York: Academic Press 1975
14. Mehring, M.: High resolution NMR spectroscopy in solids. Heidelberg: Springer Verlag 1976
15. Haeberlein, U.: High resolution NMR in solids. New York: Academic Press 1976

b) Pulse and Fourier methods in nuclear magnetic resonance

16. Farrar, T. C., and Becker, E. D.: Pulse and Fourier transform NMR. New York: Academic Press 1971
17. Ziessow, D.: On-line Rechner in der Chemie. Berlin: Walter de Gruyter u. Co. 1973
18. Gillies, D. G., Shaw, D.: Ann. Rev. NMR Spectrosc. *5A*, 560 (1972)
19. Cooper, J. W.: The computer in Fourier transform NMR. In: Topics in carbon-13 NMR spectroscopy. Levy, G. L. (ed.), vol. 2, p. 392. New York: J. Wiley 1974
20. Redfield, A. G.: NMR, Grundlagen u. Fortschritte *13*, 137 (1976)
21. Shaw, D.: Fourier transform nuclear magnetic resonance spectroscopy. Amsterdam: Elsevier, Publ. Co. 1976
22. Müllen, K., Pregosin, P. S.: Fourier transform NMR techniques: A practical approach. New York: Academic Press 1976

c) Some selected reviews about infrared Fourier transform spectroscopy

23. Bell, R. J.: Introductory Fourier transform spectroscopy. New York: Academic Press 1972
24. Geick, R.: Meßtechnik *2*, 43 (1974)
25. Genzel, L.: Fresenius Z. Anal. Chem. *273*, 391 (1975)
26. Geick, R.: Topics in Current Chemistry *58*, 75 (1975)
27. Geick, R.: Fresenius Z. Anal. Chem. *288*, 1 (1977)

B. References for nuclear magnetic resonance in general

28. Bloch, F., Siegert, H.: Phys. Rev. *57*, 522 (1940)
29. Purcell, E. M., Torrey, H. C., Pound, R. V.: Phys. Rev. *69*, 37 (1946)

30. Bloch, F., Hansen, W. W., Packard, M.: Phys. Rev. *69*, 127 (1946)
31. Bloch, F.: Phys. Rev. *70*, 460 (1946)
32. Bloch, F., Hansen, W. W., Packard, M.: Phys. Rev. *70*, 474 (1946)
33. Purcell, E. M., Pound, R. V., Bloembergen, N.: Phys. Rev. *70*, 986, 988 (1946)
34. Rollin, B. V.: Nature *158*, 669 (1946)
35. Rollin, B. V., Hatton, J.: Nature *159*, 201 (1947)
36. Rollin, B. V., et al.: Nature *160*, 457 (1947)
37. van Fleck, J.: Phys. Rev. *74*, 1168 (1948)
38. Bloembergen, N., Purcell, E. M., Pound, R. V.: Phys. Rev. *73*, 679 (1948)
39. Jacobsohn, B. A., Wangsness, R. K.: Phys. Rev. *73*, 942 (1948)
40. Karplus, R., Schwinger, J.: Phys. Rev. *73*, 1020 (1948)
41. Karplus, R.: Phys. Rev. *73*, 1027 (1948)
42. Pake, G. E., Purcell, E. M.: Phys. Rev. *74*, 1184 (1948)
43. Torrey, H. C.: Phys. Rev. *76*, 1056 (1949)
44. Torrey, H. C.: Phys. Rev. *85*, 365 (1952)
45. Andrew, E. R., Eades, R. G.: Proc. Roy. Soc. *A 216*, 398 (1953)
46. Wangsness, R. K., Bloch, F.: Phys. Rev. *89*, 728 (1953)
47. Bloch, F.: Phys. Rev. *94*, 496 (1954)
48. Bloembergen, N., Pound, R. V.: Phys. Rev. *95*, 8 (1954)
49. Bloembergen, N., Rowland, T. J.: Phys. Rev. *97*, 1679 (1955)
50. Bloch, F.: Phys. Rev. *102*, 104 (1956)
51. Bruce, C. R., Norberg, R. E., Pake, G. E.: Phys.Rev. *104*, 419 (1956)
52. Torrey, H. C.: Phys. Rev. *104*, 563 (1956)
53. Anderson, W. A.: Phys. Rev. *104*, 850 (1956)
54. Williams, G. A., Gutowsky, H. S.: Phys. Rev. *104*, 278 (1956)
55. Bloch, R.: Phys. Rev. *105*, 1206 (1957)
56. Kaplan, J. I., Maiboom, S.: Phys. Rev. *106*, 499 (1957)
57. Pound, R. V.: Rev. Sci. Instr. *28*, 966 (1957)
58. Andrew, E. R., Bradbury, A., Eades, R. G.: Nature *182*, 1659 (1958)
59. Clough, S., Gray, K. W.: Proc. Phys. Soc. *79*, 457 (1962)
60. Szöke, A., Maiboom, S.: Phys. Rev. *113*, 585 (1959)
61. Yatsiv, S.: Phys. Rev. *113*, 1522 (1959)
62. Anderson, W. A.: Rev. Sci. Instr. *33*, 1160 (1962)
63. Goldburg, W. I., Lee, M.: Phys. Rev. Lett. *11*, 255 (1963)
64. Lee, M., Goldburg, W. I.: Phys. Rev. *140*, A 1261 (1965)
65. Ernst, R. R., Anderson, W. A.: Rev. Sci. Instr. *36*, 1689, 1696 (1965)
66. Ernst, R. R.: Rev. Sci. Instr. *39*, 998 (1968)

C. References for pulse methods in NMR and spin echoes

67. Hahn, E. L.: Phys. Rev. *77*, 297 (1950)
68. Hahn, E. L.: Phys. Rev. *80*, 580 (1950)
69. Hahn, E. L., Maxwell, D. E.: Phys. Rev. *84*, 1246 (1951)
70. Gutowsky, H. S., McCall, D. W., Slichter, C. P.: Phys. Rev. *84*, 589 (1951)
71. Ramsey, N. F., Purcell, E. M.: Phys. Rev. *85*, 143 (1952)
72. Carr, H. Y., Purcell, E. M.: Phys. Rev. *88*, 415 (1952)
73. Hahn, E. L., Maxwell, D. E.: Phys. Rev. *88*, 1070 (1952)
74. Ramsey, N. F.: Phys. Rev. *91*, 303 (1953)
75. Gutowsky, H. S., McCall, D. W., Slichter, C. P.: J. Chem. Phys. *21*, 279 (1953)
76. Carr, H. Y., Purcell, E. M.: Phys. Rev. *94*, 630 (1954)
77. Lowe, I. J., Norberg, R. E.: Phys. Rev. *107*, 46 (1957)
78. Carr, H. Y.: Phys. Rev. *112*, 1693 (1958)
79. McConnel, H. M.: J. Chem. Phys. *28*, 430 (1958)
80. Maiboom, S., Gill, D.: Rev. Sci. Instr. *29*, 688 (1958)
81. Solomon, I.: C.R. Acad. Sci. Paris *248*, 92 (1959)
82. Solomon, I.: Phys. Rev. Lett. *2*, 301 (1959)
83. Emshwiller, M., Hahn, E. L., Kaplan, D.: Phys. Rev. *118*, 414 (1960)

84. Alexander, S.: Rev. Sci. Instr. *32*, 1066 (1961)
85. Powles, J. G., Hartland, A.: Proc. Phys. Soc. *77*, 273 (1961)
86. Alexander, S.: J. Chem. Phys. *37*, 967, 974 (1962)
87. Powles, J. G., Strange, J. H.: Proc. Phys. Soc. *82*, 6 (1963)
88. Powles, J. G., Strange, J. H.: Mol. Phys. *8*, 169 (1964)
89. Allerhand, A., Gutowsky, H. S.: J. Chem. Phys. *41*, 2115 (1964)
90. Allerhand, A., Gutowsky, H. S.: J. Chem. Phys. *42*, 1587 (1965)
91. Bloom, M., Reeves, L. W., Wells, E. J.: J. Chem. Phys. *42*, 1615 (1965)
92. Allerhand, A., Gutowsky, H. S.: J. Chem. Phys. *42*, 4203 (1965)
93. Wells, E. J., Gutowsky, H. S.: J. Chem. Phys. *43*, 3414 (1965)
94. Gutowsky, H. S., Vold, R. L., Wells, E. J.: J. Chem. Phys. *43*, 4107 (1965)
95. Allerhand, A.: J. Chem. Phys. *44*, 1 (1966)
96. Ostroff, E. D., Waugh, J. S.: Phys. Rev. Lett. *16*, 1097 (1966)
97. Cunningham, A. C., Day, S. M.: Phys. Rev. *152*, 287 (1966)
98. Kessemeier, H., Norberg, R. E.: Phys. Rev. *155*, 321 (1967)
99. Tokuhiro, T., Fraenkel, G.: J. Chem. Phys. *49*, 3998 (1968)
100. Freeman, R., Witteboek, S.: J. Magn. Res. *1*, 238 (1969)
101. Wells, E. J., Abramson, K. H.: J. Magn. Res. *1*, 378 (1969)

D. References for Fourier transform nuclear magnetic resonance

102. Ernst, R. R., Anderson, W. A.: Rev. Sci. Instr. *37*, 93 (1966)
103. Ernst, R. R.: J. Magn. Res. *3*, 10 (1970)
104. Kaiser, R.: J. Magn. Res. *3*, 28 (1970)
105. Freeman, R., Jones, R. C.: J. Chem. Phys. *52*, 465 (1970)
106. Ernst, R. R.: J. Magn. Res. *4*, 280 (1971)
107. Freeman, R., Hill, H. D. W.: J. Magn. Res. *4*, 366 (1971)
108. Jonas, D. E., Sternlicht, H.: J. Magn. Res. *6*, 167 (1972)
109. Jonas, D. E.: J. Magn. Res. *6*, 183, 191 (1972)
110. Kaplan, J. I.: J. Chem. Phys. *57*, 5615 (1972)
111. Ernst, R. R.: J. Chem. Phys. *59*, 989 (1973)
112. Kaplan, J. I.: J. Chem. Phys. *59*, 990 (1973)
113. Tomlinson, B. L., Hill, H. D. W.: J. Chem. Phys. *59*, 1775 (1973)
114. Bartholdi, E., Ernst, R. R.: J. Magn. Res. *11*, 9 (1973)
115. Stejskal, E. O., Schaefer, J.: J. Magn. Res. *14*, 160 (1974)
116. Campbell, I. D., et al.: J. Magn. Res. *11*, 172 (1973)
117. Stejskal, E. O., Schaefer, J.: J. Magn. Res. *13*, 249 (1974)
118. Moniz, W. B., Poranski, C. F., Sojka, S. A.: J. Magn. Res. *13*, 110 (1974)
119. Ernst, R. R., et al.: Pure Appl. Chem. *37*, 47 (1974)
120. Dadok, J., Sprecher, R. F.: J. Magn. Res. *13*, 243 (1974)
121. Gupta, R. K., Feretti, J. A., Becker, E. D.: J. Magn. Res. *13*, 275 (1974)
122. Pajer, R. T., Armitage, I. M.: J. Magn. Res. *21*, 365 (1976)
123. Redfield, A. G., Kunz, S. D.: J. Magn. Res. *19*, 250 (1975)
124. de Marco, A., Wüthrich, K.: J. Magn. Res. *24*, 201 (1976)
125. Ferretti, J. A., Ernst, R. R.: J. Chem. Phys. *65*, 4283 (1976)
126. Vega, S., Shattuck, T. W., Pines, A.: Phys. Rev. Lett. *37*, 43 (1976)
127. Grussmann, S. B., Scheuzle, A., Brewer, R. G.: Phys. Rev. Lett. *38*, 275 (1977)
128. Wouters, J. M., Peterson, G. A.: J. Magn. Res. *28*, 81 (1977)
129. Wouters, J. M., et al.: J. Magn. Res. *28*, 93 (1977)
130. Fujiwora, S.: J. Magn. Res. *29*, 201 (1978)
131. Ferrige, A. G., Lindon, J. C.: J. Magn. Res. *31*, 337 (1978)
132. Akitt, J. W.: J. Magn. Res. *32*, 311 (1978)
133. Clin, B., at al.: J. Magn. Res. *33*, 457 (1979)
134. Marshall, A. G., Ree, D. Ch.: J. Magn. Res. *33*, 551 (1979)
135. Kühne, R. O., et al.: J. Magn. Res. *35*, 39 (1979)

E. Special pulse methods in FTNMR (Determination of relaxation times, solvent peak suppression etc.)

136. Vold, R. L., et al.: J. Chem. Phys. *48*, 3831 (1968)
137. Freeman, R., Hill, H. D. W.: J. Chem. Phys. *51*, 3140 (1969)
138. Becker, E. D., Ferretti, J. A., Farrar, T. C.: J. Amer. Chem. Soc. *91*, 7784 (1969)
139. Freeman, R., Hill, H. D. W.: J. Chem. Phys. *53*, 4103 (1970)
140. Allerhand, A., Cochran, D. W.: J. Amer. Chem. Soc. *92*, 4482 (1970)
141. Wough, J. S.: J. Mol. Spectr. *35*, 298 (1970)
142. Wallace, W. E.: J. Chem. Phys. *54*, 1425 (1971)
143. Waldstein, P., Wallace, W. E.: Rev. Sci. Instr. *42*, 437 (1971)
144. Freeman, R., Hill, H. D. W.: J. Chem. Phys. *55*, 1985 (1971)
145. Markley, J. L., Horsley, W. J., Klein, M. P.: J. Chem. Phys. *55*, 3604 (1971)
146. Schwenk, A.: J. Magn. Res. *5*, 376 (1971)
147. Freeman, R., Hill, H. D. W.: J. Chem. Phys. *54*, 3367 (1971)
148. Redfield, A. G., Gupta, R. K.: J. Chem. Phys. *54*, 1418 (1971)
149. Vold, R. L., Chan, S. O.: J. Magn. Res. *4*, 208 (1971)
150. Freeman, R., Hill, H. D. W.: J. Chem. Phys. *54*, 301 (1971)
151. Tokuhiro, T., Fraenkel, G.: J. Chem. Phys. *55*, 2797 (1971)
152. Patt, S. L., Sykes, B. D.: J. Chem. Phys. *56*, 3182 (1972)
153. Freeman, R., Hill, H. D. W., Kaptein, R.: J. Magn. Res. *7*, 82 (1972)
154. Benz, F. W., Feeney, J., Roberts, G. C. K.: J. Magn. Res. *8*, 114 (1972)
155. Boden, N., Mortimer, M.: Chem. Phys. Lett. *21*, 538 (1973)
156. Boden, N., et al.: Phys. Lett. *A46*, 329 (1974)
157. Boden, N., et al.: J. Magn. Res. *16*, 471 (1974)
158. Kaiser, R., Bartholdi, E., Ernst, R. R.: J. Chem. Phys. *60*, 2966 (1974t
159. Demco, P. E., van Hecke, P., Waugh, J. S.: J. Magn. Res. *16*, 467 (1974)
160. Bleich, H. E., Glasel, J. A.: J. Magn. Res. *18*, 401 (1975)
161. Hoult, D. I.: J. Magn. Res. *21*, 337 (1976)
162. Kumar, A., Ernst, R. R.: Chem. Phys. Lett. *37*, 162 (1976)
163. Cutnell, J. D., Bleich, H. E., Glasel, J. A.: J. Magn. Res. *21*, 43 (1976)
164. Krishna, N. R.: J. Magn. Res. *22*, 555 (1976)
165. Kumar, A., Ernst, R. R.: J. Magn. Res. *24*, 425 (1976)
166. Gupta, R. K.: J. Magn. Res. *24*, 461 (1976)
167. Kronenbitter, J., Schwenk, A.: J. Magn. Res. *25*, 147 (1977)
168. Maricq, M. M., Waugh, J. S.: Chem. Phys. Lett. *47*, 327 (1977)
169. Stejskal, E. O., Schaefer, J., McKay, R. A.: J. Magn. Res. *25*, 569 (1977)
170. Waugh, J. S., Maricq, M. M., Cantor, R.: J. Magn. Res. *29*, 183 (1978)
171. Maricq, M. M., Waugh, J. S.: J. Chem. Phys. *70*, 3300 (1979)
172. Gupta, R. K., Gupta, P.: J. Magn. Res. *34*, 657 (1979)
173. Hochmann, J., Rosanske, R. C., Levy, G. C.: J. Magn. Res. *33*, 275 (1979)

F. References for nuclear magnetic double resonance

174. Bloom, A. L., Shoolery, J. N.: Phys. Rev. *97*, 1261 (1955)
175. Solomon, I.: Phys. Rev. *99*, 559 (1955)
176. Ramsey, N. F.: Phys. Rev. *100*, 1191 (1955)
177. Solomon, I., Bloembergen, N.: J. Chem. Phys. *25*, 261 (1956)
178. Feher, G.: Phys. Rev. *103*, 834 (1956)
179. Anderson, W. A.: Phys. Rev. *102*, 151 (1956)
180. Sarles, L. R., Cotts, R. M.: Phys. Rev. *111*, 853 (1958)
181. Kaiser, R.: Rev. Sci. Instr. *31*, 963 (1960)
182. Freeman, R., Whiffen, D. H.: Proc. Phys. Soc. *79*, 794 (1962)
183. Hartmann, S. R., Hahn, E. L.: Phys. Rev. *128*, 2042 (1962)
184. Anderson, W. A., Freeman, R.: J. Chem. Phys. *37*, 85 (1962)
185. Anderson, W. A.: J. Chem. Phys. *37*, 1373 (1962)
186. Anderson, W. A., Freeman, R.: J. Chem. Phys. *37*, 2053 (1962)
187. Anderson, W. A., Nelson, F. A.: J. Chem. Phys. *39*, 183 (1963)

188. Anderson, W. A., Freeman, R., Reilly, C. A.: J. Chem. Phys. *39*, 1518 (1963)
189. Primas, H., Ernst, R. R.: Helv. Phys. Acta *36*, 583 (1963)
190. Forsén, S., Hoffmann, R. A.: J. Chem. Phys. *39*, 2892 (1963)
191. Forsén, S., Hoffmann, R. A.: Acta Chem. Scand. *17*, 1787 (1963)
192. Forsén, S., Hoffmann, R. A.: J. Chem. Phys. *40*, 1189 (1964)
193. Lurie, F. M., Slichter, C. P.: Phys. Rev. *133*, A 1108 (1964)
194. Baldeschwieler, J. D.: J. Chem. Phys. *40*, 459 (1964)
195. Anderson, W. A., Freeman, R.: J. Chem. Phys. *42*, 1199 (1965)
196. Anders, L. R., Baldeschwieler, J. D.: J. Chem. Phys. *43*, 2147 (1965)
197. Gordon, S. L., Baldeschwieler, J. D.: J. Chem. Phys. *43*, 76 (1965)
198. Freeman, R.: J. Chem. Phys. *43*, 3087 (1965)
199. Ferretti, J. A., Freeman, R.: J. Chem. Phys. *44*, 2054 (1966)
200. Ernst, R. R.: J. Chem. Phys. *45*, 3845 (1966)
201. Gordon, S. L.: J. Chem. Phys. *45*, 1145 (1966)
202. Freeman, R., Ernst, R. R., Anderson, W. A.: J. Chem. Phys. *46*, 1125 (1967)
203. Gordon, S. L.: J. Chem. Phys. *48*, 2129 (1968)
204. McArthur, D. A., Hahn, E. L., Walstedt, R.: Phys. Rev. *188*, 609 (1969)
205. Freeman, R.: J. Chem. Phys. *53*, 457 (1970)
206. Kuhlmann, K. F., Grant, D. M., Harris, R. K.: J. Chem. Phys. *52*, 3439 (1970)
207. Yang, P. P., Gordon, L.: J. Chem. Phys. *54*, 1779 (1971)
208. Bleich, H. E., Redfield, A. E.: J. Chem. Phys. *55*, 5405 (1971)
209. Mansfield, P., Grannell, P. K.: J. Phys. *C4*, L 197 (1971)
210. Mansfield, P., Grannell, P. K.: J. Phys. *C5*, L 226 (1972)
211. Freeman, R., Hill, H. D. W., Dadok, J.: J. Chem. Phys. *58*, 3107 (1972)
212. Grannell, P. K., Mansfield, P., Whitaker, M. A. B.: Phys. Rev. *B8*, 4149 (1973)
213. Field, R. W., et al.: J. Chem. Phys. *59*, 2191 (1973)
214. Krishna, N. R.: J. Chem. Phys. *63*, 4329 (1975)
215. Grutzner, J. B., Santini, R. E.: J. Magn. Res. *19*, 173 (1975)
216. Stoll, M. E., Vega, A. J., Vaughan, R. W.: J. Chem. Phys. *67*, 2029 (1977)
217. Basus, V. J., et al.: J. Magn. Res. *35*, 19 (1979)
218. Kaplan, J. I., Carter, R. E.: J. Magn. Res. *33*, 437 (1979)

G. References about none-equilibrium states

219. Overhauser, A. W.: Phys. Rev. *92*, 411 (1953)
220. Redfield, A. G.: Phys. Rev. *98*, 1787 (1955)
221. Slichter, C. P., Holton, W. C.: Phys. Rev. *122*, 1701 (1961)
222. Anderson, A. C., Hartmann, S. R.: Phys. Rev. *128*, 2023 (1962)
223. Kaiser, R.: J. Chem. Phys. *39*, 2435 (1963)
224. Noggle, J. H.: J. Chem. Phys. *43*, 3304 (1965)
225. Kaiser, R.: J. Chem. Phys. *42*, 1838 (1965)
226. Hoffmann, R. A., Forsén, S.: J. Chem. Phys. *45*, 2049 (1966)
227. Freeman, R., Gestblom, B.: J. Chem. Phys. *47*, 2744 (1967)
228. Bargon, J., Fischer, H., Johnson, U.: Z. Naturf. *A22*, 1551 (1967)
229. Bargon, J., Fischer, H.: Z. Naturf. *A22*, 1556 (1967)
230. Freeman, R., Gestblom, B.: J. Chem. Phys. *48*, 5008 (1968)
231. Freeman, R., Wittekoek, S., Ernst, R. R.: J. Chem. Phys. *52*, 1529 (1970)
232. Fischer, H., Lehnig, M.: Z. Naturf. *A25*, 1957 (1970)
233. Rhim, W. K., Pines, A., Waugh, J. S.: Phys. Rev. Lett. *25*, 218 (1970)
234. Mansfield, P., Grannell, P. K.: J. Phys. *C4*, L 197 (1971)
235. Rhim, W. K., Kessemeier, H.: Phys. Rev. *B3*, 3655 (1971)
236. Rhim, W. K., Pines, A., Waugh, J. S.: Phys. Rev. *B3*, 684 (1971)
237. Pines, A., Rhim, W. K., Waugh, J. S.: J. Magn. Res. *6*, 457 (1972)
238. Krishna, N. R., Gordon, S. L.: Phys. Rev. *A6*, 2059 (1972)
239. Pines, A., Gibby, M. G., Waugh, J. S.: J. Chem. Phys. *56*, 1776 (1972)
240. Schäfer, J.: J. Magn. Res. *6*, 670 (1972)

241. Pachler, K., Wessels, P.: J. Magn. Res. *12*, 337 (1973)
242. Campbell, I. D., Freeman, R.: J. Chem. Phys. *58*, 2666 (1973)
243. Pines, A., Gibby, M., Waugh, J. S.: J. Chem. Phys. *59*, 569 (1973)
244. Krishna, N. R., Yang, P. P., Gordon, S. L.: J. Chem. Phys. *58*, 2906 (1973)
245. Müller, L., et al.: Phys. Rev. Lett. *32*, 1402 (1974)
246. Schäublin, S., Hohner, A., Ernst, R. R.: J. Magn. Res. *13*, 196 (1974)
247. Vold, R. L., Vold, R. R.: J. Chem. Phys. *61*, 2525 (1974)
248. Freeman, R., et al.: J. Chem. Phys. *61*, 4466 (1974)
249. Henrichs, P. M., Schwartz, L. J.: J. Magn. Res. *28*, 477 (1977)
250. Schäublin, S., Wokaun, A., Ernst, R. R.: J. Magn. Res. *27*, 273 (1977)
251. Bain, A. D., Martin, J. S.: J. Magn. Res. *29*, 125 (1978)
252. Bain, A. D., Martin, J. S.: J. Magn. Res. *29*, 137 (1978)
253. Kasper, J. V. V., Lowe, R. S., Curl, R. F.: J. Chem. Phys. *70*, 3350 (1979)
254. Henrichs, P. M., Schwartz, L. J.: J. Chem. Phys. *69*, 622 (1978); Erratum: J. Chem. Phys. *70*, 586 (1979)

H. References for special multiple pulse experiments

255. Powles, J. G., Mansfield, P.: Phys. Lett. *2*, 58 (1962)
256. Mansfield, P.: Phys. Rev. *137*, A 961 (1965)
257. Mansfield, P., Ware, D.: Phys. Lett. *22*, 133 (1966)
258. Waugh, J. S., Huber, L. M.: J. Chem. Phys. *47*, 1862 (1967)
259. Waugh, J. S., Wang, C. H.: Phys. Rev. *162*, 209 (1967)
260. Waugh, J. S., Huber, L. M., Haeberlein, U.: Phys. Rev. Lett. *20*, 180 (1968)
261. Haeberlein, U., Waugh, J. S.: Phys. Rev. *175*, 453 (1968)
262. Waugh, J. S., et al.: J. Chem. Phys. *48*, 662 (1968)
263. Haeberlein, U., Waugh, J. S.: Phys. Rev. *185*, 420 (1969)
264. Ellet jr., J. D., Waugh, J. S.: J. Chem. Phys. *51*, 2851 (1969)
265. Mansfield, P.: Phys. Lett. *A32*, 485 (1970)
266. Mehring, M., et al.: J. Chem. Phys. *54*, 3239 (1971)
267. Mansfield, P.: J. Phys. *C4*, 1444 (1971)
268. Haeberlein, U., Ellet jr., J. D., Waugh, J. S.: J. Chem. Phys. *55*, 53 (1971)
269. Mehring, M., Waugh, J. S.: Phys. Rev. *B5*, 3459 (1972)
270. Pines, A., Waugh, J. S.: J. Magn. Res. *8*, 354 (1972)
271. Rhim, W. K., Elleman, D. D., Vaughan, R. W.: J. Chem. Phys. *59*, 3740 (1973)
272. Mansfield, P., et al.: Phys. Rev. *B7*, 90 (1973)
273. Rhim, W. K., et al.: J. Chem. Phys. *60*, 4595 (1974)
274. Hester, R. K., et al.: Phys. Rev. Lett. *34*, 993 (1975)
275. Sabinov, R. Kh.: Sov. Phys. Solid State *18*, 1455 (1976)
276. Bodenhausen, G., Freeman, R., Morris, G.: J. Magn. Res. *23*, 171 (1976)
277. Yamoni, C. S., Vieth, H. M.: Phys. Rev. Lett. *37*, 1230 (1976)
278. Gerstein, B. C., et al.: J. Chem. Phys. *66*, 361 (1977)
279. Stoll, M. E., Rhim, W. K., Vaughan, R. W.: J. Chem. Phys. *64*, 4808 (1976)
280. Morris, G. A., Freeman, R.: J. Magn. Res. *29*, 433 (1978)

I. References for two-dimensional Fourier transform nuclear magnetic resonance

281. Ernst, R. R.: Chimia *29*, 179 (1975)
282. Müller, L., Kumar, A., Ernst, R. R.: J. Chem. Phys. *63*, 5490 (1975)
283. Aue, W. P., Bartholdi, E., Ernst, R. R.: J. Chem. Phys. *64*, 2229 (1976)
284. Bodenhausen, G., Freeman, R., Niedermeyer, R.: J. Magn. Res. *24*, 291 (1976)
285. Bodenhausen, G., Freeman, R., Turner, D. L.: J. Chem. Phys. *65*, 839 (1976)
286. Aue, W. P., Karhan, J., Ernst, R. R.: J. Chem. Phys. *64*, 4226 (1976)
287. Bodenhausen, G., et al.: J. Magn. Res. *25*, 559 (1977)
288. Wokaun, A., Ernst, R. R.: Chem. Phys. Lett. *52*, 407 (1977)
289. Maudsley, A. A., Ernst, R. R.: Chem. Phys. Lett. *50*, 368 (1977)
290. Nagayama, K., et al.: Naturwissenschaften *64*, 581 (1977)
291. Bodenhausen, G., et al.: J. Magn. Res. *26*, 133 (1977)

292. Freeman, R., Morris, G., Turner, D. L.: J. Magn. Res. *26*, 373 (1977)
293. Bodenhausen, G., et al.: J. Magn. Res. *28*, 17 (1977)
294. Bachmann, P., et al.: J. Magn. Res. *28*, 29 (1977)
295. Bodenhausen, G., Freeman, R., Turner, D. L.: J. Magn. Res. *27*, 511 (1977)
296. Müller, L., Kumar, A., Ernst, R. R.: J. Magn. Res. *25*, 383 (1977)
297. Bodenhausen, G., Freeman, R.: J. Magn. Res. *28*, 303 (1977)
298. Maudsley, A. A., Müller, L., Ernst, R. R.: J. Magn. Res. *28*, 463 (1977)
299. Bodenhausen, G., Freeman, R.: J. Magn. Res. *28*, 471 (1977)
300. Niedermeyer, R., Freeman, R.: J. Magn. Res. *30*, 617 (1978)
301. Nagayama, K., et al.: J. Magn. Res. *31*, 133 (1978)
302. Aue, W. P., Bachmann, P., Wokaun, A., Ernst, R. R.: J. Magn. Res. *29*, 523 (1978)
303. Bodenhausen, G., et al.: J. Magn. Res. *31*, 75 (1978)
304. Kumar, A.: J. Magn. Res. *30*, 227 (1978)
305. Freeman, R., Kempsell, St. P., Levitt, M. H.: J. Magn. Res. *34*, 663 (1979)
306. Levitt, M. H., Freeman, R.: J. Magn. Res. *34*, 675 (1979)
307. Bodenhausen, G.: J. Magn. Res. *34*, 357 (1979)

K. References for spin mapping and zeugmatography

308. Damadian, R. V.: Science *171*, 1151 (1971)
309. Weisman, I. D., et al.: Science *178*, 1288 (1972)
310. Lauterbur, P. C.: Nature *242*, 190 (1973)
311. Mansfield, P., Grannell, P. K.: J. Phys. *C6*, L 422 (1973)
312. Hinshaw, W. S.: Phys. Lett. *48A*, 87 (1974)
313. Knispel, R. R., Thompson, R. T., Pintar, M. M.: J. Magn. Res. *14*, 44 (1974)
314. Lauterbur, P. C.: Pure Appl. Chem. *40*, 149 (1974)
315. Garroway, A. N., Grannell, P. K., Mansfield, P.: J. Phys. *C7*, L 457 (1974)
316. Kumar, A., Welti, D., Ernst, R. R.: Naturwissenschaften *62*, 34 (1975)
317. Mansfield, P., Grannell, P. K.: Phys. Rev. *B12*, 3618 (1975)
318. Hinshaw, W. S.: J. Appl. Phys. *47*, 3709 (1975)
319. Kumar, A., Welti, D., Ernst, R. R.: J. Magn. Res. *18*, 69 (1975)
320. Lauterbur, P. C., et al.: J. Amer. Chem. Soc. *97*, 6866 (1975)
321. Damadian, R., et al.: Science *194*, 1430 (1976)
322. Hoult, D. I.: J. Magn. Res. *26*, 165 (1976)
323. Hester, R. K., et al.: Phys. Rev. Lett. *36*, 1081 (1976)
324. Mayne, C. L., Grant, D. M., Alderman, D. W.: J. Chem. Phys. *65*, 1684 (1976)
325. Mansfield, P., Maudsley, A. A., Baines, T.: J. Phys. *E9*, 271 (1976)
326. Hinshaw, W. S.: J. Appl. Phys. *47*, 3709 (1976)
327. Mansfield, P., Maudsley, A. A.: J. Phys. *C9*, L 409 (1976)
328. Mansfield, P., Maudsley, A. A.: J. Magn. Res. *27*, 101 (1977)
329. Mansfield, P.: J. Phys. *C10*, L 55 (1977)
330. Hinshaw, W. S., Bottomley, P. A., Holland, G. N.: Nature *270*, 722 (1977)
331. Damadian, R., et al.: Naturwissenschaften *65*, 250 (1978)
332. Mansfield, P., Pykett, I. L.: J. Magn. Res. *29*, 355 (1978)
333. Hoult, D. I., Lauterbur, P. C.: J. Magn. Res. *34*, 425 (1979)
334. Hoult, D. I.: J. Magn. Res. *33*, 183 (1979)
335. Brunner, P., Ernst, R. R.: J. Magn. Res. *33*, 83 (1979)
336. Mansfield, P., et al.: J. Magn. Res. *33*, 261 (1979)
337. Hoult, D. I.: J. Magn. Res. *35*, 69 (1979)

Analytical Isotachophoresis

Petr Boček

Institute of Analytical Chemistry, Czechoslovak Academy of Sciences, Leninova 82, 611 42 BRNO, Czechoslovakia

Table of Contents

1 Introduction

Isotachophoresis is an electrophoretic technique. It is used in the field of inogenic compounds in solutions. With the use of adequate instrumentation the separations can be performed at a considerable speed (3–5 min). For both qualitative and quantitative analysis easily measurable parameters of the record (height and length of the step) are available.

The study is aimed at making the readers acquainted with the basic theory, instrumentation and application possibilities of analytical isotachophoresis. The article also includes advanced knowledge of the method itself and simultaneously outlines problems of the present basic research and prospects for further development.

In the whole article, the literature cited was selected to give a brief guideline to different stages of the development of isotachophoresis on the one hand and to draw the attention to some papers of basic significance and to some techniques and applications of practical interest on the other hand. An exhaustive chronical review of the literature has been published elsewhere.[1] However, the review[2] of common electrophoretical techniques and of their applications in analytical chemistry is worth/ mentioning. Isotachophoresis was also compiled monographically[3] and there exists a number of reviews[4–9].

2 Basic Principles

A basic feature which differentiates isotachophoresis from the other electrophoretical techniques is that zones migrate at the same velocity from the moment the equilibrium has established. By this the name iso-tachos is explained. Its simplest version is the moving boundary technique applied to the measurement of transference numbers (known since Nernst[10], Whetham[11] and Kohlrausch[12]). Theoretical, experimental and instrumental elaboration of this technique was described in detail by MacInnes and Longsworth[13]. Based on the example of this simple method, basic features and characteristics of isotachophoretical migration and its terminology can be described and explained.

The state prior to the passage of electric current is illustrated in Fig. 1a. The system is composed of two solutions designated as phases $\lambda(L^-, R^+)$ and $\tau_0(T^-, R^+)$ separated by a phase boundary. The ions under investigation, e.g. univalent anions L^-, T^-, possessing identical signs, are placed in such a way that in the direction of assumed movement in the electric field the front of the migration is formed by the ion with higher mobility, i.e. ion L^- in zone λ, and is followed by the less mobile ion T^- in zone τ_0. Ion L^-, forming the migration front, is called the leading ion and phase λ the leading electrolyte. Ion T^-, forming the migration rear part, is called the terminating ion and phase τ_0 the terminating electrolyte. Both electrolytes contain an identical counter-ion, e.g. cation R^+. In addition to the above mentioned ions L^-, T^- and R^+, no other ionic components leading electric current are present in

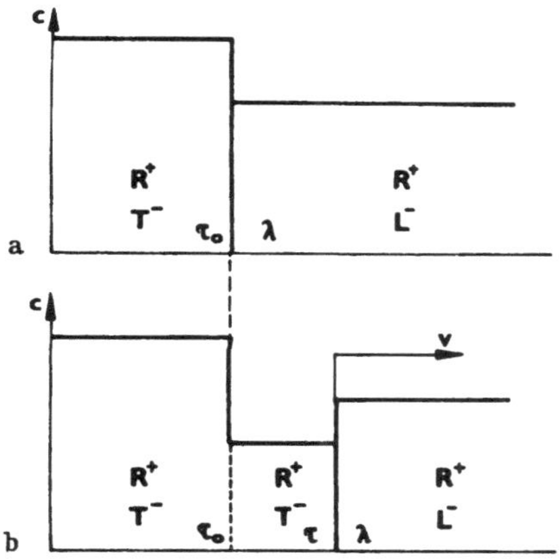

Fig. 1. Scheme of the moving boudary method. **a** Situation prior to the passage of electric current, **b** migration of zone λ and formation of isotachophoretically migrating adjusted zone τ, under the influence of d.c. current

the system or the contribution of such components to the total conductivity of the solutions is negligible.

If direct current passes through the system, then the state, after a certain time elapse, is characterized by Figure 1b. The boundary between the leading and the terminating ions migrates toward the respective electrode (in the present case toward the cathode). Phase λ formed by the leading electrolyte appears at the front of this boundary, and on the other side of the boundary a new phase τ — the isotachophoretic zone — containing the terminating electrolyte is formed. The concentration of the terminating electrolyte T^-R^+ in zone τ is not optional but is determined by the composition of the leading electrolyte and is called the adjusted concentration. It is characteristic of the given ion T^- and independent of the initial concentration of ion T^- in zone τ_0. The less mobile ion forms the zone with the concentration lower than that of the more mobile, leading ion.

Leading ion L^- in the zone of leading electrolyte λ and terminating ion T^- in adjusted zone τ migrate with the same velocity. Adjusted zone τ is separated from initial zone τ_0 of the terminating electrolyte by a stationary concentration boundary. It is characterized by the same qualitative composition on both sides of the boundary. However, the concentrations of ion T^- are different.

2.1 Concentrating Effect

As already mentioned, the adjusted concentration of ions T^- in isotachophoretically migrating zone τ does not depend on the optionally selected concentration of ions T^- in zone τ_0. This means that dilution takes place at the concentration of electrolyte T^-R^+ selected initially higher than it corresponds to the adjusted value. On the other hand, the electrolyte becomes more concentrated in zone τ for a lower initial concentration of T^-R^+ in zone τ_0.

This phenomenon has a considerable practical significance which is particularly distinct in the case when a third electrolyte A^-R^+, containing anion A^- of intermediate mobility, $u_T < u_A < u_L$, is placed between leading L^-R^+ and terminating

T^-R^+ electrolytes in a suitable capillary tube. Ion A^- will also form a zone with the adjusted concentration in the course of electromigration. If the initial concentration of A^- were lower than it would correspond to the adjusted value, then concentrating of ion A^- would take place. This effect is illustrated by Fig. 2 in which investigated ions L^-, A^- and T^- are only drawn for simplification, counter-ion R^+ being omitted.

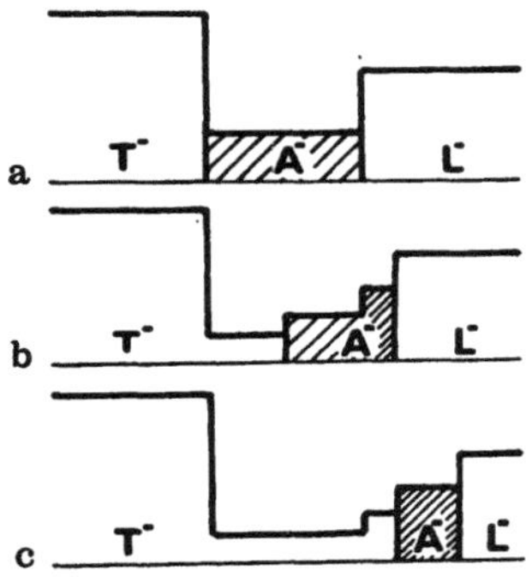

Fig. 2. Concentrating effect. **a** Situation prior to the passage of electric current, **b** situation after the passage of an amount of electricity, **c** situation where adjusted zone of A^- has been completely formed

Figure 2a describes the initial situation when the solution of intermediate ion A^- is placed between the leading and the terminating electrolytes, L^- and T^-, respectively, and the concentration of A^- is lower than it would correspond to the adjusted value.

Figure 2b illustrates the state at a certain moment during the passage of electric current. It can be seen that an adjusted zone with a higher concentration of ion A^- is formed behind the zone of the leading electrolyte.

Figure 2c depicts the state with the adjusted zone of ion A^- already completely formed — the initial solution of ion A^- (sample) has become more concentrated and occupies a considerably smaller part of the capillary than in the initial state.

Behind the adjusted zone of ion A^-, a zone of terminating ion T^- is generated, also adjusted to the composition of the leading electrolyte. In the initial position of sample A^-, a low-concentration region remains in the terminating electrolyte, bounded from both sides by a stationary concentration boundary, i.e. by a stepwise change in the concentration and with a qualitative composition of the electrolyte being identical on both sides of this boundary.

2.2 Characteristics of Zones

In order to describe isotachophoretic zones, it is necessary to start with basic electrolyte transport equations, first thoroughly investigated by Nernst[14] and Planck[15] and later by Kohlrausch[12], Weber[16,17], Laue[18], MacInnes[13] and Longsworth[19,20].

A general equation relating concentration, c_j, to time, t, and position, x, for an ion species, j, of charge z_j and mobility u_j moving in the x direction in a tube of uniform cross section under the influence of gradients of chemical and electrical potential, $\partial\mu_j/\partial x$ and $\partial\varphi/\partial x$, may be written (cf. [19,20,21])

$$\frac{\partial c_j}{\partial t} = \frac{\partial}{\partial x}\left[\frac{c_j u_j}{|z_j|\,F}\left(\frac{\partial \mu_j}{\partial x} + z_j F \frac{\partial \varphi}{\partial x}\right)\right] \tag{1}$$

and the expression for the electric current density in a solution containing s ionic species

$$i = -F \sum_{k=1}^{s} \frac{c_k |z_k| u_k}{z_k}\left[\frac{1}{F}\frac{\partial \mu_k}{\partial x} + z_k \frac{\partial \varphi}{\partial x}\right]. \tag{2}$$

In these equations, the concentrations ($mol \cdot cm^{-3}$) and the mobility ($cm^2\ V^{-1}\ s^{-1}$) are positive values. The valence of an ion, account being taken of its sign, is denoted by z_j whereas $|z_j|$ indicates the magnitude only. The gradients of the chemical and electrical potentials, $\partial\mu/\partial x$ and $\partial\varphi/\partial x$, respectively, are both expressed in $V \cdot cm^{-1}$. F is the Faraday constant ($C \cdot mol^{-1}$) and i is the current density ($A \cdot cm^{-2}$).

In the case of n ionic species, n equations of type (1) are obtained of which one can be eliminated by means of the law of electroneutrality

$$\sum_{j=1}^{n} c_j z_j = 0. \tag{3}$$

By describing steady-state migration of isotachophoretic zones, a good approximation may be carried out by neglecting the diffusion, i.e. all terms comprising gradient $\partial\mu/\partial x$ may be omitted.

Further, an ideal case can be investigated (as has been done already by Kohlrausch[12]) and Weber[17]) where solutions of two strong electrolytes with a common counter-ion, e.g. L^-R^+ and A^-R^+, are separated from one another by the phase boundary which moves at constant velocity under the influence of a constant current density and does not change with time.

As already shown by Kohlrausch[12]) and Weber[16,17]) such a case corresponds to the particular solution of equations (1)–(3) in the form

$$c_j = f(x - vt), \tag{4}$$

where v ($cm \cdot s^{-1}$) is the boundary velocity; this particular solution exists under the following conditions:

- it must hold for ion A^- migrating behind leading ion L^- that $u_A < u_L$,
- the concentrations in both zones cannot be optional but they must exhibit an entirely defined ratio. Under the assumption that all mobilities are constants throughout the system, this ratio can be explicitly expressed in the form

$$\frac{c_A}{c_L} = \frac{u_A}{u_A + u_R} \cdot \frac{u_L + u_R}{u_L}. \tag{5}$$

The condition for concentration follows from the character of the so-called "beharrliche Funktion" or the Kohlrausch regulating function, ω, the value of which is independent of time and entirely defined by the initial state prior to starting electric current. This function is defined under the assumption of constant mobilities as

$$\omega(x) = \sum_{j=1}^{n} \frac{c_j}{u_j} . \tag{6}$$

For our case, where at the beginning of the experiment it is assumed that the entire separation capillary is filled with the homogeneous solution of leading electrolyte L^-R^+, it holds

$$\omega(x) = \frac{c_L}{u_L} + \frac{c_R}{u_R} = \text{constant} . \tag{7}$$

The above presented knowledge is summarized for the case of isotachophoretic zones λ, α and τ, containing ions L^-, A^- and T^-, respectively, migrating along the capillary with a constant cross section and schematically illustrated in Fig. 3.

Figure 3a schematically describes individual zones where the common counter-ion is omitted for the sake of simplification.

Figure 3b illustrates the demand on the mobilities

$$u_L > u_A > u_T . \tag{8}$$

Figure 3c gives the values of the adjusted concentrations for which, if ions with higher valencies are considered (cf. [4]), Eq. (9) holds

$$\frac{c_X}{c_L} = \frac{u_X}{u_X + u_R} \cdot \frac{u_L + u_R}{u_L} \cdot \frac{|z_L|}{|z_X|} , \tag{9}$$

where X = A, T.

Figure 3d represents the specific conductivities of individual zones $\varkappa_\lambda$, $\varkappa_\alpha$ and $\varkappa_\tau$; Figure 3e describes electric gradients E_λ, E_α and E_τ in zones λ, α and τ, respectively.

These values satisfy the condition of the constancy of the density of electric current, i

$$E_\lambda \varkappa_\lambda = E_\alpha \varkappa_\alpha = E_\tau \varkappa_\tau = i \tag{10}$$

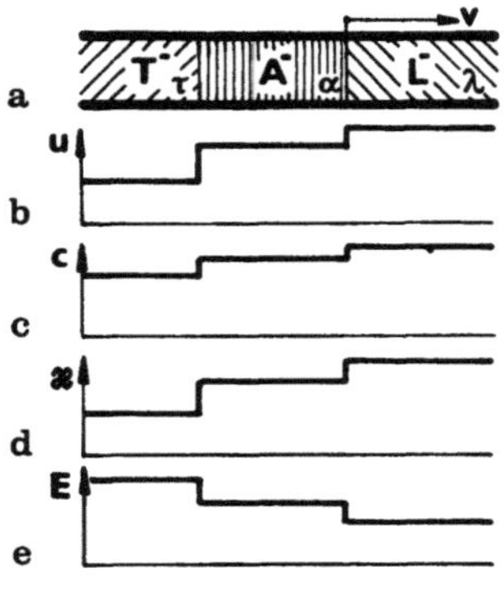

Fig. 3. Characteristics of isotachophoretically migrating zones λ, α and τ. **a** Qualitative composition of zones, **b** distribution of mobilities of anions, **c** distribution of concentrations of anions, **d** course of electric conductivity, **e** course of electric gradient

and the condition of the same migration velocity, v, of all zones (of the ions under investigation)

$$E_\lambda u_\lambda = E_\alpha u_\alpha = E_\tau u_\tau = v\,. \tag{11}$$

If the data on the leading electrolyte, i.e. the concentrations and the mobilities of ions L^- and R^+ and further the density of electric current, i, are known then for the given value of u_A or u_T the isotachophoretic migration of the corresponding zones is defined entirely by Eqs. (9) to (11), supplemented by the law of neutrality

$$\sum c_j z_j = 0 \tag{12}$$

and with the expression for the specific conductivity

$$\varkappa = F \sum c_j |z_j| \, u_j \tag{13}$$

where subscript j denotes couples L^- and R^+, A^- and R^+, and T^- and R^+ for zones λ, α, and τ, respectively. Specific conductivity, $\varkappa$, is expressed in $\Omega^{-1}\ cm^{-1}$.

The preceding solution of the electrolyte transport equations was derived for strong electrolytes. Solving these equations in an explicit form for weak electrolyte systems is practically impossible. However, for the description of the steady-state migration, even in such a case, an approach can be adopted successfully where the relationships valid for isotachophoresis are applied to elementary formulated equations of the mass balance, the density of electric current and the electroneutrality in isotachophoretic zones.

First, the concept of mobility must be defined for weak electrolytes. The initial Tiselius' perception[22)] serves as the basis and it can be expressed as follows: the substance, present in the solution in more forms, whose molar fractions are $x_0, x_1, \dots x_n$, mobilities $u_0, u_1, \dots u_n$ and individual forms are in a rapid dynamic equilibrium with one another, migrates through the electric field as the only substance with a certain effective mobility, $\bar{u}$, defined by the relationship

$$\bar{u} = x_0 u_0 + x_1 u_1 + \dots + x_n u_n\,. \tag{14}$$

From the macroscopic point of view, this mixture of different forms of the given substance (ions or neutral molecules) thus appears during electromigration as a uniform substance with a defined mobility and a defined charge.

For the mixture mentioned above, appearing as the only uniform substance, the concept of "ion constituent" was introduced[13)]. The ion constituent (for simplification, the term "constituent" will be used) is regarded as an ionic component of an electrolyte, being both in the form of already existing ions and in the form of potential sources of ions, created by different complexes and neutral molecules (cf. [23)]). The "phosphate" constituent or constituent "PO_4", present in the solution in the form of ions PO_4^{3-}, HPO_4^{2-}, $H_2PO_4^-$ and neutral molecule H_3PO_4 can serve as an example.

In isotachophoresis, the constituent can also comprise the particles formed by the association equilibrium with the counter-ion. For example, in the zone of sulfates, if Cd^{2+} serves as a counter-ion, the sulfate constituent is formed by particles H_2SO_4, HSO_4^-, SO_4^{2-} and $CdSO_4$. Frequently, when speaking about zones, shorter terms are used, e.g. instead of zone of the sulfate constituent the term sulphate zone is employed, etc.

The concentration of constituent A, present in the solution in different forms as species A_j at concentrations c_{Aj}, where $j = 1, 2, \ldots n_A$, represents, as a matter of fact, the analytical, i.e. the total concentration of this substance, $\bar{c}_A$,

$$\bar{c}_A = \sum_{j=1}^{n_A} c_{Aj} . \tag{15}$$

For the mobility of constituent A, $\bar{u}_A$, migrating in the electric field as the uniform substance from the macroscopic point of view, it holds[24)]

$$\bar{u}_A = \frac{1}{\bar{c}_A} \cdot \sum_{j=1}^{n_A} c_{Aj} u_{Aj} , \tag{16}$$

where u_{Aj} are the mobilities of various species of constituent A. Different terms were used for mobility $\bar{u}_A$, e.g. net mobility[25)], constituent mobility[23)] or effective mobility[3)]. In isotachophoresis, "effective mobility" is the expression used most widely.

A basic equation giving a true picture of the migration of weak electrolytes was derived independently by Svensson[26)] and Alberty[24)]. This moving boundary equation is valid for any constituent A present in zones α and β which are separated from one another by a moving boundary $\alpha\beta$ formed by the passage of electric current. It can be expressed as follows[27)]

$$\frac{\bar{c}_{A,\alpha}\bar{u}_{A,\alpha}}{\varkappa_\alpha} - \frac{\bar{c}_{A,\beta}\bar{u}_{A,\beta}}{\varkappa_\beta} = v_{\alpha\beta}(\bar{c}_{A,\alpha} - \bar{c}_{A,\beta}) . \tag{17}$$

$\bar{c}_A$ and $\bar{u}_A$ are concentration and effective mobilities of constituent A, respectively, in zones denoted by subscripts α and β. Specific conductivities of zones α and β are denoted $\varkappa_\alpha$ and $\varkappa_\beta$, respectively. $v_{\alpha\beta}$ is the volume in cm^3 swept out by boundary $\alpha\beta$ during the passage of 1 coulomb of electricity.

For the case of isotachophoretic migration, Eq. (17) can be rearranged by taking into consideration the fact that each constituent under separation is present in one zone only (cf. [28)]). For our case (cf. p. 136) of zone λ, α, τ of substances L^-, A^-, T^-, respectively, it can be written

$$\frac{\bar{u}_L}{\varkappa_\lambda} = \frac{\bar{u}_A}{\varkappa_\alpha} = \frac{\bar{u}_T}{\varkappa_\tau} = v_{\lambda\alpha} = v_{\alpha\tau} . \tag{18}$$

In order to calculate concentration $\bar{c}_A$ in zone α, an equation expressing the specific conductivity is necessary. If in zone α constituent R is present as a counter-ion in the form of species R_k, where $k = 1, 2, \ldots n_R$, the concentrations and the ionic mobilities of which are c_{Rk} and u_{Rk}, respectively, then it holds for the specific conductivity

$$\varkappa_\alpha = F \sum_{j=1}^{n_A} c_{Aj} |z_{Aj}| u_{Aj} + F \sum_{k=1}^{n_R} c_{Rk} |z_{Rk}| u_{Rk} . \tag{19}$$

Analogous expressions are valid for $\bar{u}_L$ and $\varkappa_\lambda$. In case that besides constituents A, L and counter-ion R also H^+ and OH^- ions contribute to the conductivities of zones (i.e. the separation is performed in markedly acidic or basic medium), it is necessary to add their contributions $F \cdot [H^+] \cdot u_H$ and $F \cdot [OH^-] \cdot u_{OH}$, respectively, to the right side of Eq. (19). By combining Eqs. (16), applied to $\bar{u}_L$ and $\bar{u}_A$, and (18), the relationship for adjusted concentration $\bar{c}_A$ is obtained.

$$\bar{c}_A = \frac{\sum_{j=1}^{n_A} c_{Aj}u_{Aj}}{\sum_{j=1}^{n_L} c_{Lj}u_{Lj}} \cdot \frac{\varkappa_\lambda}{\varkappa_\alpha} \cdot \bar{c}_L . \tag{20}$$

Eq. (20) can be considered as a form of the Kohlrausch regulating function extended to systems of weak electrolytes (cf. [29]).

Eq. (20) either alone or combined with Eq. (19) is obviously not sufficient for the calculation of $\bar{c}_A$. Further equations are therefore required which describe: a) the mass balance for the counter-ion expressed in the form given by the moving boundary equation for the counter-ion

$$\frac{\bar{c}_{R,\lambda}\bar{u}_{R,\lambda}}{\varkappa_\lambda} - \frac{\bar{c}_{R,\alpha}\bar{u}_{R,\alpha}}{\varkappa_\alpha} = v_{\lambda\alpha}(\bar{c}_{R,\alpha} - \bar{c}_{R,\lambda}) , \tag{21}$$

b) the principle of electroneutrality in the zones, c) dissociation equilibria of subspecies of constituents L, A, R.

For the solution of the resulting system of equations, routine computer programs, some of which take into consideration necessary corrections for the influence of ionic strength and temperature, are available today. However, sufficient knowledge of the input data, i.e. of ionic mobilities and the dissociation constants, is still problematic. For a more detailed analysis of the problem and the review of the literature see [30].)

2.3 Self-Sharpening Effect of the Zone Boundary

The boundary between the two isotachophoretic zones is very sharp. Its width is constant for a given composition of the solution and for a given density of electric current and it does not change with time. This, at first sight supprising fact, is caused by a self-sharpening effect of isotachophoretic boundary[13], which can simply be explained as follows: If leading ion L^- penetrates, as a result of molecular diffusion from its zone λ, through the zone boundary into adjoining zone α, it will occur in the zone with an electric gradient higher than that in zone λ. Due to the higher gradient, ion L^- is forced to move with a velocity higher than that corresponding to the isotachophoretic migration. Ion L^- therefore passes the boundary and returns to its zone λ. On the other hand, if ion A^- diffuses into zone λ, its migration velocity in the zone of a lower gradient will decrease and zone α will reach its ion A^-. The width of the zone boundary is obviously the result of the compromise between the action of the molecular diffusion in the direction of the boundary layer spreading and the sharpening effect of the electric field.

In order to describe the structure of the boundary zone Eqs. (1) to (3) were solved already in 1910 by Weber[17)] who gave an explicit solution for two-salt boundary with a common counter-ion. Later, the structure of the boundary zone was investigated theoretically and experimentally by MaxInnes[13)] and Longsworth[19,20)].

Based upon Weber's theory, these authors proved that a two-salt boundary zone with a common counter-ion (i.e. the simplest case of neighboring isotachophoretic zones) shows a certain concentration distribution through the boundary and does not change with time while migrating at a constant velocity under the influence of a constant current density.

Similar as in the preceding case, a particular solution has the form $c_j = f(x - vt)$. It can be expressed explicitly under the assumption of constant mobilities.

The explicit solution for boundary $\lambda\alpha$ between the zones of univalent ions L^- and A^-, where the origin $x = 0$ is located at point $c_L = c_A$, has the following form [13,20)]:

$$\ln = \frac{c_L}{c_A} = \frac{F \cdot v}{RT} \cdot \frac{u_L - u_A}{u_L u_A} \cdot x\,, \tag{22}$$

where R and T are the universal constant and temperature, respectively. If the width of the zone boundary in which the ratio c_L/c_A changes symmetrically from the value e^2 to $1/e^2$ is denoted by Δx (cm), thent it holds

$$\Delta x = \frac{4RT}{Fv} \cdot \frac{u_L u_A}{u_L - u_A}\,. \tag{23}$$

This means that the width of the zone boundary is inversely proportional to the velocity of the migration and thus inversely proportional to the density of electric current. Moreover, the width of the zone boundary diminishes with increasing difference in the mobilities of ions in the respective neighboring zones.

2.4 Isotachophoretic Analysis

A sample for the isotachophoretic analysis is introduced between the leading and the terminating electrolytes. For the successful separation of all the components in the sample, their mobilities must fulfil the condition:

$$u_L > u_1 > u_2 \dots u_n > u_T\,.$$

The course of the isotachophoretic analysis can be divided into two stages — separation and isotachophoretic migration. During the separation individual components of the sample are separated according to their effective mobilities. Individual species migrate at different velocities, separate from one another and form individual zones until the total separation is reached. Since that moment, each zone contains one constituent only and all of them have a common counter-ion. The zones are separated from one another by the phase boundary, joined closely to one another and migrate at the same velocity (isotachophoretic migration).

Isotachophoretic analysis will be described best by an actual example of an anionic analysis of a mixture of orthophosphate (o-P) and pyrophosphate (p-P) in a liquid NP fertilizer, schematically described in Fig. 4. The solution of 0.01 M HCl + 0.02 M histidine, where Cl^- is the leading anion and protonized histidine (His^+) the counter-ion, serves as the leading electrolyte. Before the start of the analysis, a reservoir (1), an electrode chamber (2) and a separation capillary (3) (Fig. 4a) are filled with the leading electrolyte. The electrode chamber is separated from the separation capillary (3) by a semipermeable membrane (4). A terminator chamber (5) and a three-way valve (6) (Fig. 3b) are filled with 0.01 M glutamic acid as the terminating electrolyte. A two-way valve (7) is then closed to prevent the movement of the leading electrolyte in the capillary. By turning the three-way valve (6), a boundary is formed between the leading and the terminating electrolytes at the place of an injection equipment (8). Then, a sample is introduced (Fig. 3c). Thus, everything is ready for the beginning of the separation. A stabilized direct current supply (9) is connected to electrodes (10) and (11); then, migration and separation occur (Fig. 3d). Leading ions Cl^-, anions from the sample and glutamic acid anions (glu^-) of the terminating electrolyte move toward the anode. Ortho- and pyrophosphates begin to migrate as a mixed zone of substances with different effective mobilities. In the course of migration, owing to different mobilities, both substances separate from one another, pure zones of phosphates of both types separate from the mixed zone. The mixed zone between them diminishes until the separation is finished. The zone has then disappeared entirely. The cations present move in a direction opposite to that of the zone under investigation. In the course

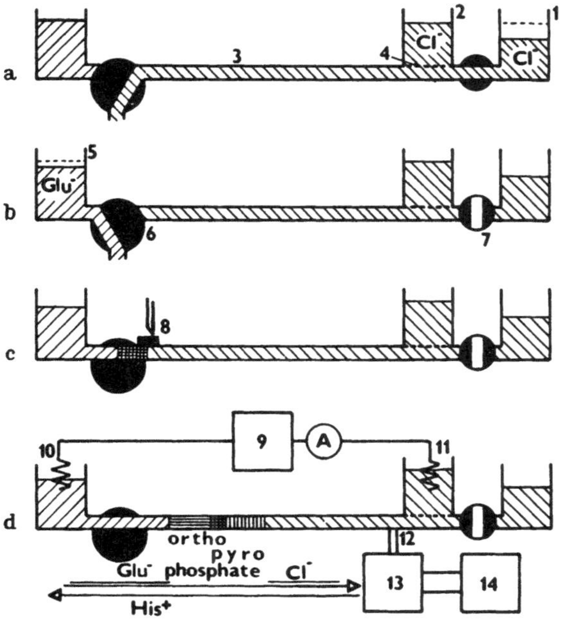

Fig. 4. Scheme of the anionic analysis of a liquid fertilizer sample containing ortho- and pyrophosphate. **a** Filling with the leading electrolyte, **b** filling with the terminating electrolyte, **c** injection of the sample, **d** separation process

of the migration the cation of the leading electrolyte, His^+ (protonized histidine) will thus become the only counter-ion, common to all the zones. The separated substances form the system of isotachophoretic zones migrating along the separation capillary in close contact to one another and arranged according to descending values of the mobilities. In the present case, the zone of pyrophosphate thus migrates behind the zone of the leading electrolyte Cl^-, then the zone of orthophosphate and at last the zone of glutamate since in this case it holds for the mobilities that $u_{Cl} > u_{pyro} > u_{ortho} > u_{glu}$. All these zones follow that of the leading ions of the electrolyte, i.e. the zones of pyrophosphate, orthophosphate and glutamate possess adjusted concentrations determined by the composition of the leading electrolyte and are independent of the amount of the sample injected. The length of the zones is then given by the amount of the given substance taken for the analysis and by its adjusted concentration. Consequently, this lengh represents a quantitative parameter.

The migrating system of zones will then pass through a detection cell (12) where a suitable characteristic of zones is sensed by a detection equipment (13). The signal of the detector is recorded by a line recorder (14) as an isotachophoregram.

A stepwise change in the signal corresponds to the passage of the front boundary of the given zone through the detection cell. A constant value of the signal (plateau), corresponds to the zone. A stepwise change shows the subsequent zone.

In the time record of the signal — the isotachophoregram — the step corresponds to the substance. The isotachophoretic step is characterized by its height and its length. The step height (h) represents the value of the effective signal of the detector relative to a given zone measured from a certain base line. It is determined by the quality of these substance in the respective zone. The step height is thus a qualitative characteristic of the component separated in the respective zone. The quantitative evaluation of the isotachophoregram is based on the measurement of the step length utilizing calibration with standard solutions of the components under investigation. An example of the isotachophoregram of a liquid fertilizer is shown in Fig. 5. Detection was performed by sensing the electric gradient in zones.

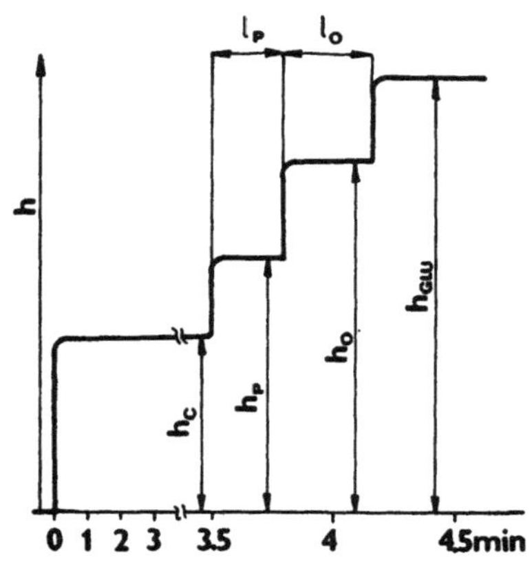

Fig. 5. Isotachophoregram of a liquid fertilizer sample (as mentioned in Fig. 4). l_P, l_O — steplengths of pyrophosphate and orthophosphate, h_P, h_O — stepheights of pyrophosphate and orthophosphate, h_C — stepheight of the leading electrolyte (leading anion Cl^-), h_{GLU} — stepheight of the terminating electrolyte (terminating anion glutamate, GLU^-)

2.5 Instrumentation

The development of the instrumentation for analytical isotachophoresis has played a leading role in the extension of the knowledge of the technique itself and in its applications. Although a detailed historical review has been reported[4], it is expedient to note, at least briefly in chronological sequence, some of the contributions to instrumentation and applications and to mention the previous terms for the present analytical isotachophoresis.

In 1928 Kendall[31] described experiments involving the separation of ions by means of the "ionic migration technique". In 1953 Longsworth[32] successfully separated alkaline earth ions, some amino acids and low-molecular organic acids by "moving boundary technique". He also used the names "leading and trailing electrolytes" for the first time.

In 1963 Konstantinov[33] described an application of the "moving boundary method" to rapid analyses of metal cations. He performed the separation in a thin-walled glass capillary, the detection of the ions being based on the differences in the refractive indices of zones. In 1966 Konstantinov and Oshurkova[34] published the description of "the analyzer of electrolyte solutions according to ionic mobilities" where the separation of substances proceeded in a thin horizontally placed glass capillary. A hydrodynamic counter-flow of the leading electrolyte was simultaneously applied by a suitable adjustment of the levels in electrode compartments and the migration of the boundaries fronts toward the separation capillary was stopped. At this stage, the detection was carried out by irradiating the capillary with a narrow light beam and recording the diffraction image of the zones on dry plate. Having used the above described equipment, the authors reported a number of separations of about 40 cations and anions. In 1964 Schumacher[35] in a fundamental study "Elektrophorese in pH-Gradienten" drew most of the basic conclusions of the Kohlrausch regulating function and clearly pointed principles of qualitative and quantitative analysis.

In 1966 Preetz[36] published the principle and the theoretical background of "Gegenstromionophorese", i.e. of "counterflow isotachophoresis". In 1967 Preetz and Pfeifer[37] described the equipment used for this method. They carried out the separation in a capillary, the detection of zones by means of a series of metallic contacts protruding into the capillary, the sensing of electric gradient, and the regulation of the counter-flow by utilizing the difference in the levels in the electrode compartements.

Martin and Everaerts published a paper in 1967[38] which gave a new impulse. Their capillary equipment for "displacement electrophoresis" had already the character of the present devices. They used as a detector a thermocouple glued on the outside wall of a thin-walled separation capillary. The principle of and the equipment for the "moving boundary analysis" with a detection performed potentiometrically was reported by Hello[39] in 1968. One year later, Fredriksson[40] developed the analytical apparatus for the "displacement electrophoresis". He used a conductivity detector, successfully separated low-molecular fatty acids and performed quantitative analyses by measuring the lengths of zones.

In 1969, Martin[41] outlined substantial features of this technique and estimated its future analytical usefulness.

A more extensive study on the "displacement electrophoresis" was reported by Martin and Everaerts[42] in 1970. In this study they covered substantial parts of the theory, the instrumentation and the application of this technique. The year 1970 is a certain milestone in the nomenclature since the name "isotachophoresis" was then introduced and adopted (cf. [4]).

The introduction of the UV detector by Arlinger and Routs[43], by means of which the authors demonstrated the sharpness of isotachophoretic boundaries and the resolution power of the isotachophoretic separation was an outstanding event in the development of the instrumentation.

Instrumentation developed in 1970 and in subsequent years has been used till nowadays and has created the basis of the present instrumentation. Intensive efforts have been devoted to the development of more sensitive detectors than the thermocouple[38] or the thermistor detector[44]. Thus, the currently available very sensitive high-resolution detectors have been obtained. These include, the contact conductivity detector[45–50], which senses the electric conductivity of zones by means of two metallic (Pt) microelectrodes protruding into the separation capillary and being in direct contact with the electrolyte; the potential gradient detector[51–55] in which the electric gradients in zones are sensed with the aid of two similar electrodes placed in at certain small distance from one another in the direction of migration; the UV detector[5,43,55a,56] where a narrow beam of UV light passes perpendicularly through a narrow section of the separation capillary and changes in its intensity, caused by different absorption of UV light in different zones, are sensed. A very promising detector is the contactless high-frequency detector[57] which detects conductivity of zones by means of an microelectrode system placed on the outside surface of the separation capillary.

The present state of the instrumentation used for analytical isotachophoresis can be characterized by the fact that both commercial devices[57a–60] and fairly advanced home-made devices are being used for analytical and preparative purposes. (For a description see [3,52,53,61,69].)

The basic instrumental parts of isotachophoresis are as follows:
a high-voltage stabilized d.c. current supply,
an isotachophoretic column and
a detection equipment with a recorder.

The heart of the isotachophoretic column is a separation capillary, equipped with an injection device and a detection cell, connecting two electrode compartments. Common working conditions are the following:
a capillary (0.1–0.2 mm^2), 15–60 cm long;
electrolyte concentrations of 10^{-2}–10^{-3} M;
electric current 20–400 μA and voltage 2–30 kV;
analysis time 4–30 min;
amounts of substances taken for analysis approx. 10^{-9} mol.

3 Qualitative and Quantitative Analysis

The operation procedures of the isotachophoretic analysis can be roughly divided into four stages — selection of the separation conditions, performance of the total separation and its recording, qualitative and quantitative interpretation of the record.

3.1 Selection of Separation Conditions

Selection assumes that such conditions should be found under which all substances of the same sign (anions or cations) present in the sample are separated and form the corresponding zones during analysis. A basic demand is that all the components considered should be sufficiently soluble and that possible interfering reactions such as hydrolysis or precipitation are eliminated.

The second question is the separability of all the components expected to be present in the sample, i.e. the selection of conditions under which all the components of the sample differ sufficiently from each other with respect to their effective mobilities.

Changes required in the effective mobilities may be obtained either by variation of the equilibrium between various subspecies of the constituents to be analyzed or by influencing the ionic mobilities of these subspecies.

The variation of pH is the most significant way of affecting the dissociation equilibria and thus the mobilities of weak electrolytes. In the case of the classic zone or the Tiselius electrophoresis, the required pH is readily adjusted and determined by the selection of a suitable buffer as the background electrolyte. In isotachophoresis, where there is no background electrolyte, the pH value in the zones is adjusted by appropriate choice of the pH of the leading electrolyte, pH_L, and by the selection of a suitable counter-ion R which has a sufficient buffering capacity in the range of the required pH_L. For the selected pH_L values and R, the values of pH_A, pH_B, ... pH_X, pH_T, and thus also those of the effective mobilities, $\bar{u}_A$, $\bar{u}_B$, ... $\bar{u}_X$, $\bar{u}_T$, in the zones of substances A, B, ... X, T, respectively, are then already given.

A very effective aid for the selection of a suitable pH_L is the calculation and tabulation of the effective mobility values for a series of suitably selected R and pH_L values using routine computer programs[29)]. However, a prerequisite of such a calculation is the knowledge of sufficiently precise values of all the ionic mobilities and the dissociation constants. The data required have, however, mostly not yet been available, particularly in the case of biochemically interesting substances and suitable conditions must be determined experimentally.

For one of this cases there was suggested a simple procedure[70)] based on electric gradient detection and on the calculation of the relative mobilities by using a reference substance whose mobility is practically independent of pH. The procedure was verified by investigating the conditions for the separation of a complicated mixture of acids from the Krebs cycle; chloride was used as a reference substance and simultaneously served as a leading anion. If the electric gradients in the zone of substance X and that in the zone of the chlorides are denoted by E_X and E_{Cl}, respectively, then the isotachophoretic condition of the identical velocity of the migration (see Eq. (11)) is valid in the form

$$E_X\bar{u}_X = E_{Cl}\bar{u}_{Cl} = v\,. \tag{24}$$

If electric gradients are recorded in the isotachophoregram in the form of step heights h_X and h_{Cl}, then relative mobility U_X is defined by

$$U_X = \frac{\bar{u}_X}{\bar{u}_{Cl}} = \frac{h_{Cl}}{h_X}. \qquad (25)$$

From the compilation of the dependences $U_X = f(pH_L)$ for different substances X the suitable working conditions can be selected. For simplification, Fig. 6 illustrates these dependences only for some of the acids. In addition, this fig. also gives the relative mobility of carbonate which can interfere with the analysis of anions. Its presence is due to the absorption of atmospheric CO_2 in the electrolytes used. The intersections of the curves mean identical relative mobilities at the given pH which results in the formation of stable mixed zones. On the basis of the diagram, pH = 3.8 was selected as suitable. At this pH the effective mobilities of all the components differ sufficiently from one another and the presence of carbonate does not interfere with the separations. The result is shown in Fig. 7.

In order to influence effective mobilities, complex-forming equilibria[71,72,72a] can also be utilized. The selection of the working conditions is again carried out by choosing a suitable composition of the leading electrolyte which contains the complex-forming counter-ion. These method could be utilized, for instance for the isotachophoretic analysis of chlorides and sulfates. Under the usual conditions, chlorides and sulfates are the most mobile anions and there is practically no leading anion available which is suitable for them. However, if Cd^{2+} ions, which establish a complex-forming equilibrium by the formation of $CdSO_4$, $CdCl^+$ or $CdCl_2$, are used as counter-ions, the effective mobilities of chlorides and sulfates are reduced selectively in comparison with e.g. nitrates. Nitrates can then be employed as suitable leading anions and the leading electrolyte $Cd(NO_3)_2$ thus produced

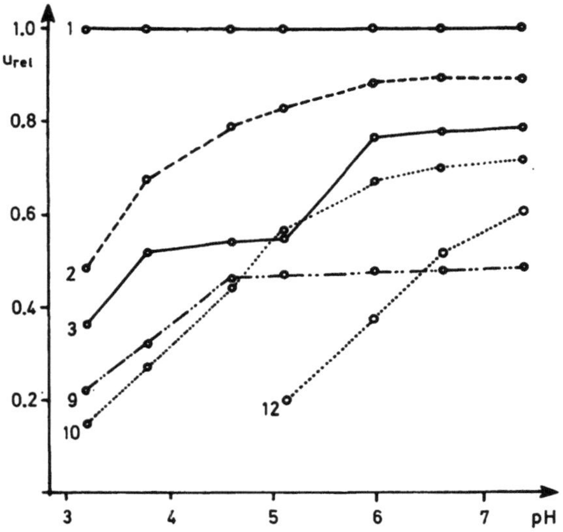

Fig. 6. Dependence of relative mobilities of some acids from the Krebs cycle on pH of the leading electrolyte. 1 — chloride, 2 — oxalate, 3 — oxalolacetate, 9 — lactate, 10 — succinate, 12 — carbonate

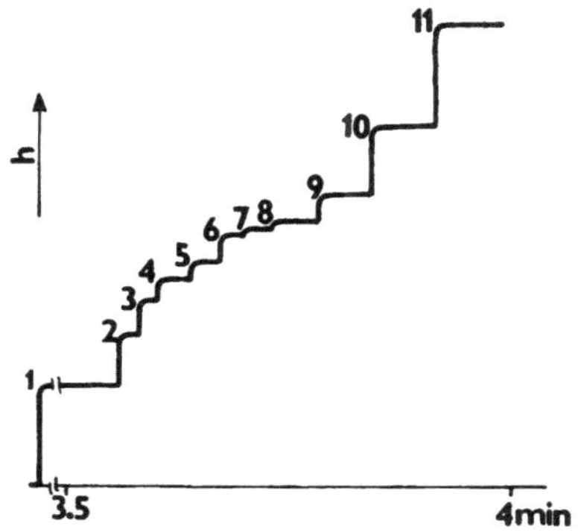

Fig. 7. Isotachophoregram of a model mixture of some acids from the Krebs cycle (injection of 4 μl, concentrations of acids 0.4–1.0 · 10^{-3} M). 1) chloride (the leading anion), 2) oxalate, 3) oxalolacetate, 4) fumarate, 5) α-ketoglutarate, 6) citrate, 7) malate, 8) isocitrate, 9) lactate, 10) succinate, 11) acetate (terminator)

permits to perform the effective isotachophoretic analysis of chlorides and sulfates (see Sect. 6, Fig. 24).

Similarly, in order to separate sulfates and nitrates more efficiently, Ca^{2+} was used as a complex-forming cation. Sulfates and nitrates are poorly separated under common conditions since their mobilities are close and the sequence of zones is given by $\bar{u}_{SO_4} > \bar{u}_{NO_3}$. By the addition of Ca^{2+} to the leading electrolyte, the mobility of sulfates is reduced selectively, the sequence is reversed and their separation may readily be performed (see Sect. 6, Fig. 26).

The effects of pH and a complex-forming counter-ion can also be combined to achieve the required separation. The analysis of a mixture of antiherpetically active substances (phosphonoformate and phosphonoacetate) and the admixtures from their synthesis (formate, acetate and phosphate) can serve as an example (Fig. 8).

The formation of ionic associates provides an additional possibility of influencing effective mobilities. As follows from the character of association equilibria, this possibility will mainly be applied to multivalent ions since the higher the charge of the ions, the stronger the resulting association. The data on relative mobilities of some polyamines[73] illustrate these effects (Figs. 9 and 10). Figure 9 describes

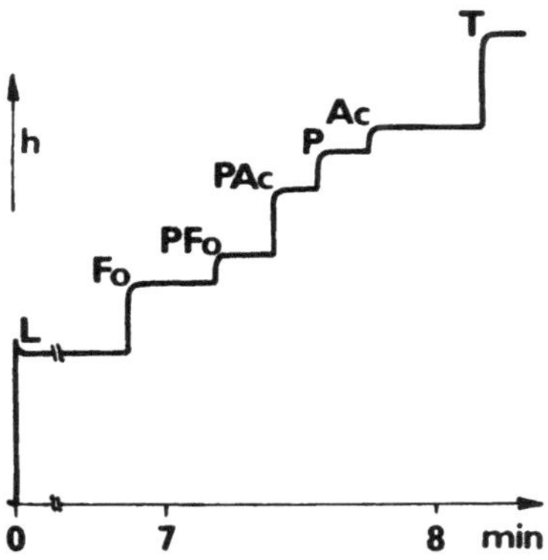

Fig. 8. Separation of the model mixture containing formate (Fo), phosphonoformate (PFo), phosphonoacetate (PAc), phosphate (P) and acetate (Ac) in the amounts 12, 8, 8, 10 and 18 μmol, respectively. Leading electrolyte 0.01 M HCl + 0.019 M urotropine + 0.003 M $CaCl_2$; terminator 0.015 M glutamic acid, leading anion (L) Cl^-, and terminating anion (T) glutamate

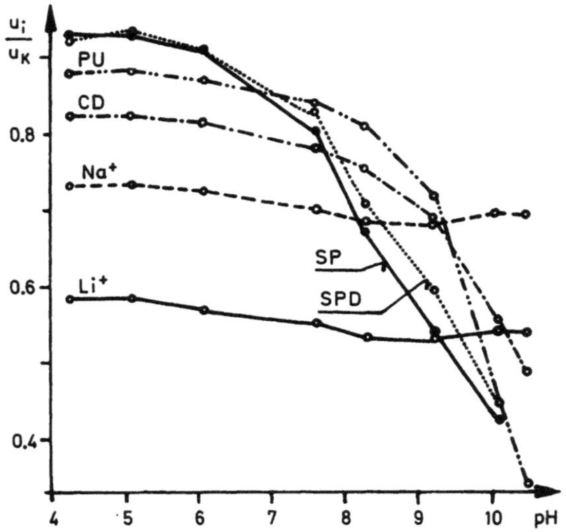

Fig. 9. Dependence of relative mobilities of some polymines on pH of the leading electrolyte using univalent anionic species as counterions. In all cases 0.01 M K^+ served as the leading cation. As anionic counterions propionic acid, morpholinoethanesulfonic acid, veronal, and glycine were employed. PU — putrescine, CD — cadaverine, SP — spermine, and SPD — spermidine

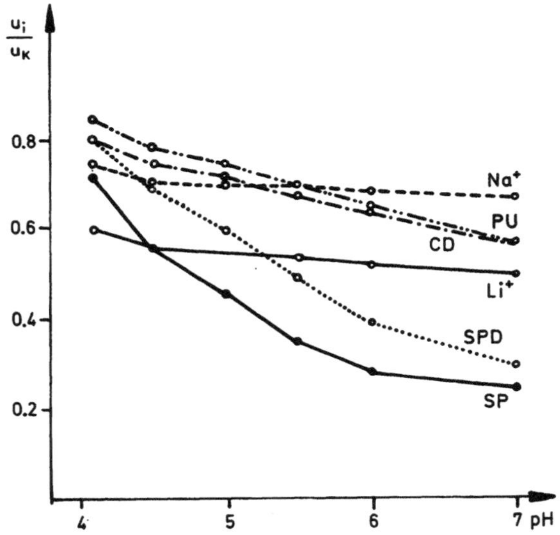

Fig. 10. Dependence of relative mobilities of some polyamines on pH of the leading electrolyte consisting of 0.01 M KOH + citric acid

the relative mobilities of putrescine, cadaverine, spermidine, and spermine, migrating as cations, as a function of pH under conditions at which the effective charge of the counter-ion is either less or equal to one (i.e., monovalent weak acids served as counter ions). The mobility of the leading cation K^+ was used as a reference unit. For a better orientation, relative mobilities of Na^+ and Li^+ are also shown in the figure. It can be seen that at a pH less than 6, spermidine and spermine display the largest relative mobilities which is obviously a consequence of their ionization. At pH higher than 6, the ionization and consequently also the relative mobilities of spermine and spermidine decrease. In the above range of pH, the mobility of cation Na^+ is lower than that of any other polyamine mentioned and practically constant. The application of citric acid as a counter-ion (Fig. 00) causes that the univalent counter-ion H_2Citr^- predominates in the zones at pH = 4. With increasing pH, $HCitr^{2-}$ prodominates and at pH = 7, mostly $Citr^{3-}$ is present. It can be seen that with increasing contents of bi and trivalent counter-ions, the mobilities of spermidine and spermine decrease distinctly. This is understandable because spermidine and spermine are present in the involved range of pH as cations with charges +3 and +4, respectively, and association effects reducing their effective mobilities are most pronounced. Less pronounced association occurs in the case of putrescine and cadaverine, the maximum degree of ionization of which is +2. At a pH of about 6, cation Na^+, which does not practically exhibit association, is already more mobile than all polyamines. Moreover, the order of migration of polyamines is reversed to that obtained with univalent counter-ions (cf. Fig. 9) where only weak associations of ions can be expected. A successful separation of polyamines and Na^+ occurring in biological samples is demonstrated in Fig. 11.

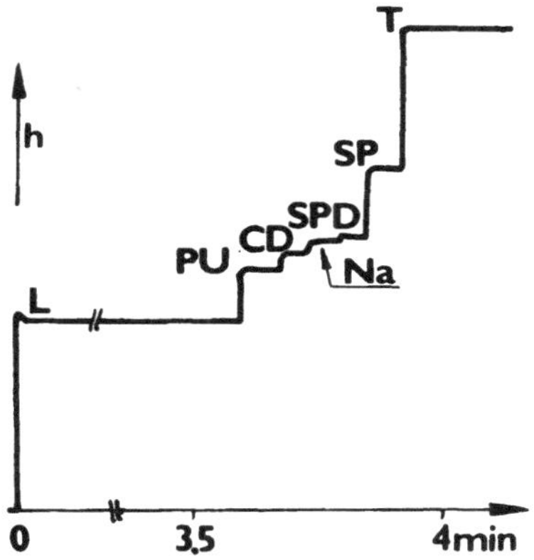

Fig. 11. Separation of a model mixture of putrescine (PU), cadaverine (CD), sodium (Na), spermidine (SPD) and spermine (SP), containing ca. 2 nmol of each substance. 0.01 M KOH + citric acid at pH = 4.40 served as the leading electrolyte (L) and creatinine as the terminator (T)

A further possibility of influencing the effective mobility is the affection of ionic mobilities. The mobility of the ions themselves is fairly dependent on their solvation and the variation in the mobilities can thus be caused by changing the solvent.

An example is the successful separation of K^+ and NH_4^+ by isotachophoresis in methanol[73a)]. In water, on the other hand, the mobilities of these ions are almost identical so that they cannot practically be separated.

3.2 Separation and its Record

If two components of different effective mobilities are to be separated completely from one another, a definite migration path, which is directly proportional to the total amount of the components, is necessary[42)]. Until the separation of these two components is complete, a system also containing a mixed zone of the two components is migrating along the column. This fact must always be considered since a number of steps can appear in the isotachophoregram which is greater than the number of the components separated in the sample. Hence, the evaluation whether total separation of the given amount of the sample with the expected composition can be reached under the given working conditions is important for the selection of the separation conditions. For this purpose, the concept of the so-called separation capacity[56,74] was introduced. This is defined as the maximum equimolar mixture of a couple of selected components which can be separated completely from one another under the given conditions. An approximate estimation of the separation capacity is performed experimentally by preparing an equimolar mixture of the selected couple of components and by injecting increasing amounts of this mixture. The maximum amount of the mixture (in moles) that can be separated defines the separation capacity. By a further increase of the injected amounts, the record in which a new step appears is obtained, corresponding to a mixed zone. Obviously, the separating power thus determined is valid for the given working conditions and the given couple of components only. Nevertheless, it provides the information permitting the estimation of the separation possibilities in many practical cases. In order to evaluate the separation possibilities of a multicomponent sample, the separating power determined for the pair of the most difficulty separable components can be used.

A more general procedure[74] for the characterization of the separation capacity is based on the investigation of the amount of the electricity passed through the mixture to be separated. It was derived from the dynamics of the separation in which the amounts of the ionic species separated from one another in a given mixture are proportional to the amount of the electricity passed through this mixture regardless of the migration path. In order to achieve a complete separation of a binary mixture of N_A and N_B moles of ions A and B with mobilities u_A and u_B and charges z_A and z_B, respectively, in the isotachophoretic arrangement with counter-ion R having mobility u_R, it is necessary that the following amount of the electricity, Q_S, called "separation factor", passes through the column

$$Q_S = F \cdot \frac{N_A|z_A|\, u_A + N_B|z_B|\, u_B + u_R(N_A|z_A| + N_B|z_B|)}{|u_A - u_B|}. \tag{26}$$

From this point of view, the so-called "column hold-up", Q_L, which defines the amount of the electricity that passes through the column from the start to the moment of the passage of the first separated boundary through the detector (i.e. to the passage of the rear boundary of the zone of the leading electrolyte) is a basic parameter of the separation column with the given system of electrolytes. Then, the evaluation of the separation capacity for the given case consists in comparing Q_S and Q_L. The case $Q_S \leqq Q_L$ implies successful separation. A more detailed analysis, taking into account that separation also takes place during the passage of the first zone of the sample through the detector, provides the following expression for the separation capacity of the equimolar mixture of univalent components A and B, $N_A = N_B = N_S$, where $u_A > u_B$,

$$N_S = \frac{u_A - u_B}{u_R\left(1 + \dfrac{u_B}{u_A}\right) + 2u_B} \cdot \frac{Q_L}{F}. \tag{27}$$

It is possible to verify that the steps in the record really correspond to the isotachophoretic zones of various components by investigating the character of the isotachophoregram provided by a universal detector upon changes in the injected amounts of the sample or the changes in Q_L. The character of the isotachophoregram implies a set of data concerning the number of steps, their mutual lengths and heights according to the separation sequence. For instance, the first step length is twice the size of the third step length, the height of the second step is three times the height of the first step etc. If complete separation is always achieved, the character of the isotachophoregram for the given sample is not variable and does not depend on the amount of the sample injected.

A comparison of the records of the two detectors mounted in the given column at a certain distance from one another may also be very useful[75].

3.3 Qualitative Interpretation

There is no universal procedure for the qualitative evaluation of the steps in the record; the interpretation is mainly based on the comparison of the data obtained by the analysis of standard substances and of the samples under the same conditions. The significance of either agreement or disagreement between the qualitative parameters of the records of the standard mixture and the sample must be taken into consideration. If a known standard substance provides a step which does not coincide with any step height of the sample, then it can be stated that the standard substance is not present in the sample. If the step height of the standard coincides with one of the steps of the sample, the presence of a substance identical with the standard substance in the sample can be considered as probable only.

Significant possibilities are provided by the application of selective detectors in combination with a universal detection, e.g. by simultaneous record by conductivity and UV detectors[76]. Two step heights are thus obtained for one zone, i.e. two data of qualitative character, derived from different analytical properties of the given substance. The agreement of both data on the given zone with those of the standard substance already represents the identity of the corresponding substances with high probability.

The measurement of the relative mobilities of substances, using the gradient detection of zones and the comparison of the data obtained with tabulated values, may serve as a useful and simple procedure[53] for the qualitative orientation. The qualitative index

$$\Delta_X(S) = \frac{h_S}{h_X}, \tag{28}$$

is compared with the relative mobility (see Eq. (25))

$$U_X(S) = \frac{\bar{u}_X}{\bar{u}_S}. \tag{29}$$

As long as the the temperatures in the zones do not markedly differ from thermostating temperature T_0 and tabulated values u_X and u_S at temperature T_0 are available, this procedure can easily be applied. It is, however, based on the fact that the step heights measured from the base line are directly proportional to electric gradient in the zone.

In connection with the application of the gradient detector, another qualitative index, the so-called potential unit value (PU value), was suggested[77]. This index is defined by means of the step heights of the two reference substances, the leading (h_L) and the terminating (h_T) zones.

Using the conductivity detector, the detector signal is proportional to the reciprocal of the conductance between the measuring electrodes. The response of the detector to the leading electrolyte is usually used as the base line in the record; from this line the step heights are measured. For the identification with the conductivity detector, the qualitative index is applied[73] in which the step height, measured from the line of the leading electrolyte, is related to the analogously measured step height of chlorate (ClO_3^-).

3.4 Quantitative Interpretation

To interpret the isotachophoregram quantitatively, it is necessary to start with the relationship between the parameters of the zone in the column and the amount of the given substance present in this zone under given constant working conditions (composition of the leading and terminating electrolytes and temperature). In general, the value of the concentration, $\bar{c}_X$, at the given place in the column is adjusted to the composition of the electrolyte which took this place in the column before the start of the electrophoretic migration.

During the analytical isotachophoresis (with the exception of the cascade variant, see p. 161), the entire separation capillary is filled with homogeneous leading electrolyte prior to the beginning of separation. $\bar{c}_X$ is then adjusted to the composition of this electrolyte and is constant in the entire capillary. The theory of the migration of moving boundaries[26] necessitates certain conditions concerning the type of the concentration scale for expressing $\bar{c}_X$, it should only be expressed by means of values related to volume. The above fact and the requirement of the consistency with the common way of expressing the specific electrolytic conductivity in the literature on electrophoresis have led to the expression for the concentration of substances in zones, $\bar{c}$ (mol · cm^{-3}). The amount of substances in zones, N, is logically expressed in moles.

The zone of a given substance X is represented by the solution of this substance at concentration $\bar{c}_X$ which occupies a certain volume of the capillary, ΔV_X. Additional idealizing assumptions are fulfilled in common practice. These imply that the phase boundaries of the given zone represent a negligible part of the entire zone and that the concentration of the given substance is constant within the entire volume of the zone. Thus, the volume of the given zone is its quantitative parameter since it holds

$$N_X = \bar{c}_X \cdot \Delta V_X , \tag{30}$$

i.e. the amount of the given substance in the zone that is determined is directly proportional to the volume of the adjusted zone. A direct measurement of the volume of the migrating zone is, of course, not commonly carried out. Instead of that, the time interval required for the passage of the investigated zone through the detector is measured. Denoting this interval Δt_X(s) and the driving current I(A), it holds

$$N_X = v \cdot \bar{c}_X \cdot I \cdot \Delta t_X \tag{31}$$

where v is defined by Eq. (17).

In the record of the signal provided by a line recorder at a chart speed b, the step length, l_X, corresponds to the passage of the zone through the detector, and the following relationship holds

$$N_X = \frac{v \cdot \bar{c}_X \cdot I}{b} \cdot l_X . \tag{32}$$

In comparison with elution techniques, it is remarkable that Eq. (32) does not include either the property which is sensed by the detector or the way of signal amplification. The only demand is that the detector should resolve two neighboring zones.

Providing that the experimental conditions are constant, the corresponding values in Eq. (32) can be included into calibration constant K_X and the direct proportion

$$N_X = K_X \cdot l_X \tag{33}$$

is valid. Eq. (33) is applied to quantitative evaluations. Calibration constant K_X differs for various components and different working conditions. Based on relationship (33), the quantitative analysis is carried out by the direct comparison of the step length of the known amount of the sample and the step length of the standard, both analyzed under the same experimental conditions.

An interesting way of quantifying the record, eliminating the necessity of maintaining constant driving electric current I, was suggested by the authors[78]. Their procedure is based on the coulometric principle according to which the amount of electricity passed through the column is converted into pulses that control the chart speed. Under these circumstances, the given step length corresponds to a definite amount of the substance, regardless of variability of the driving current.

Besides the above calibration procedures, the application of universal calibration constant, K, was suggested[79] according to the relationship

$$N_X = K \cdot \bar{c}_X \cdot \Delta t_X , \tag{34}$$

in which the required absolute values of the concentration, $\bar{c}_X$, are determined for every optional component X under the given experimental conditions by the calculation.

Quantitative interpretation by means of the relative correction factors[28] is based on the consideration that the components under investigation, X, are separated and detected simultaneously with a suitable reference standard substance, S. By applying the relationships mentioned above, we obtain, after rearrangement,

$$l_X \doteq K_A \cdot D_{X,S} \cdot N_X , \tag{35}$$

where K_A is the apparatus constant for the given working conditions and the reference substance, and the correction factor $D_{X,S}$ is the value depending on substance X only. The determination of the correction factor $D_{X,S}$ is performed according to Eq. (36):

$$D_{X,S} = \frac{L_X/N_X}{L_S/N_S} \tag{36}$$

with the parameters L_X and L_S representing the lengths of the steps in the record of the analysis of the mixture of N_X and N_S moles of components X and S, respectively. A more detailed analysis[28] shows that the value of $D_{X,S}$, once measured for the components whose mobilities are influenced by acidobasic equilibria, are valid for different experimental conditions as long as the pH of the leading electrolyte is constant and the counter-ion is the same, i.e. $D_{X,S}(R, pH_L) = \text{const.}$

Values $D_{X,S}$ allow to get a rapid orientation regarding the ratios of the components of the sample since their values express relative step lengths proper of the equimolar mixture of the analyzed substances. They additionally permit the internal standard method to be used, thus enabling to perform the quantitative evaluation with the aid of the only analysis without knowing the injected volumes. Volume V_S at molarity m_S of a suitable standard substance S is added to a defined volume of sample V_X at molarity m_X which is to be determined. Then, a suitable amount of the mixture thus obtained is injected and the step lengths, L_X and L_S, are evaluated. Molarity m_X, which is determined, is then given by the relationship

$$m_X = \frac{L_X}{L_S} \cdot \frac{1}{D_{X,S}} \cdot \frac{V_S}{V_X} \cdot m_S \,. \tag{37}$$

If the idealized assumptions are not fulfilled, i.e. the volume of the zone boundary and the effective volume of the detection cell are not negligible as compared with the detected zone, then a special procedure is required for the quantitative interpretation. This problem was studied in detail by a number of authors[56,80,81] for the case of the UV detector. If a sufficiently long zone is determined by the UV detector, then a rectangular shaped step is obtained. Its height (step plateau) corresponds to the characteristic intensity of the absorption of UV radiation in the given zone and is a qualitative parameter. For the zones shorter than the width of the detector slit the absorption of UV radiation does not attain the characteristic value (plateau) and the step has the character of a peak instead of a rectangular shape. In this case, the peak height is not a qualitative information any longer. It becomes a quantitative parameter and can be used for the quantitative evaluation.

4 Analytical Aspects of the Joule Heat

With respect to the strong dependence of the effective mobilities on temperature, the effects associated with the generation of the Joule heat in the separation system are of primary analytical significance. The generation of the Joule heat results not only in the increase of the zone temperatures (related to the temperature of the thermostat or to the initial currentless state) but also in the formation of temperature gradients. The generation of heat, which is different in various zones, as described by Kendall[31] already many years ago, is a feature characteristic of the isotachophoretic separation. By different heat generation in various zones, the temperature increases stepwise and longitudinal gradients are created in the boundary region.

In the development of the method itself, the increase in the temperature in the isotachophoretic zones played an important role since temperature measurement was the first universal detection procedure with sufficient sensitivity in the capillary isotachophoresis[38]. In connection with the detection by means of a thermocouple, more attention was devoted[42,50,82,83,83 a] to the study of interrelations between the longitudinal distribution of the temperature on the outside wall of the isotachophoretic column and the width and the position of the zone boundary inside the column. At present, the thermocouple detector lost greater significance; however, the temperature regime in the isotachophoretic column still requires adequate attention.

In order to describe the mean temperature of the isotachophoretic zone $\bar{T}$(K) (with respect to the temperature of the thermostat, T_0(K)), for the electric power, P($W \cdot cm^{-1}$), quotient $\bar{Q}$ was introduced[84] by the definition

$$\bar{Q} = \frac{\bar{T} - T_0}{P}. \tag{38}$$

Quotient $\bar{Q}$ is a constant characteristic of the given type of the separation capillary and thermostating system. Once determined, $\bar{Q}$ allows to ascertain the increase in the mean temperatures of the zones under the experimental conditions given. Quotient $\bar{Q}$ is, as a matter of fact, a measure of the thermostatic imperfectness since if the separation capillary was thermostated ideally, then $\bar{Q} = 0$. The product $\bar{Q} \times S$, where S is the cross section of the capillary filled with the electrolyte, corresponds to the increase in the mean temperature related to the electric power dissipated in the unit volume. This product permits to compare the efficiency of the thermostating of the capillaries with different shapes and cross sections.

The values of Q and QS for columns of different types (Fig. 12) are compiled in Table 1 (cf. [85]). This table also includes the values of electric current, I, electric power, P, and the corresponding increase in temperature, $\bar{T} - T_0$, calculated for the glutamate zone using 0.01 M HCl + 0.02 M β-alanine as the leading e'ectrolyte. The migration velocity was considered to be the same in all instances (equal to 2.5 cm/min).

The data show that the increase in the temperature in the isotachophoretic capillary must be taken into account since heating by 5 K, e.g. with strong electrolytes, implies a change in the mobilities by 10%.

This has serious consequences for both qualitative and quantitative analysis. For instance, the character of the record of the analysis provided by a universal detector, which senses electric conductivity or the potential gradient, can vary significantly even with small changes in the driving current since the heating is approximately proportional to the square power of the electric current. The expression

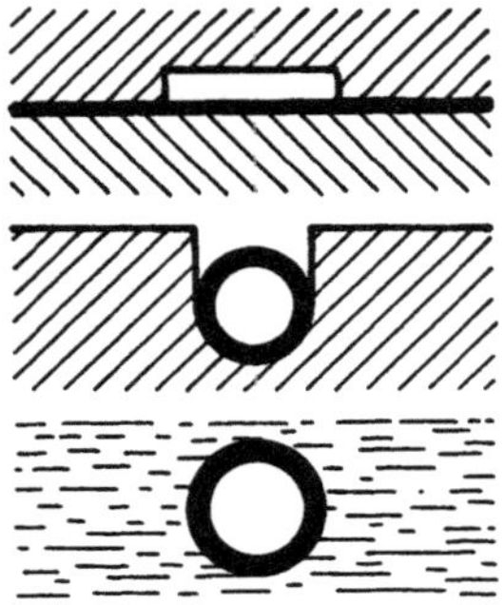

Fig. 12. Schematic representation of the cross sections of the three types of the separation capillaries. **a** Rectangular groove (1 × 0.2 mm), bored (deepened) in a block of perspex glass, firmly pressed against a metallic, thermostated block covered by a PTFE foil, ca. 0.2 mm thick. (For a detailed description see [52].). **b** PTFE capillary of a circular cross section; I.D. 0.45 mm and wall thickness 0.12 mm wound in the groove in the thermostated aluminum cylinder. (For a detailed description see [95].) **c** PTFE capillary of the LKB 2127 Tachophor (LKB, Bromma, Sweden). Inner diameter of the capillary, which is immersed in a cooling liquid, is 0.8 mm

Table 1. Comparison of the values $\bar{Q}$, $\bar{Q}S$, electric current I, electric power dissipated over a unit column length P, and the mean temperature increase relative to the termostat temperature $\bar{T} - T_0$, calculated at the same migration velocities

Column	$\bar{Q}$ [K cm W^{-1}]	$\bar{Q}S$ [K cm^3 W^{-1}]	I [μA]	P [W cm^{-1}]	$\bar{T} - T_0$ [K]
A	180	0.39	110	0.027	5.1
B	510	0.92	100	0.025	13
C	140	0.32	130	0.033	4.5

"approximately" implicity includes the fact that the heating increases the specific conductivity in the zones and thus considerably decreases the degree of the heating.

For qualitative analysis, it is necessary to take into account in the first place the fact that the heating in various zones is different and step heights h_X and h_S correspond to reciprocal mobilities $\bar{u}_X$ and $\bar{u}_S$ of not only different substances X and S but also to various temperatures of the zones, T_X and T_S. These also differ from the thermostat temperature, T_0, i.e. qualitative index $\Delta_X(S)$ represents the ratio (cf. Eq. (28))

$$\Delta_X(S) = \frac{h_S}{h_X} = \frac{\bar{u}_X(T_x)}{\bar{u}_S(T_S)} \,. \tag{39}$$

In order to eliminate the effect of the Joule heat on the values of index $\Delta_X(S)$, the standardization procedure was suggested[86]. This is based on the extrapolation of the data measured at different driving currents to the given standard temperature (T_0) and to negligible Joule heating, i.e. to the standard state at which the temperature of all the zones is the same. The standardized index $\Delta_X^0(S)$ is then defined by the ratio

$$\Delta_X^0(S) = \frac{h_S^0}{h_X^0} = \frac{\bar{u}_X(T_0)}{\bar{u}_S(T_0)} . \tag{40}$$

Two isotachophoregrams are recorded at two different values of current, I_1 and I_2, and step heights $h_{X,1}$ and $h_{S,1}$ and $h_{X,2}$, $h_{S,2}$ are measured. The extrapolated value of $\Delta_X^0(S)$ is then given by the relationship ([86])

$$\Delta_X^0(S) = \frac{h_{S,1}}{h_{X,1}} \cdot \frac{h_{S,2}}{h_{X,2}} \cdot \frac{h_{X,1}^2 - h_{X,2}^2}{h_{S,1}^2 - h_{S,2}^2} \cdot \frac{\dfrac{h_{S,1}}{I_2} - \dfrac{h_{S,2}}{I_1}}{\dfrac{h_{X,1}}{I_2} - \dfrac{h_{X,2}}{I_1}} . \tag{41}$$

The standardized value of $\Delta_X^0(S)$ is already directly comparable with the ratio of the tabulated values of the mobilities for temperature T_0 and for the given ionic strength and can be used for the qualitative interpretation of isotachophoregram.

Figures 13 and 14 illustrate the influence of the driving current on the increase in the mean temperature of the zones and on the qualitative characteristics of the isotachophoregram of a mixture of bromide, nitrate, chlorate, bromate and iodate, recorded by the gradient detector. 0.005 M NaBr served as the leading and 0.0025 M picric acid as the terminating electrolytes. (For the type of the capillary used see Fig. 12a and for a more detailed description of the equipment see [52].)

Figure 13 illustrates various zones and the increase of their mean temperatures for $I = 350\ \mu A$ and $T_0 = 15\ °C$. Figure 14 schematically depicts experimentally determined isotachophoregrams of the same mixture at different values of driving current I and, for comparison, the theoretical shape of the isotachophoregram, determined from the standardized indices, is also shown.

It can be seen that the driving current considerably affects the qualitative character of the isotachophoregram. The lower the mobility of the substance in the given zone, the greater the effect. It can further be seen that the measurements made at small values of the Joule heat fairly converge toward the standardized values.

In addition to the increase in the mean temperature of the zones, the radial temperature profiles, which can cause a curvature of zone boundaries and thus

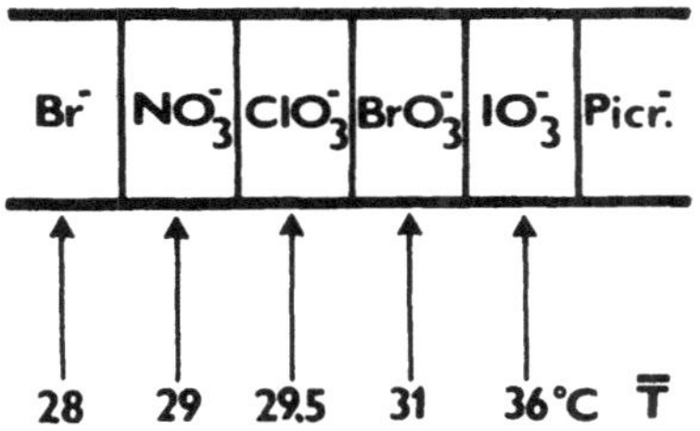

Fig. 13. Schematic representation of the zones and of the increase in their mean temperatures (for further details see text)

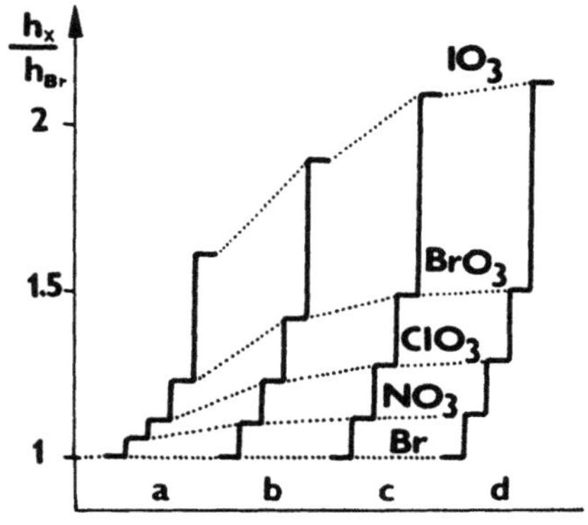

Fig. 14. Effect of the driving current on the qualitative characteristics of an isotachophoregram. Experimental values of h_X/h_{Br} were obtained at driving currents I: **a** 350 μA, **b** 175 μA, **c** 87.5 μA. Theoretical value of $h_X^0/h_{Br}^0 = 1/\Delta_X^0(Br)$, corresponding to $I \rightarrow 0$ described by (**d**)

deteriorate their detection, are also important for analytical isotachophoresis. The problems of both transversal and radial temperature profiles have been discussed by a number of authors[87–90] (for the analytical point of view these problems see [85]).

The radial temperature profile in the capillary of the circular cross section (type C, Fig. 12) under the conditions given in Table 1 (for further details see [85]) is illustrated in Fig. 15. The value $R = r/R_1$ where r is the actual distance from the center of the capillary and R_1 the inner radius of the capillary. It can be seen that the temperature difference in the center of the capillary and at its inner wall is 0.44 K while the mean temperature $\bar{T} - T_0$ increases to 4.5 K. It can thus be said that under the common working conditions, the changes in the mobilities in the radial direction, caused by the influence of the temperature gradient, are negligible with respect to the influence of the mean temperature.

Zones, migrating along the capillary, possess different mean temperatures and thus also longitudinal temperature gradients exist and zones exhibit different longitudinal temperature distributions (temperature profiles). This is important for zone identification that is based on the measurements of conductivity, potential gradient or UV absorption. At the ideal state, the concentration and the temperature in the entire zone are constant. The actual state is, however, characterized by

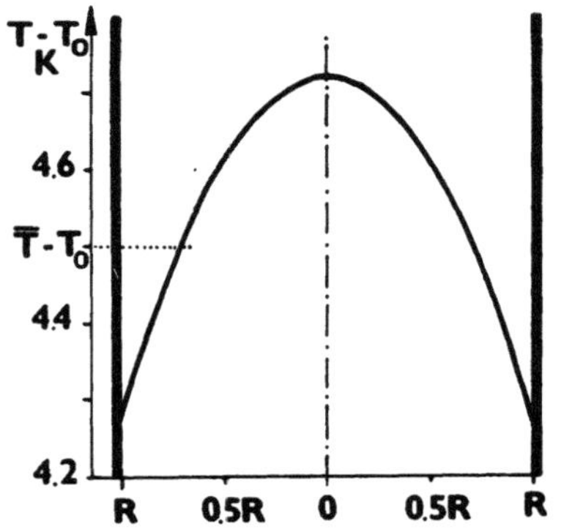

Fig. 15. Radial distribution of the temperature increase, $T - T_0$ (K), at the stationary state inside the separation capillary of type C (see Fig. 22); R is the inner radius of the capillary

curved concentration and temperature profiles at the boundary layer. If the zone is sufficiently long, the plateau of both the concentration and temperature is reached and the detector signal also attains the characteristic plateau. Only then does the height of the plateau provide a qualitative information. However, if the zone is short, the temperature does not reach the plateau and inside the entire short zone, the temperature profile is enforced by the temperature of the neighboring zones.

The question is how long the zone must be in order that its qualitative characteristics may be described by the plateau. This problem was therefore dealt in detail[91]. Figures 16 and 17 can illustrate the longitudinal temperature profiles calculated for bromide, bromate and iodate zones under conditions analogous to those of the preceding cases, depending on the length of the zone of the bromate. Figure 16 schematically illustrates the respective zones and Fig. 17 the graphs of the normalized function

$$\vartheta = \frac{T(l) - T_1^{\infty}}{T_2^{\infty} - T_1^{\infty}}, \tag{42}$$

where T(l) is the temperature at a given length, l, in the capillary. T_2^{∞} and T_1^{∞} are mean temperatures (corresponding to the plateaux) in infinitely long zones of bromate and bromide, respectively, and a is the length of the bromate zone selected as a parameter.

For short zones of bromate, the temperature profile is very steep; the difference in the temperature between the both ends of this zone can be up to 4 K. Unless the bromate zone is at least 10 mm long (curve 5 in Fig. 17), the temperature of the zone will not reach a constant value. With shorter zones the temperature profile shows an inflexion at temperatures lower than it corresponds to that of a sufficiently long zone. Thus, the short bromate zone migrates at under a different temperature regime than does a sufficiently long zone. Hence, it follows that the effective mobility of one substance can acquire different values owing to longitudinal temperature profiles. For the qualitative analysis, this implies that the zones of different lengths that correspond to one substance only can appear as the zones of different substances.

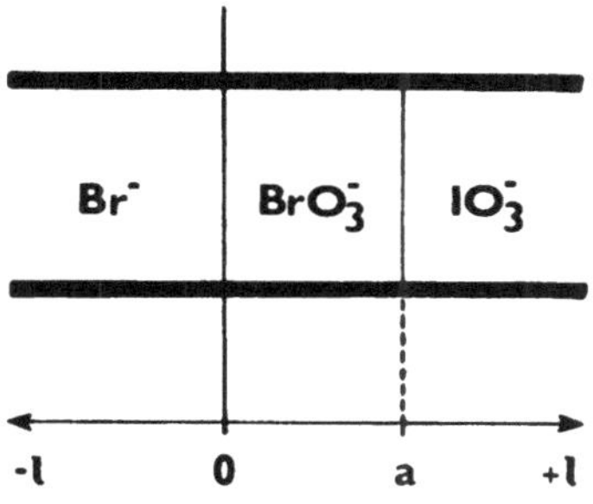

Fig. 16. Schematic diagram of bromide, bromate and iodate zones. l — longitudial distance in the capillary, a — length of bromate zone

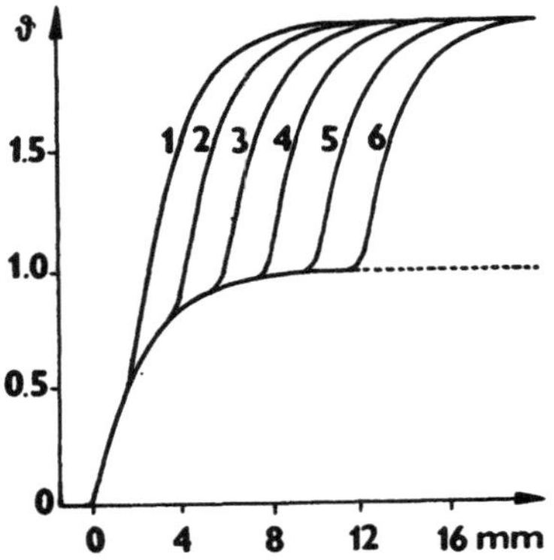

Fig. 17. Distribution of temperature in bromide, bromate and iodate zones expressed by normalized function ϑ (see Eq. (42)); for bromate zones of different lengths a (mm) see also Fig. 16: 1) 2, 2) 4, 3) 6, 4) 8, 5) 10, and 6) 12 mm

5 Advanced Techniques and Procedures

This section deals with the working techniques that extend the possibilities of applying isotachophoresis to the samples which, analyzed by simple procedures, provide mixed zones (counter-flow technique, cascade technique). It also describes the techniques which facilitate the analysis of very dilute samples (continuous sampling technique) or of small amounts of substances in the presence of a large excess of other components (column coupling technique). Furthermore, the spacer technique which provides a more efficient fractionation of complicated samples, e.g. in protein separations, is dealt with.

At the end of this section, attention is paid to the so-called "bleeding zone technique" which permits the analysis of the complexes which are partially degraded during migration.

5.1 Counter-Flow Isotachophoresis

Counter-flow technique is a well-known technique in electrophoresis that permits the extension of the effective length of the separation path. It was introduced into isotachophoresis[36,37,92] in order that the separation capacity of the column is increased under the same detection conditions and without enormous increase in high-voltage requirements. The diagram of the arrangement for the counter-flow analysis is shown in Fig. 18. Flow rates of the counter-flow which are commonly used are 10^{-8} to $10^{-7}\ l \cdot s^{-1}$. Some of the first counter-flow instruments employed control the level of the leading electrolyte in the reservoir connected with the column by a float[93] or overpressure of the gas above this level[94,95]. There is further described a pump forcing out the leading electrolyte by the movement of an elastic membrane to which the pressure of the electrically generated gas[96] is applied and of an electroosmotic pump[97] creating the flow of the leading electrolyte by the passage of electric current through the two membranes displaying different electro-osmotic activities.

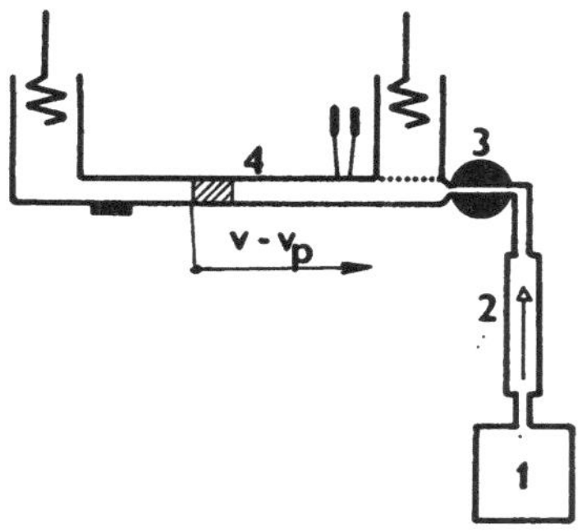

Fig. 18. Arrangement at counter-flow isotachophoresis. Pump (1) pushes out the leading electrolyte from reservoir (2) through valve (3) into separation capillary (4) in the direction opposite to the electromigration of zones. The zone migrates at the velocity given by the difference of electromigration velocity (v) and counterflow (v_p)

5.2 Cascade Isotachophoresis

The application of "cascade isotachophoresis" [62] permits to increase the separation capacity by chemical means, the detection conditions remaining unaffected.

The principle of cascade isotachophoresis consists in the establishment of the two concentration levels of the leading electrolyte in the separation capillary. The higher level of the electrolyte concentration begins at the injection port and reaches up to a certain point in the capillary. There, it is separated by the stationary concentration boundary from the low-concentration leading electrolyte. This electrolyte fills the rest of the capillary with the detection cell up to the membrane of the electrode compartment. The course of the cascade isotachophoresis is illustrated in Fig. 19. In the range of higher concentration of the

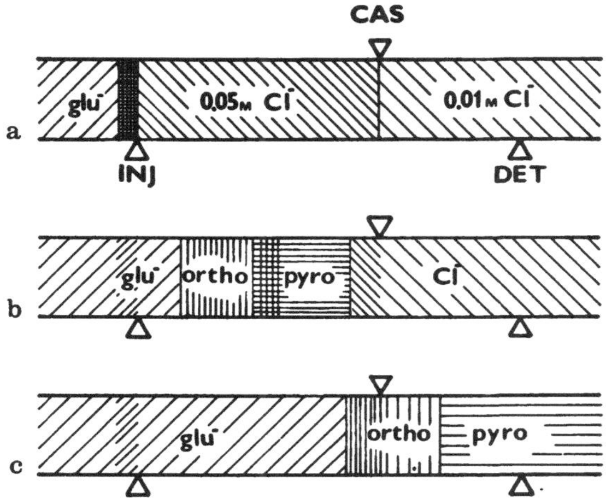

Fig. 19. Cascade isotachophoresis of a mixture of pyro- and orthophosphates. Density of hatched areas represents the concentration in zones. **a** State prior to the passage of current. The concentration cascade of the leading electrolyte (0.05 M HCl + 0.1 M urotropine and 0.01 M HCl + 0.02 M urotropine) is formed in the capillary. The boundary layer between high and low concentration is established in a certain place (CAS). The sample is injected at the place denoted by INJ. Glutamate (Glu^-) serves as the terminator, **b** course of separation at a higher concentration, **c** passage of pyro zone through the detector (DET) and passage of ortho zone through cascade boundary (CAS) with subsequent concentration and zone length changes

electrolyte (and thus also higher separation capacity of the column) an efficient separation occurs (per unit of length). However, at the same time, also short zones are established, and adjusted to the high concentration of the leading electrolyte. This is disadvantageous from the viewpoint of the detection. Having been separated, the short zones enter the section of the column filled with the low-concentration leading electrolyte and are adjusted to the low concentration, too. The length of zones extends and the detection is performed under favorable circumstances.

The arrangement for cascade electrophoresis is simple and its description has been reported[62]. The record of the analyses of the same sample of the liquid fertilizer performed by both simple and cascade procedures is described in Fig. 20. The presence of a mixed zone in the former case and a complete separation under the same detection conditions using the cascade are obvious from the figure.

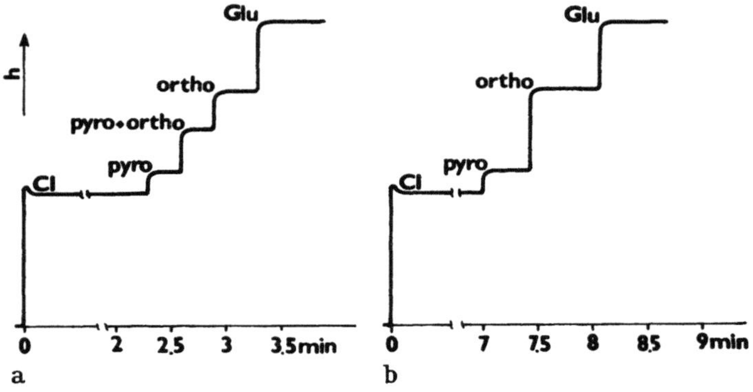

Fig. 20. Analysis of a sample of liquid phosphate fertilizer performed by **a** simple procedure, **b** cascade technique. In both cases, the same samples were separated and the same driving currents applied. For composition of electrolytes see Fig. 19

5.3 Continuous Sampling Technique

In some cases, when the concentration of the component in the sample is very low, the volumes commonly sampled (ca. 10 μl) are not sufficient for the establishment of a zone that is sufficiently long and thus well detectable. In such cases, the method of continuous sampling[98] can be used to advantage. In this method, the sample is pumped into the column in the injection part during the electromigration with simultaneous counter-flow of the leading electrolyte. The arrangement of the experiment is illustrated in Fig. 21. The components to be analyzed are concentrated in this procedure in the column and establish isotachophoretic zones with adjusted concentrations. The experimental conditions can be selected such that the growth of zones of the components of the sample may be roughly compensated for by their migration velocity in the separation capillary (i.e. counter-flow may not completely compensate electromigration). An excess of solvent, corresponding

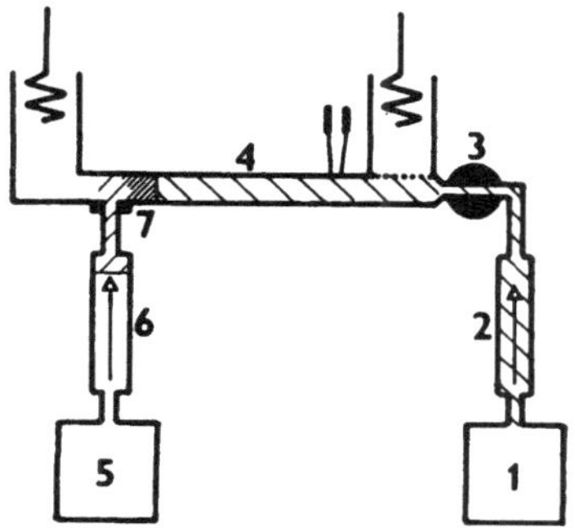

Fig. 21. Scheme of the continuous sampling technique. With this technique, using counter-flow applied during the migration (by means of pump (1) from reservoir (2) through valve (3) into separation capillary (4)), the rear boundary of the leading electrolyte zone is practically stopped. The solution to be analyzed is continuously sampled by means of pump (5) from calibrated reservoir (6) at point of injection (7) into separation capillary (4). The ions from the sample gradually form a zone with the adjusted concentration at the injection point; the sample is concentrated (denoted by hatching). After introducing the required amount of the sample, both counter-flow and sampling is switched off and the analysis proceeds in the common way

to the pumped volume of the sample and to the counter-flow of the leading electrolyte, is forced into the only loose direction, i.e. into the terminator chamber.

5.4 Column Coupling Technique

Column coupling technique[99] is based on the utilization of the two separation capillaries with different inner diameters. The isotachophoretic separation proceeds first in the capillary with the larger inside diameter having a high separation capacity and allows to inject larger volumes of the sample and to apply higher values of the driving current. A pre-separation takes place in this column, permitting the separation of large amounts of the major components of the sample from small zones of the investigated components. With the aid of a T-piece, the second, narrower separation capillary is coupled with the end of the pre-separation capillary. In this capillary, the required analytical separation and the qualitative and quantitative detection of the selected zones take place.

5.5 Spacer Technique

This technique allows to use selective detectors even in the case of zones which can only poorly be distinguished by these detectors[100-103]. It permits a better orientation in the isotachophoretic record of complex mixtures. Moreover, it provides better fractioned separation profiles of complex mixtures, particularly of proteins [104,105], and a more effective qualitative orientation of the separation profiles as far as the identification of various subfractions[106] is concerned.

The principle of spacer technique consists in the mutual spatial separation of poorly distinguished isotachophoretic zones in the separation capillary by forming zones of suitable substances (spacers), which are added to the sample prior to separation, in between of sample zones.

The development of the spacer technique in isotachophoresis has been associated in the first place with its application in the field of proteins as a "spacing mobility gradient"[4,104,105,106 a)] established with the aid of "carrier ampholytes".

Carrier ampholytes are complex mixtures of a large number of acids with a wide range of different pK values. If such a mixture is added to the sample, these acids then arrange in the separation capillary according to their mobilities and thus create a migrating gradient of mobilities. Zones of the analyzed substances arrange according to their mobilities in the corresponding places in the established mobility gradient and are not adjacent any longer. The separation profile of the sample is extended to a larger length in the separation capillary and both qualitative and quantitative detection of zones is easier to perform.

5.6 "Bleeding Zone" Technique

The basic feature of the isotachophoretic zone is that both its front and rear boundary migrate at the same velocity, i.e. the length of the zone does not change in the course of the migration and the whole amount of the given substance is always contained in the respective zone.

A particular situation occurs, if e.g. a kinetically labile anionic complex MY^- (the signs mentioned in the further text are of symbolic meaning only and do not denote the number of electric charges) is placed into an anionic isotachophoretic system, i.e. $\bar{u}_T < \bar{u}_{MY} < \bar{u}_L$. Then, between the zones of leading substance L^- and terminator T^-, a zone of complex MY^- is established which also contains a certain amount of free cation of metal M^+ and free ligand Y^- produced by the dissociation of complex MY^-. Cation M^+, with respect to the sign of its charge, will migrate in a direction opposite to that of the zone of the complex and will leave this zone via its rear boundary. The zone of MY^- decomposes part by part during the migration since it leaves behind itself a trace of cation M^+.

The above ceoncept of the decomposing zone has led to the term of "bleeding zone" at which the method and its application were described[6)].

The analytical application of this technique assumes that such working conditions should be found under which the total decomposition of the investigated zone during the migration should be negligible, i.e. less than a certain limit determined in advance and acceptable analytically, e.g. 0.1%. Under such conditions, it can then be said that the zone will have migrated into the detector "quantitatively" and, in spite of its "bleeding", it can be considered as an isotachophoretic zone.

By chosing suitable working conditions, a selective behavior of various complexes can be reached so that in the course of one analysis some complexes decompose while the others migrate isotachophoretically.

A more detailed study of this technique[107)] revealed that the behavior of free ligand Y^-, produced in addition to cation M^+, by dissociation of complex MY^-, plays a significant role in the migration of the zone of complex MY^-. This free ligand Y^- leaves the investigated zone of the complex and creates its own anionic zone. According to the relationship between mobilities $\bar{u}_Y$ and $\bar{u}_{MY}$, two cases may occur as illustrated in Fig. 22a and b. Fig. 22a shows the case $\bar{u}_Y > \bar{u}_{MY}$ when free ligand Y^- leaves the zone of the complex via its front boundary to form here its own independent zone of Y^-. From the detailed analysis of this case[6,108] it follows that the amount of the complex decomposing in the course of the analysis particularly depends on the degree of dissociation of the complex in the zone,

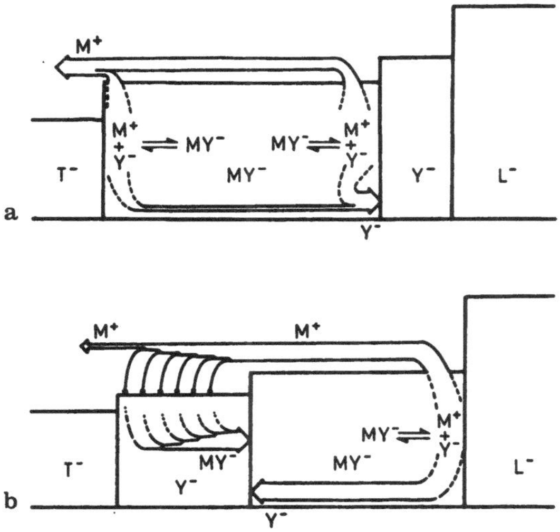

Fig. 22. Diagram of migration of MY^- complex. The leading and the terminating anions are denoted by L^- and T^-, respectively. For simplification, the common counter-ion from the leading electrolyte is not indicated in the zones. M^+ and Y^- denote free cation and free ligand anion, respectively, formed by dissociation of complex $MY^- \rightleftharpoons M^+ + Y^-$. The signs of the ions have only symbolic meaning and do not denote the number of charges. The arrows symbolize movement of the participating ions. **a** $\bar{u}_Y > \bar{u}_{MY}$, **b** $\bar{u}_Y < \bar{u}_{MY}$. For explanation see text

the working parameters of the isotachophoretic column and the composition of the leading electrolyte. These factors are decisively affected by the pH of the leading electrolyte. Figure 22b illustrates the case $\bar{u}_Y < \bar{u}_{MY}$ for which free ligand Y^- leaves the zone of the complex via the rear boundary and forms its own independent zone behind the zone of the complex. This means that in the migration from the zone of the complex, cation M^+ passes through the zone of the free ligand and recombines with it in the direction of the complex-forming equilibrium. Complex MY^- is again produced in the zone of the ligand in an amount proportional to the length of the zone of ligand Y^- and to the rate constant of the reversed reaction $M^+ + Y^- \rightarrow MY^-$. Having been produced, MY^- returns into its zone, thus retarding the decomposition of the zone of the complex. Even a short zone of the free ligand behind the zone of the complex can cause a quantitative migration of the poorly stable complex MY^- since its isotachophoretic stability is enforced (enforced stable zone). This case can be expected in practice, particularly in strongly acidic systems where the free ligand is protonized to a considerable extent, its mobility being thus markedly reduced.

The above cases of the migration are demonstrated in Fig. 23, showing a record of the separation of a mixture containing Al, Cu, Mn and Co in the form of complexes with EDTA. The various steps in the record correspond to the zones of the complexes exhibiting different migration behavior:

— zone of kinetically stable (inert) Al(III)-EDTA complex which migrates without any decomposition,
— zone of kinetically labile Cu(II)-EDTA complex having a mobility lower than that of free EDTA. Owing to sufficient stability of the complex at given pH, the zone is isotachophoretically stable and migrates quantitatively,
— zone of free EDTA, produced by the total decomposition of the poorly stable complex Mn(II)-EDTA. The zone of this complex "bleeds" till complete decomposition in the course of the analysis and the zone of the free ligand of EDTA only migrates into the detector,
— zone of low stability of the Co(II)-EDTA complex displaying a mobility higher than that of free EDTA. Due to the zone of EDTA behind it, the Co(II)-EDTA complex forms an enforced stable zone and migrates practically quantitatively.

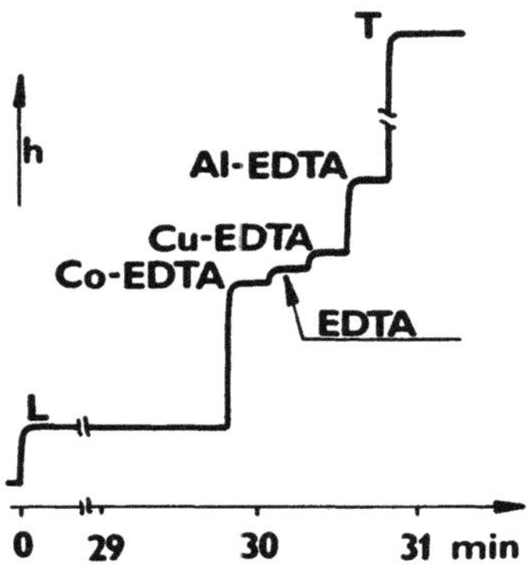

Fig. 23. Separation of a model mixture of EDTA complexes. The sample injected contained Co(II)-EDTA, Mn(II)-EDTA, Cu(II)-EDTA and Al(III)-EDTA 2 nmol of each substance). The leading electrolyte consisted of HCl + KCl, pH = 2.2; the leading anion (L) was 0.015 M Cl^-. Glutamate served as terminator (T)

From the above example follows the possibility of the application of the bleeding zone technique to the quantitative analysis of complicated mixtures of cations existing as anionic chelates. This technique may also be applied to the study of the formation and stability of complexes.

6 Analytical Applications

The application possibilities of analytical isotachophoresis cover the range from simple separations of inorganic ions to separations of proteins. This can be proved by a number of published separations (cf. [1]).

This section summarizes the author's experience made in isotachophoretic analyses of samples used in practice, where the application of other methods is either laborious or fails. This survey also lists some other practical applications roughly classified according to the origin of the samples.

Compared with other methods, isotachophoretic analysis of anions in water is very time-saving, as proved by Fig. 24 describing the simultaneous determination

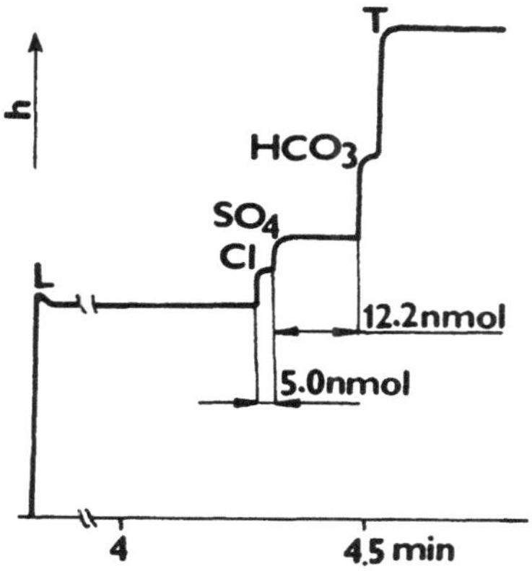

Fig. 24. Anionic analysis of 10 μl of mineral water. Nitrate and tartarate served as leading (L) and terminating (T) anions, respectively. Cd^{2+} was used as the counter-ion. The sample contained 5.0 nmol chloride, 12.2 nmol sulfate, and carbonate

of chlorides and sulfates[71]. Figure 25 depicts the analysis of sulfate water from mines carried out by cascade technique. Obviously, even with great differences in the concentrations of the components to be analyzed the analysis may be carried out within an acceptible period of time.

Isotachophoretic analysis of liquid fertilizers, i.e. the determination of the ortho- and pyrophosphate content[62,110] (see Fig. 5) and that of the nitrate, sulfate and phosphate[72] content in a combined fertilizer (see Fig. 26), is significant in agriculture. In both cases, the short time required for the analysis is the main advantage. Similarly, isotachophoretic analysis of silage extracts[111] rapidly provides reliable information on the quality of the silage, i.e. the determination of lactate, acetate and interfering propionate and butyrate (Fig. 27).

In the field of food analysis, a number of successful applications of analytical isotachophoresis have been reported (e.g. determination or organic acids in juices [9,76,99,112–114], fruit yoghourts[9,112], wines[115], and tea[116]. The short time required for the separation and the minimum necessary treatment of the samples are the main advantages of these analyses. Thus both preservatives (sorbic acid and benzoic acid) and the initial components of the samples (ascorbic, isoascorbic, citric, lactic, aconitic, aspartic and glutamic acids, theanine etc.) may be determined.

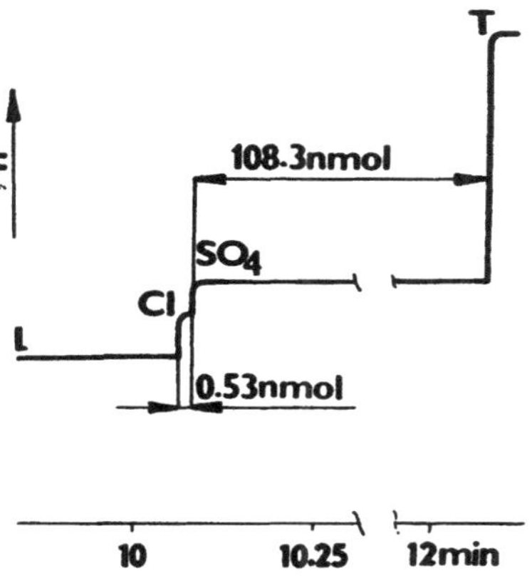

Fig. 25. Determination of chloride and sulfate in a sample of 10 μl of mine water performed by use of the cascade technique. $Cd(NO_3)_2$ solutions of concentrations 0.01 M and 0.006 M served as high- and low-concentration leading electrolyte, resp. Nitrate and tartrate were employed as leading (L) and terminating (T) anions, resp.

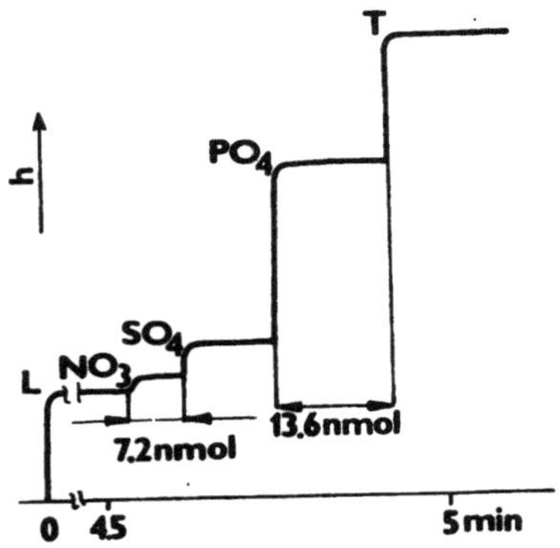

Fig. 26. Determination of soluble nitrate, sulfate and phosphate in solid N-P type fertilizer. Injection of 3 μl of aqueous extract (1 g of a sample extracted by 500 ml of water). Chloride and tartrate served as leading (L) and terminating (T) anions, resp.

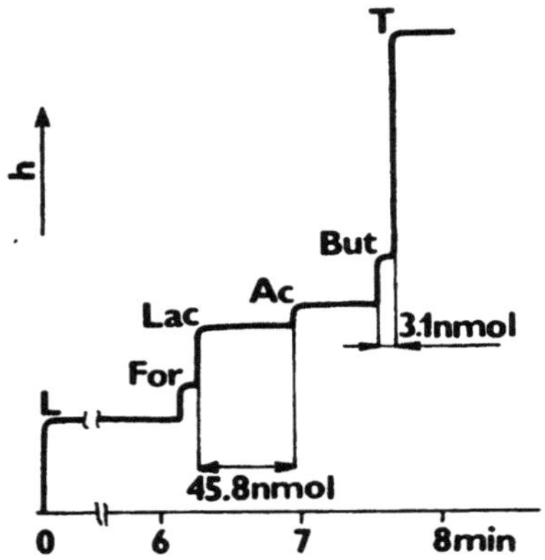

Fig. 27. Anionic analysis of 2.6 μl of a silage extract. Chloride and bicarbonate served as leading (L) and terminating (T) anions, resp. The extract contained formate (For), lactate (Lac), acetate (Ac) and butyrate (But)

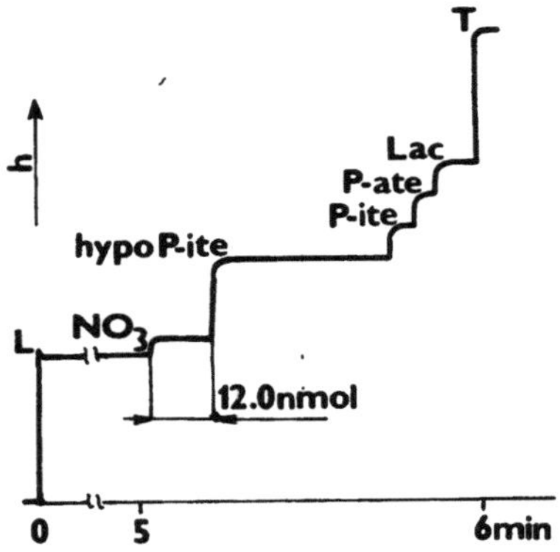

Fig. 28. Determination of interfering nitrates in a nickel-plating bath. Leading (L) and terminating (T) anions; chloride and glutamate, resp. Other components of the bath, namely hypophosphite (hypo P-ite), phosphite, (P-ite), phosphate (P-ate), and lactate (Lac) are also separated

In the future, analytical isotachophoresis will find wide application in analytical control in industry. Particularly in the field of anions, this technique may bring about progress, due to its rapid application and easy interpretation of the record as demonstrated by Figs. 28 and 29. Figure 28 illustrates the determination of interfering nitrates in the presence of an active component (hypophosphite) in chemical nickel-plating baths[117)] where the contents of the oxidation products (phosphite and phosphate) and buffering components (lactate) may also be simultaneously determined. Figure 29 describes the determination of the degradation products of tributyl phosphate[118)] which is used as an excellent reagent for the extraction of heavy metals from the aqueous phase, particularly in the regeneration of fuel cells in nuclear industry. By radiolysis and hydrolysis, tributyl phosphate is degraded to dibutyl phosphate, monobutyl phosphate and phosphate which reduce the extraction yield so that their contents must be controlled analytically.

The control of pharmaceutics is the field where analytical isotachophoresis has already proved to be advantageous, particularly due to its rapid and simplicity. Inorganic and organic components may be determined in one analysis only. This is illustrated by the analysis[119)] of a pharmaceutical preparation in which the sodium, calcium and ethyl morphine content must be controlled (Fig. 30) and by the analysis of an infusion solution in which the sodium, calcium and procaine contents are controlled[119)] (Fig. 31).

Figure 32 shows a control cationic analysis[119)] of a selected batch of artificial sweetener Aspartam (*L*-aspartylphenylalanine methyl ester hydrochloride). In one analysis both the main component and the admixtures from the technological

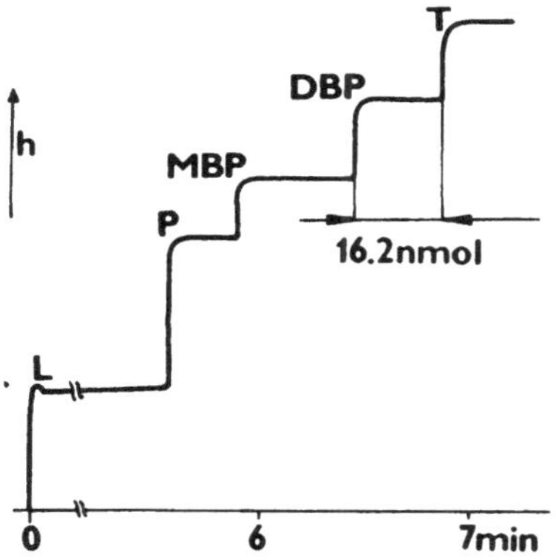

Fig. 29. Determination of the degradation products of tributyl phosphate. Analysis of a 3 μl sample of an aqueous extract of tributyl phosphate. Leading (L) and terminating (T) anions: Chloride and morpholinoethanesulfonic acid, resp. The sample contained 15, 24.3 and 16.2 nmol of phosphate (P), monobutyl phosphate (MBP) and dibutyl phosphate (DBP), respectively

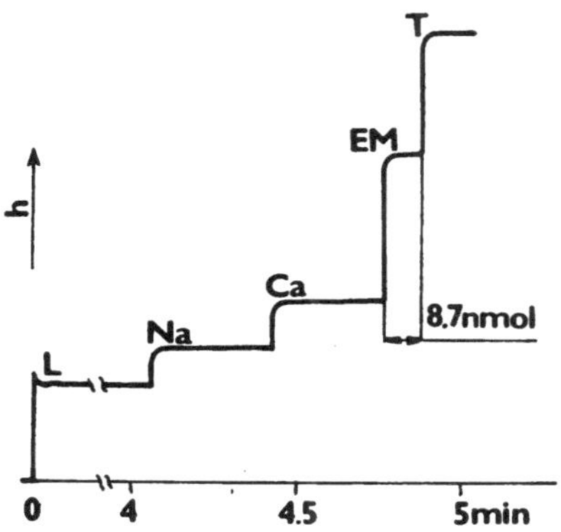

Fig. 30. Control of the contents of Na, Ca and ethylmorphine (EM) in a pharmaceutical preparation (0.5 μl of the sample was analyzed). Leading (L) and terminating (T) cations; potassium and histidine, resp.

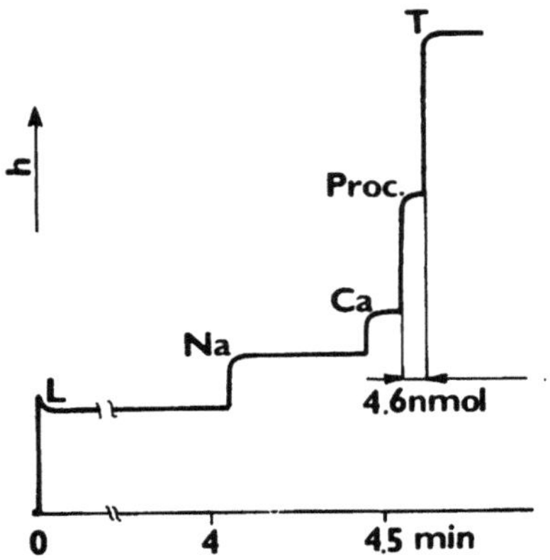

Fig. 31. Control of the contents of Na, Ca and procaine (Proc.) of an infusion solution (injection of 0.5 μl). Potassium and histidine served as the leading (L) and terminating (T) cations, resp.

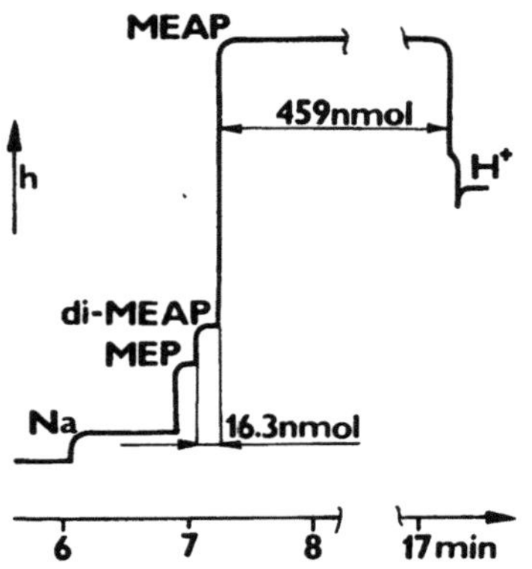

Fig. 32. Cationic analysis of a selected batch of artificial sweetener aspartam. 10 μl of the sample solution (97 mg/5 ml H_2O) were analyzed, and the main component, the methyl ester of aspartyl-phenylalanine (MEAP) as well as the admixtures, sodium, methyl ester of phenylanine (MEP), and dimethyl ester of aspartyl-phenylalanine (di-MEAP) were separated. Leading and terminating cations; $NH_4^{\oplus}$ and $H^{\oplus}$, resp. The counterion was acetate

procedure are determined. The determination of anionic admixtures is described in Fig. 33. Figure 34 depicts the anionic analysis of the selected batch of the pharmaceutical preparation of disodium phosphonoacetate used as a herpeticum. It can be seen that the interfering phosphate content can also be easily determined. Moreover, isotachophoretic control has been exploited for the control of the purity of antibiotics of the penicillin and tetracyclin type[9,120].

A significant application[77,121–124] of analytical isotachophoresis involves the control of synthesis, isolation and purification of peptides. Since in many cases, direct determination of admixtures is not involved, one can thus monitor various isolation stages by controling the extension of the length of the investigated zone of the peptide in relation to the zones of the other admixtures. A number of biologically active peptides such as oxytocin, vasopressin, adrenocorticotropic hormones, somatistatin, secretin, angiotensin, bacitracin, gluthathione etc., have thus been investigated.

The investigation of enzymatic processes often requires laborious and complicated treatment of samples. A number of publications have proved that the main advatages of analytical isotachophoresis in this field are the minimum, sometimes none at all, treatment of samples prior to analysis and the possibility of simul-

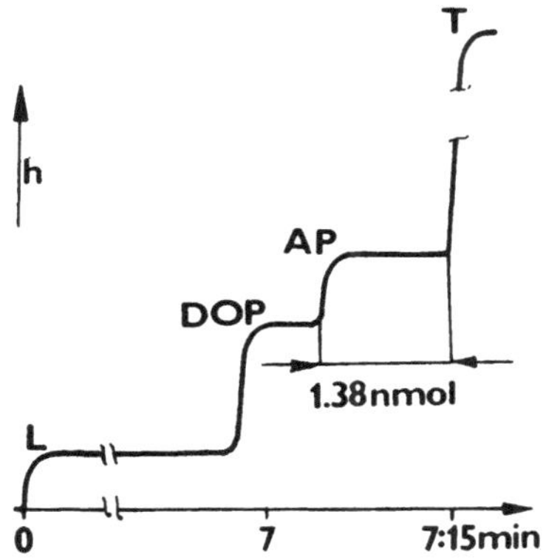

Fig. 33. Analysis of anions of a selected batch of artificial sweetener aspartam. 10 μl of the sample solution (14 mg/5 ml H_2O) were analyzed and impurities 2,5-dioxopiperazine (DOP) and aspartyl-phenylalanine (AP) separated. Chloride and morpholinoethanesulfonic acid served as the leading (L) and terminating (T) anions, resp.

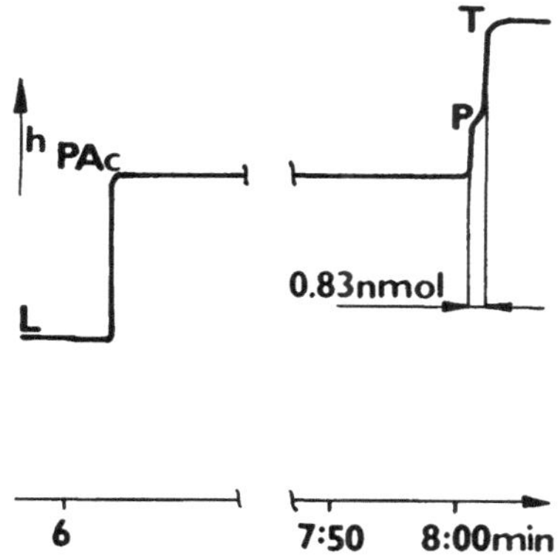

Fig. 34. Analysis of a pharmaceutical preparation of sodium phosphonoacetate. 10 μl of the sample solution (18.5 mg/10 ml H_2O) were analyzed and the bulk component, phosphonoacetate (PAc), as well as the impurity, phosphate (P), separated. Leading (L) and terminating (T) anions; chloride and morpholinoethanesulfonic acid, resp.

taneous investigation of a larger number of reactants and reaction products. Studies on enzymatic conversions of pyruvate into succinate[125)], pyruvate into lactate[126)] and glucose into 6-phosphonogluconate[127)] have been reported. In the analysis (taking about 30 min.) of these conversions, one can detect simultaneously e.g. ATP, ADP, $NADP^+$, NADPH, glucose-6-phosphate, and 6-phosphonogluconate. Analytical isotachophoresis was further applied successfully to the investigation of the enzymatic hydrolysis of UDP glucuronic acid to UMP and glucuronic acid-1-phosphate[128)]. The above examples also include the study of the contents of organic acids (formic, phosphoric, lactic, and acetic acid) in the bacterial fermentation products[129)] and the analysis of the crude fermentation broth from the production of citric acid[9)].

Isotachophoresis may widely be applied to clinical analyses of urine, plasma, serum or tissues. Its main advantages include rapid and accurate determination of all charged molecules in a non-destructive way with minimum demands on the amount of the sample and on its preliminary treatment. In many cases, isotachophoresis can prospectively replace analytical procedures generally based at present on a combination of a suitable colorimetric and suitable chromatographic method.

Isotachophoresis has already been successfully applied to the analysis of urine of persons exposed to styrene, toluene, and xylene, for the contents of mandelic, phenylglyoxylic, hippuric and methylhippuric acids[130,131]. For the clinical disgnostic of inborne metabolic disorders of purines and pyrimidines, it has been elaborated[132,133], permitting the identification of different inborne disorders of the metabolism of these bases by the contents of characteristic metabolites excreted in urine (adenine, uric acid, xanthin, deoxyinosin, deoxyguanosin etc.).

Applications of analytical isotachophoresis in clinical biochemistry, concentrating on blood, plasma or serum analysis, are of topical interest to a number of research laboratories. Promising results have already been published, concerning both analyses of specific substances and isotachophoretical profiles of human serum which are diagnostically characteristic of different diseases. The knowledge of the concentration of theophylline in blood plasma is important for the therapy of asthma at which effective concentrations acquire 10–20 μl/ml. The determination of theophylline by isotachophoresis[134] only necessitates a simple treatment of the sample (precipitation and centrifugation). The advantage of this simple sample treatment is also reflected by the procedure[135] used for the isotachophoretic determination of the levels of aspartic and glutamic acids and asparagin and glutamin in the serum for the diagnosis of metabolic disorders. Further applications, which serve the same purpose, have been reported for the determination of uric acid in the serum[136] using microliter amounts without any preliminary treatment (see also determination of purines and pyrimidines in the serum[137] and of phenylalanine in the serum in the case of phenylketouria[138].

Additional important results have been obtained in the monitoring of proteins from human serum or plasma where pathological cases showed characteristic changes in the separation profiles in comparison with normal serum samples. The utilization of spacers[106], mostly amino acids, added to the samples in such as a way that easily identifiable zones of these spacers separate various protein fractions (create the space between them) is an outstanding feature of these applications. A suitable choice of such spacers can prevent overlapping of the investigated fractions or their cross-contamination through the zone of the spacer without any dilution or without affecting all the other zones (cf. [106]). Characteristic changes in the separation profiles (separation patterns) were found for human serum in the case of immunoglobulin synthesis[139] abnormalities and for plasma at uremia[140].

Other diagnostically significant applications of analytical isotachophoresis concern separation profiles of proteins in cerebrospinal fluid at multiple sclerosis. By using spacer technique, the profiles were found to show a remarkable growth of subfractions of γ-globulins in all cases of multiple sclerosis[139,141] and other neurological diseases. High reproducibility with small amounts of samples is the oustanding feature of this analytical method. The resulting separation profile can be obtained within a short time (ca. 25 min.)[142].

In biochemical research, analytical isotachophoresis has already proved to be a relatively inexpensive tool providing a good reproducibility within short analysis times. It has already been applied to the analysis of muscle tissue[80] in which, after adequate treatment of the sample, separation of the metabolites can be carried out within ca. 20 min, (determination of combined ATP, Pi, PCr, ADP, NADH, IMP, lc.-AMP, AMP, and NAD). This has been proved by the application of isotachophoresis to the analysis of skeletal muscle biopsis of a man at rest and after exercise[143] where ATP, CP, Pi, ADP, G-6-P, lactate and pyruvate concentrations were determined.

Of other applications in biochemical research, the investigation of characteristic changes in the separation profiles of proteins from eye lenses of mouse during ageing[9, 144, 145] and the study on interactions of proteins with detergents[146] and pharmaceuticals[147] are worth mentioning.

Selectivity and minimum treatment of samples prior to analysis indisputably belong to the advantages of analytical isotachophoresis in these fields. High selectivity is known to be the advantage of all chromatographic techniques. However, biological samples containing proteins and lipids, rapidly deteriorate the separation efficiency of the chromatographic columns and sometimes even irreversibly contaminate the column packing. Therefore, chromatographic procedures often necessitate very laborious preliminary treatment of samples. From this standpoint capillary isotachophoresis is only slightly sensitive to non-ionogenic admixtures since they remain in the injection port and are washed out from the capillary after each analysis. Refilling of the capillary with the leading electrolyte leads to the readjustment of exactly defined initial conditions.

7 Conclusions

The theoretical basis of isotachophoresis has been elaborated to such an extent that relationships which permit the calculation of pH, mobilities, composition of zones, level of the separation reached etc., are available. These relationships have even been developed to routine computer procedures. Thus, not only a great deal of information on the substances to be separated can be gained but also theoretical predictions of the optimum electrolytic systems enabling successful separations can be made.

Analytical isotachophoresis has proved to be a valuable routine method for the rapid analysis of a wide scale of substances and a useful method for both analytical and physico-chemical research.

From the analytical point of view, the concentrating effect of isotachophoresis is of great significance, it allows to analyze minute amounts of ionic components in both electrolytic and non-electrolytic sample mixtures. The self-sharpening effect causes that the isotachophoretic zone boundaries, having once been formed remain very sharp and do not change with time. This enables even very small amounts of the substances that form very narrow zones to be analyzed.

Constant composition and constant volume of the zone during the isotachophoretic migration in the steady state permit to select the time optimum for the given analysis so that the substances with small differences in their mobilities may well be separated from one another. This possibility, together with the self-sharpening effect of the boundary, ensures an efficient separation of the substances to be analyzed.

The fundamental inherent property of isotachophoretic zones, i.e. the fact that each zone contains one substance only at a given concentration, means that the relationships between the composition of the zones and the qualitative data of the detectors are well established, which is of considerable significance for qualitative analysis. The constant concentrations of the substances in the zones permit an easy and well defined quantitative interpretation.

In comparison with common zone electrophoresis and with chromatographic techniques, capillary isotachophoresis does not employ any supporting material so that permanent stability and reproducibility of the working conditions can easily be secured. It is only slightly affected by accompanying non-ionic substances that often cause deterioration of chromatographic columns. In isotachophoresis, non-ionic accompanying compounds remain at the injection part and, are washed out from the separation capillary after analysis has been performed.

An advantageous characteristic of isotachophoresis is the easy separation of inorganic, organic, simple and complex ions in one run only.

Finally, it should be mentioned that the instrumentation for analytical isotachophoresis has at present been advanced enough so that all the possibilities, described above may be used to advantage.

8 Acknowledgement

The author is grateful to his co-workers Ing. M. Deml, Ing. B. Kaplanová, Dr. P. Gebauer, and Dr. V. Dolník for their kind assistance in the preparation of the manuscript. The author is furthermore indebted to Dr. J. Janák for his kind reviewing of the manuscript and for his interest in this work.

9 References

1. Acta Isotachophoretica 1967–1979, Literature reference list, LKP-Produkter AB, Bromma, Sweden
2. Preetz, W.: Fortschr. Chem. Forsch. *11*, 375 (1969)
3. Everaerts, F. M., Beckers, J. L., Verheggen, Th. P. E. M.: Isotachophoresis: theory, instrumentation and applications. Amsterdam, Oxford, New York: Elsevier 1976
4. Haglund, H.: Sci. Tools *17*, 2 (1970)
5. Arlinger, L. In: Protides of biological fluids (Peters, H. (ed.)) vol. 22, p. 661. Oxford, New York: Pergamon Press 1975
6. Boček, P., Deml, M., Janák, J.: Laborpraxis *1979*, May, pp. 18, 21–23
7. Hollaway, W. L., Ball, J.: Internat. Lab. *1977*, July/August, pp. 41–48
8. Nagayanagi, Y.: ibid. *1977*, Nov./Dec., pp. 33–41
9. Delmotte, P.: J. Chromatogr. (Chromatogr. Rev.) *165*, 87 (1979)
10. Nernst, W.: Z. Elektrochem. *3*, 308 (1897)
11. Whetham, W. C. D.: Phil. Trans. *A184*, 337 (1893)
12. Kohlrausch, F.: Ann. Phys. Chem., N.F. *62*, 209 (1897)
13. MacInnes, D. A., Longsworth, L. G.: Chem. Rev. *11*, 171 (1932)
14. Nernst, W.: Z. Phys. Chem. *4*, 129 (1889)
15. Planck, M.: Ann. Phys. Chem., N.F. *40*, 561 (1890)

16. Weber, H.: Sitz. Preuss. Akad. Wiss. Berlin, Sitzungsber. 1897, p. 936
17. Weber, H.: Die Partiellen Differential-Gleichungen der Mathematischen Physik, 5th edit., vol. I., pp. 503–527. Braunschweig 1910
18. v. Laue, M.: Z. Anorg. Chem. *93*, 329 (1915)
19. Longsworth, L. G.: J. Am. Chem. Soc. *65*, 1755 (1943)
20. Longsworth, L. G.: ibid. *66*, 449 (1944)
21. Levine, H. A., Harris, D. K., Nichol, J. C.: J. Phys. Chem. *77*, 2989 (1973)
22. Tiselius, A.: Nova Acta Regiae Soc. Sci. Uppsaliensis *7*, (4) (1930)
23. Longsworth, L. G. In: Electrophoresis. Theory, methods and applications. Bier, M. (ed.), pp. 92–136. New York: Academic Press 1959
24. Alberty, R. A.: J. Am. Chem. Soc. *72*, 2361 (1950)
25. Consden, R., Gordon, A. H., Martin, A. J. P.: Biochem. J. *40*, 33 (1946)
26. Svenson, H.: Acta Chem. Scand. *2*, 841 (1948)
27. Dismukes, E. B., Alberty, R. A.: J. Am. Chem. Soc. *76*, 191 (1954)
28. Boček, P., Deml, M., Janák, J.: J. Chromatogr. *91*, 829 (1974)
29. Everaerts, F. M., Routs, R. J.: ibid *58*, 181 (1971)
30. Vacík, J.: D. Sc. Thesis, Prague University 1980
31. Kendall, J.: Science *67*, 163 (1928)
32. Longsworth, L. G.: Nat. Bur. Stand. Circ. *1953*, No. 524, p. 59
33. Konstantinov, B. P., Oshurkova, O. V.: Dokl. Akad. Nauk. USSR *148*, 1110 (1963)
34. Konstantinov, B. P., Oshurkova, O. V.: Zh. Tekhn. Fiz. *36*, 942 (1966)
35. Schumacher, E., Studer, T.: Helv. Chim. Acta *47*, 957 (1964)
36. Preetz, W.: Talanta *13*, 1649 (1966)
37. Preetz, W., Pfeifer, H. L.: Anal. Chim. Acta *38*, 255 (1967)
38. Martin, A. J. P., Everaerts, F. M.: ibid *38*, 233 (1967)
39. Hello, O.: J. Electroanal. Chem. *19*, 37 (1968)
40. Fredriksson, S.: Acta Chem. Scand. *23*, 1450 (1969)
41. Martin, A. J. P. In: Column chromatography. Kovats, E. (ed.), pp. 16–22. Aarau, Switzerland: Sauerländer AG 1970
42. Martin, A. J. P., Everaerts, F. M.: Proc. Roy. Soc. London *A316*, 493 (1970)
43. Arlinger, L., Routs, R.: Sci. Tools *17*, 21 (1970)
44. Vacík, J., et al.: Chem. Listy *66*, 545 (1972)
45. Verheggen, Th. P. E. M., et al.: J. Chromatogr. *64*, 185 (1972)
46. Stankoviansky, D.: ibid. *106*, 131 (1975)
47. Everaerts, F. M., Verheggen, Th. P. E. M.: ibid. *73*, 193 (1972)
48. Van der Steen, C., et al.: Anal. Chim. Acta *59*, 298 (1972)
49. Everaerts, F. M., Rommers, P. J.: J. Chromatogr. *91*, 809 (1974)
50. Vacík, J., Zuska, J.: ibid. *91*, 795 (1974)
51. Haruki, T., Akiyama, J.: Anal. Lett. *6*, 11 (1974)
52. Boček, P., Deml, M., Janák, J.: J. Chromatogr. *106*, 283 (1975)
53. Deml, M., Boček, P., Janák, J.: ibid *109*, 49 (1975)
54. Akiyama, J., Mizuno, T.: ibid *119*, 605 (1976)
55. Akiyama, J.: In. Electrophoresis '78. (Catsimpoolas, N. (ed.)), pp. 109–114. Amsterdam: Elsevier North Holland, Inc. 1978
55a. Arlinger, L., Lundin, H. In: Protides of Biological Fluids (Peeters, H. (ed.)) vol. 21, p. 667. Oxford, New York: Pergamon Press 1973
56. Arlinger, L.: J. Chromatogr. *91*, 785 (1974)
57. Gaš, B., Demjanénko, M., Vacík, J.: J. Chromatogr. (in press)
57a. LKB 2127 Tachophor, LKB-Produkter AB, Promma, Sweden
58. IP-1B, Shimadzu Capillary-type Isotachophoretic Analyzer, Shimadzu Seisakusha Ltd., Tokyo, Japan
59. IP-2A, Shimadzu Capillary-type Isotachophoretic Analyzer, Shimadzu Seisakusha Ltd., Tokyo, Japan
60. LKB Tachofrac, LKB-Produkter AB, Bromma, Sweden
61. Everaerts, F. M., et al.: J. Chromatogr. *119*, 129 (1976)
62. Boček, P., Deml, M., Janák, J.: J. Chromatogr. *156*, 323 (1978)
63. Ryser, P.: Thesis. Bern, Switzerland 1976

64. Schumacher, E., Ryser, P., Thormann, W.: Helv. Chim. Acta *60*, 3012 (1977)
65. Bilal, B. A.: Chem.-Ing.-Techn. *42*, 1090 (1970)
66. Blasius, E., Wenzel, U.: J. Chromatogr. *49*, 527 (1970)
67. Wagener, K., Freyer, H. D., Bilal, B. A.: Sep. Sci. *6*, 483 (1971)
68. Preetz, W., Wannemacher, U., Datta, S.: Z. Anal. Chem. *257*, 97 (1971)
69. Prusík, Z.: J. Chromatogr. *91*, 867 (1974)
70. Boček, P., et al.: ibid *117*, 97 (1976)
71. Boček, P., et al.: ibid. *137*, 83 (1977)
72. Boček, P., et al.: Collect. Czech. Chem. Commun. *43*, 2707 (1978)
72a. Kanianský, D., Everaerts, F. M.: J. Chromatogr. *148*, 441 (1978)
73. Dolník, V., Boček, P.: unpublished
73a. Beckers, J. L., Everaerts, F. M.: J. Chromatogr. *51*, 339 (1970)
74. Boček, P., et al.: ibid. *160*, 1 (1978)
75. Everarts, F. M.: ibid. *65*, 3 (1972)
76. Everaerts, F. M., Verheggen, Th. P. E. M.: ibid. *91*, 837 (1974)
77. Miyazaki, H., Katoh, K.: ibid. *119*, 369 (1976)
78. Boček, P., et al.: Panel discussion in: Prog. Chromatography. Carlsbad, Czechoslovakia, April 18–20, 1979
79. Beckers, J L., Everaerts, F. M.: J. Chromatogr. *71*, 329 (1972)
80. Gower, D. C., Woledge, R. C.: Sci. Tools *24*, 17 (1977)
81. Svoboda, M., Vacík, J.: J. Chromatogr. *119*, 539 (1976)
82. Everaerts, F. M.: Thesis, Eindhoven, Techn. Univers. Eindhoven 1968
83. Ryšlavý, Z., Vacík, J., Zuska, J.: J. Chromatogr. *114*, 315 (1975)
83a. Hinckley, J. O. N.: Biochem. Soc. Trans. *1*, 574 (1973)
84. Ryšlavý, Z., et al.: J. Chromatogr. *114*, 17 (1977)
85. Boček, P., et al.: Collection Czechoslov. Chem. Commun. *42*, 3382 (1977)
86. Boček, P., et al.: J. Chromatogr. *191*, 271 (1980)
87. Coxon, M., Binder, M. J.: ibid. *101*, 1 (1974)
88. Coxon, M., Binder, M. J.: ibid. *107*, 43 (1975)
89. Brown, J. F., Hinckley, J. O. N.: ibid. *109*, 225 (1975)
90. Brown, J. F., Hinckley, J. O. N.: ibid. *109*, 218 (1975)
91. Ryšlavý, Z., et al.: Collec. Czech. Chem. Commun. *44*, 841 (1979)
92. Everaerts, F. M., et al.: J. Chromatogr. *49*, 262 (1970)
93. Everaerts, F. M., et al.: J. Chromatogr. *60*, 397 (1971)
94. Everaerts, F. M., Verheggen, Th. P. E. M.: Sci. Tools *17*, 17 (1970)
95. Everaerts, F. M., Verheggen, Th. P. E. M.: J. Chromatogr. *53*, 315 (1970)
96. Everaerts, F. M., Verheggen, Th. P. E. M., van de Venne, J. L. M.: ibid. *123*, 139 (1976)
97. Ryšlavý, Z., et al.: ibid. *147*, 446 (1978)
98. Ryšlavý, Z., et al.: ibid. *147*, 369 (1978)
99. Everaerts, F. M., Verheggen, Th. P. E. M., Mikkers, F. E. P.: ibid. *169*, 21 (1979)
100. Vestermark, A.: Cons electrophoresis — an experimental study, Univers., Stockholm 1966
101. Vestermark, A.: Naturwiss. *54*, 470 (1967)
102. Vestermark, A.: Biochem. J. *104*, 21 (1967)
103. Vestermark, A., Wiedemann, B.: Nucl. Instr. Methods *56*, 151 (1967)
104. Svendsen, P. J., Rose, C.: Sci. Tools *17*, 13 (1970)
105. Arlinger, L.: In: Progr. in isoelectrofocusing and isotachophoresis. (Righetti, P. G. (ed.)) pp. 331–340. Amsterdam, Oxford: North-Holland Publ. Co. 1975
106. Kopwillem, A.: J. Chromatogr. *118*, 35 (1976)
106a. Arlinger, L.: In: Protides of biological fluids. Peeters, H. (ed.), vol. 22, p. 691. Oxford, New York: Pergamon Press 1975
107. Gebauer, P., et al.: J. Chromatogr. *199*, 81 (1980)
108. Kotásek, V.: Graduation report, Univers. Brno 1978
109. Gebauer, P., Boček, P.: (prepared for publication)
110. Boček, P., et al.: Chem. Průmysl *27/52*, 557 (1977)
111. Boček, P., et al.: J. Chromatogr. *154*, 356 (1978)
112. Baldesten, A., Hjalmarsson, S.-G., Neumann, G.: Z. Anal. Chem. *290*, 148 (1078)
113. Yagi, T., Shiogai, Y., Akiyama, J.: Shimadzu Rev. *34*, 229 (1977)

114. Rubach, K., Breyer, Ch., Kirchhoff, E.: Z. Lebensm. Unters. Forsch. *4*, 307 (1979)
115. Kaiser, K. P., Hupf, H.: Dtsch. Lebensm.-Rundsch. *75*, 300, 346 (1979)
116. Shiogai, Y., Yagi, T., Akiyama, J.: Bunseki Kagaku *26*, 702 (1977)
117. Boček, P., et al.: J. Chromatogr. *151*, 436 (1978)
118. Boček, P., et al.: ibid. *195*, 303 (1980)
119. Boček, P., et al.: 3. Nat. Congr. Czech Pharmaceut. Soc., Brno, Oct. 10–13, 1979
120. LKB Isotachophoresis News, No. 3, Oct. 1977. LKB, Bromma, Sweden
121. LKB Isotachophoresis News, No. 2, June 1977. LKB, Bromma, Sweden
122. Kopwillem, A., et al.: Anal. Biochem. *67*, 166 (1975)
123. Kopwillem, A., et al.: In: Protides of biological fluids (Peeters, H. (ed.)) vol. 21, p. 657. Oxford, New York: Pergamon Press 1973
124. Kopwillem, A.: In: Protides of biological fluids. Peeters, H. (ed.), vol. 22, p. 715. Oxford, New York: Pergamon Press 1975
125. Kopwillem, A.: J. Chromatogr. *82*, 407 (1973)
126. Willemsen, A. J.: ibid. *105*, 405 (1975)
127. Kopwillem, A.: Acta Chem. Scand. *27*, 2426 (1973)
128. Holloway, C. J., et al.: J. Chromatogr. *188*, 235 (1980)
129. van der Hœven, J. S., et al.: Appl. Environ, Microbiol. *35*, 17 (1978)
130. Sollenberg, J., Baldesten, A.: J. Chromatogr. *132*, 469 (1977)
131. Zschiesche, W., Schaller, K. H., Gossler, K.: Z. Anal. Chem. *290*, 115 (1978)
132. Sahota, A., Simmonds, H. A., Payne, R. H.: J. Pharmacol. Methods *2*, 263 (1979)
133. Simmonds, H. A., Sahota, A., Payne, R.: J. Clin. Chem. Clin. Biochem. *17*, 441 (1979)
134. Moberg, U., Hjalmarsson, S.-G., Mellstrand, T.: J. Chromatogr. *181*, 147 (1980)
135. Robinson, D. V., Rimpler, M.: J. Clin. Chem. Clin. Biochem. *16*, 1 (1978)
136. Oerlemans, F., et al.: ibid. *17*, 433 (1979)
137. Oerlemans, F., et al.: ibid. *17*, 432 (1979)
138. Kopwillem, A., et al.: In: Protides of biological fluids (Peeters, H. (ed.)), vol. 22, p. 737. Oxford, New York: Pergamon Press 1975
139. Delmotte, P.: Sci. Tools *24*, 33 (1977)
140. Mikkers, F., Ringoir, S., De Smet, R.: J. Chromatogr. *162*, 341 (1979)
141. Kjellin, K. G., Moberg, U., Hallander, L.: Sci. Tools *22*, 3 (1975)
142. Delmotte, P.: In: Electrofocusing and isotachophoresis (Radola, B. J., Graesslin, D. (eds.)) p. 559. Berlin, New York: W. de Gruyter Co. 1977
143. Kopwillem, A.: LKB Appl. Note 158 (1974)
144. Bours, J., Delmotte, P.: Sci. Tools *26*, 58 (1979)
145. Bours, J.: In: Interdiscipl. Topics Geront (Von Hahn, H. P. (ed.)) vol. 12, p. 196. Basel: S. Karger 1978
146. Hjalmarsson, S.-G.: Biochim. Biophys. Acta *581*, 210 (1979)
147. Sjödahl, J., Hjalmarsson, S.-G.: FEBS Lett. *92*, 22 (1978)

Bei Fragen zur Produktsicherheit wenden Sie sich bitte an:
If you have any questions regarding product safety,
please contact:

Walter de Gruyter GmbH
Genthiner Straße 13
10785 Berlin
productsafety@degruyterbrill.com